READING COMPREHENSION ACTIVITIES KIT

Ready-to-Use Techniques and Worksheets for Assessment and Instruction

Wilma H. Miller, Ed.D.

Professor of Education
Illinois State University
Normal, Illinois

**THE CENTER FOR APPLIED
RESEARCH IN EDUCATION**
West Nyack, New York 10995

To the memory of my beloved mother,
Ruth K. Miller
and
Win Huppuch, vice-president at the
Center for Applied Research in
Education and my dear friend and
adviser for many years.

10 9 8 7 6 5 4 3 2 1

Library of Congress Cataloging-in-Publication Data
Miller, Wilma H.
    Reading comprehension activities kit : ready-to-use
techniques and worksheets for assessment and instruc-
tion / Wilma H. Miller.
        p.   cm.
    Includes bibliographical references
    ISBN 0-87628-789-5
    1. Reading comprehension. 2. Reading (Elementary)—
United States. 3. Education, Elementary—United States—
Activity programs.
I. Center for Applied Research in Education. II. Title.
LB1573.7.M55   1990
372.4′1--dc20   90-43209
                                                            CIP

ISBN 0-87628-789-5

THE CENTER FOR APPLIED
RESEARCH IN EDUCATION
BUSINESS & PROFESSIONAL DIVISION
A division of Simon & Schuster
West Nyack, New York 10995

Printed in the United States of America

About the
Reading Comprehension Activities Kit

While American elementary educators have always done a fairly good job of teaching the word identification skills, I believe that we have been less successful in teaching our students to comprehend what they read. This is especially true of higher level (implicit) comprehension. For example, most of the students I have tutored in the intermediate grades demonstrate adequate knowledge of word identification skills, but have great difficulty with higher-order comprehension skills such as summarizing what is read and reading between the lines.

The *Reading Comprehension Activities Kit* is designed to give elementary and middle-upper reading teachers a store of ready-to-use techniques and activity sheets for teaching and reinforcing reading comprehension. All of these techniques and activities were selected keeping in mind the findings of contemporary research about reading comprehension, and many of them focus on interpretive (implicit) comprehension skills, traditionally the most difficult skills to teach meaningfully. The activity sheets also present interesting content material in a manner that will both interest and challenge students in grades 1 through 8.

This resource was written mainly for reading specialists, Chapter I reading teachers, and remedial reading teachers, all of whom will find a wealth of useful strategies and materials between its covers. It will also be a great help to elementary classroom teachers of reading as they seek to understand the different levels and components of reading comprehension and ways to improve their students' ability in this crucial skill. Secondary reading teachers and content teachers should find many useful techniques for improving student comprehension too.

Here are overviews of each of the seven basic sections of the *Kit*:

Section 1, "What Is Reading Comprehension?" explains the characteristics of reading comprehension in a contemporary but easy-to-understand manner. It is essential for the reading teacher to know the various subskill components of comprehension if he or she is to teach them effectively.

Section 2, "Assessing Comprehension Ability," presents many standardized and informal ways of assessing comprehension ability. Included are a variety of informal diagnostic devices the teacher can duplicate as they appear and use "as is." This section also illustrates many new assessment techniques.

Section 3, "Vocabulary Knowledge and Comprehension," is devoted to the relationship between vocabulary knowledge and reading comprehension. Most of the section presents techniques and ready-to-duplicate activity sheets which can be used to improve students' meaning vocabulary at both the primary and middle-upper levels. Also included are lists of commercially available materials, games, and computer software that can be used for vocabulary development.

Section 4, "Using Questioning Techniques for Improving Comprehension Ability," describes the various questioning techniques that can be used to improve the different aspects of reading comprehension. Each type of questioning strategy is clearly explained and illustrated.

Section 5, "Improving Comprehension Ability at the Emergent Literacy Level," presents numerous strategies and ready-to-duplicate activity sheets for improving comprehension ability at the emergent literacy level. Primary-grade teachers of reading will find it an invaluable resource for improving their pupils' comprehension at the beginning reading level.

Section 6, "Improving Comprehension Ability at the Middle-Upper Reading Levels," provides another very extensive resource for comprehension improvement at the intermediate and middle/junior high school levels. All of the many strategies and activity sheets in this section reflect contemporary research in the area and are based on interesting content (expository) materials.

The last section of the Kit—"Materials and Computer Software for Improving Reading Comprehension Ability"—contains a comprehensive list of resources that the reading teacher can use to improve students' comprehension at both the beginning and middle-upper reading levels. This section should save the teacher much time in locating appropriate instructional materials to meet individual and group reading needs.

The following are some of the reasons reading teachers will find the *Reading Comprehension Activities Kit* particularly useful in their work:

- It explains abstract concepts and the findings of contemporary research on reading comprehension in easy-to-follow, nontechnical language and translates these concepts into interesting, meaningful classroom practice.

- It is the only resource on reading comprehension that provides ready-to-duplicate activity sheets along with teaching strategies. These activity sheets have been tested with students and are ready for immediate duplication and use.

- It contains examples of the latest and most effective devices for assessing reading comprehension ready for duplication and use.

- It includes an extensive list of instructional materials and computer software for improving students' reading comprehension at both the primary and middle-upper reading levels.

The author wishes to acknowledge that her late 88-year-old mother was a continuing source of inspiration in the writing of this *Kit*, as she always had been in the past. She also wants to thank Lisa Olszta for her help in the preparation of Section 7 of this book. In addition, she wishes to thank her present and former undergraduate and graduate students at Illinois State University for some of the strategies in the *Kit*. Lastly, the author wishes to thank Win Huppuch of The Center for Applied Research in Education for his help and support over the past 19 years of professional association.

Wilma H. Miller

ABOUT THE AUTHOR

A former classroom teacher, Wilma H. Miller, Ed.D., has been teaching at the college level for the past 25 years. She completed her doctorate in reading at the University of Arizona under the direction of the late Dr. Ruth Strang, a nationally known reading authority.

Dr. Miller is a frequent contributor to professional journals and is the author of many other works in the field of reading education, including *Identifying and Correcting Reading Difficulties in Children* (1972), *Diagnosis and Correction of Reading Difficulties in Secondary School Students* (1973), *Reading Diagnosis Kit* (1974, 1978, 1986), *Reading Correction Kit* (1975, 1982), and *Reading Teacher's Complete Diagnosis & Correction Manual* (1988), all published by The Center for Applied Research in Education. She is also author of an in-service aid for teachers entitled *Reading Activities Handbook* (1980) and several textbooks for developmental reading, *The First R: Elementary Reading Today* (1972, 1977) and *Teaching Elementary Reading Today* (1983), published by Holt, Rinehart & Winston, Inc., as well as a guide to secondary reading instruction, *Teaching Reading* (1974), published by Charles C. Thomas.

CONTENTS

1

What Is Reading Comprehension?

The authors of some formal phonic approaches to reading instruction state that by using their method, any child can learn to read effectively. Do you believe that a child who can pronounce words effectively always can be described as a good reader? Although many lay people may think this to be true, most reading teachers know that it certainly is not the case. Indeed, I once tutored a junior high school girl who could pronounce all of the words in her textbooks perfectly yet could not understand one word of what she was reading. Obviously, she was not "reading" in any true sense. To be considered reading, the child must be able to understand the material well. Reading without understanding is not reading but merely word pronunciation.

In the past, reading research has focused on such areas as phonic programs and phonic analysis. A great deal of research also was done to determine what one method might be the most effective way of teaching reading to a class of children. By this time, reading specialists have determined that there *never* will be one *best* method of teaching reading to all children. Recently reading research has focused on *reading comprehension*, and this complex process undoubtedly will be the focus of most reading research for some time in the future. Reading teachers need not understand all of the complex relationships between cognition and comprehension, but they should understand the contemporary philosophy of reading comprehension.

Section 1 of the *Kit* attempts to describe comprehension in a contemporary and accurate, but understandable, manner. It is upon this definition that the strategies, activity sheets, and materials found later in this resource are based. Very briefly, the section first provides a contemporary definition of comprehension. It then emphasizes the extreme importance of prior knowledge upon adequate reading comprehension. Next the section discusses the relation of schema theory to reading comprehension. Metacognition and its relation to the improvement of reading comprehension also is mentioned briefly. The section next describes the various subskills of which effective reading comprehension is composed so that the reading teacher can understand what types of strategies and

materials can be best used to improve these various elements of reading comprehension.

Hopefully, after reading this section, the reading teacher will have a better
understanding of what constitutes the contemporary view of reading comprehension to better enable him or her to use the materials found later in this resource.

Defining Reading Comprehension

As stated before, *comprehension* is the current focus of research emphasis in
reading. Although we now know a considerable amount about what constitutes
reading comprehension, there still is a great deal that is not understood and
undoubtedly may not be understood for some time in the future. This is because
comprehension is a very complex process which is related to the brain and to
thinking, neither of which are well understood at the present time.

Much of the research which has taken place on reading comprehension
during the past decade has been done with federal funds at the Center for the
Study of Reading at the University of Illinois at Urbana under the direction of P.
David Pearson and others. These researchers and others are now trying to
translate what they have learned about reading comprehension into assessment
and teaching strategies which can be used by reading teachers at all levels to
improve children's comprehension ability. They have made some beginnings in
this very important effort. I have provided many ready-to-use assessment and
teaching strategies, including many reproducible activity sheets, in this Kit,
which I have learned, modified, and tried with children at various reading levels.
A number of them have proven to be very effective in the improvement of
children's reading comprehension. The reading teacher will find them to be
useful, time-saving aids for improving their students' reading comprehension.

Since comprehension is a very complex process, I have tried to define it here
as succinctly as possible while also being accurate and current. *I define comprehension as reconstructing and constructing meaning from the printed material.* It
must be an interactive process which requires the use of *prior knowledge (previous experiences)* which the reader brings in combination with the material that is
found on the printed page. When this definition is used, it is necessary to consider
the characteristics of both the reader and the printed material. *In the case of the
reader,* his or her prior knowledge about the material, his or her interest in
reading the material, his or her purpose for reading the material, and his or her
ability to pronounce the words in the material always must be considered. *In the
case of the printed material,* the number of difficult words must be considered, the
syntax or word order in the material, the sentence length of the material, and the
overall format of the material also must be considered.

> NOTE: I believe that in most instances *prior knowledge* is more impor-
> tant to the comprehension of the reading material than is the material
> itself. For example, a child who lacks prior knowledge of what snow is
> because he or she lives in Florida and has never seen snow normally will

not comprehend a story involving snow as well as a child who lives in northern Wisconsin where snow is abundant in the winter. It also is important to understand that the more prior knowledge a child has, the less the printed material is needed. For example, a child who has much prior knowledge about Abraham Lincoln normally will skip more words while reading about Lincoln while still retaining good comprehension than will a child with limited prior knowledge about him.

Today comprehension also can be explained in terms of the "bottom-up" theory or the "top-down" theory. The *bottom-up theory* is the more traditional and states that reading takes place in the two stages of word decoding and then of reading for meaning. The *top-down theory* is the more contemporary and states that higher-order mental structures are used to comprehend the lower-order word and sound information. Sometimes the bottom-up theory also is called the *text-driven theory*, which means that the printed material probably is the more important in reading comprehension. The top-down theory may also be called the *concept-driven theory*, meaning that the child's prior knowledge usually is the more important in reading comprehension.

> NOTE: For the most part, I believe that the top-down theory is the more accurate although I still believe that every child who is capable of doing so should learn enough sight words, phonic elements and generalizations, structural analysis elements and generalizations, and the importance of context clues to make comprehension as easy as possible for him or her.

Another aspect of contemporary research in comprehension is called *schema theory*. Schema theory tries to explain how a person stores information or knowledge in his or her mind, how the knowledge which is currently possessed is used, and how new knowledge is acquired by the person. The term *schema* (the plural is *schemata*) deals with the structure of knowledge or information in the human mind. From the aspect of schema theory, reading can be defined as the following: an active search for meaning, a constructive process, an application of different kinds of knowledge, and a strategic process.

Another useful focus of recent comprehension research tries to find the comprehension strategies which are used by mature readers. The child's own knowledge of his or her comprehension strategies or the processes being used to understand printed material currently are referred to as the *metacognitive aspect* of reading. *Metacognition* in reading, therefore, is concerned with a child's awareness of his or her own thinking as he or she is trying to understand the printed material. It is thought to be very important to teach the child to monitor his or her own comprehension while reading. A child needs to know when to use the comprehension strategies which he or she may have available to use. I have had my students use some metacognitive strategies when tutoring children recently, and they have proven to be very useful. A number of such strategies and related activity sheets for improving a child's ability in metacognition are found in later sections of the *Kit*.

The Various Levels of Comprehension

In the past, comprehension skills have been divided into four major categories by most reading specalists. They were the following: literal (factual or recall), interpretive (inferential), critical, and creative (applied). Today, however, comprehension is considered by most contemporary researchers to be a *global, language-based process* which cannot be subdivided into levels such as these. Research has discovered that reading comprehension really is composed of only two major areas: *vocabulary knowledge* (word meaning) and the *understanding* of the printed material.

Contemporary comprehension researchers sometimes say that since comprehension cannot be divided into subskills in research, the various levels of comprehension should not be taught to children. They would thus not recommend teaching such elements of comprehension as locating the directly stated and implied main ideas, locating significant and irrelevant details, learning to carry out directions, placing a number of items in correct sequence, and a number of other separate comprehension skills. Instead, as stated earlier, these researchers believe that comprehension should be taught as a global process without placing much emphasis on the separate subskills. However, I think that it is still important to attempt to teach the most important elements of comprehension separately, at least at times, to insure that both adequate and disabled readers will attain mastery in them. For example, how can a teacher be sure that a child is attaining mastery in interpretive comprehension (textually implicit comprehension) if he or she is not sure that the level of question often is being asked? As another example, how can the reading teacher be sure that the child has mastered the very important skill of learning to read and carry out directions if this element of comprehension is not taught in a fairly isolated, but meaningful manner?

Therefore, I think it is very important for the reading teacher to be aware of some of the separate subskills which comprise the various levels of comprehension. Both the contemporary and traditional names of these various levels of comprehension are included in the *Kit*, although the more modern names are generally used in later discussions. Here are the various levels of comprehension and the more important subskills of which they are comprised:

Textually Explicit (Literal or Factual) Comprehension

One important element is that of answering explicit or literal comprehension questions from the reading material. These are questions which use only the key words from the text in making the response. It may help to clarify this level of comprehension by examining the following passage from *Charlotte's Web* by E. B. White:

"Wilbur was in a panic. He raced round and round the pen. Suddenly he had an idea—he thought of the egg sac and the five hundred and fourteen little spiders that would hatch in the spring. If Charlotte herself was unable to go home to the barn, at least he must take her children along."[1]

Question: What did Wilbur want to take home with him when Charlotte herself was unable to go home to the barn?

In addition, this level of comprehension includes the following subskills:

- locating the directly stated main idea in a paragraph
- locating significant and irrelevant details in a paragraph
- placing a number of items in correct sequence or order
- reading and carrying out directions

Textually Implicit (Interpretive or Inferential) Comprehension

One important element is that of answering implicit or interpretive comprehension questions from the reading material. These are questions in which the answer is not directly stated in the text (key words from the questions do not automatically reveal its location). An effort is required to search the text for plausible answers that reflect the logical relationships between the questions and the given information. It is called "reading between the lines." It may help to clarify this level of comprehension by reading the following passage from *Charlotte's Web*:

"Wilbur's heart pounded. He began to squeal. Then he raced in circles, kicking manure into the air. Then he turned a back flip. Then he planted his front feet and came to a stop in front of Charlotte's children."[2]

Question: How did Wilbur feel when Charlotte's first baby crawled out of the sac?

In addition, this level of comprehension includes the following subskills:

- answering questions which call for interpretation
- inferring, drawing conclusions and generalization, and reading between the lines
- predicting the outcome
- sensing the author's mood and purpose
- summarizing what is read
- understanding cause-effect and comparison-contrast relationships
- locating the implied main idea

Critical (Textually Implicit or Evaluative) Reading

A number of reading specialists consider this to be an aspect of interpretive comprehension. Indeed it is very difficult to differentiate between

---

[1] E. B. White, *Charlotte's Web.* (New York: Harper & Row Pubs., Inc., 1952), p. 166.
[2] *Ibid*, p. 177.

these two levels of comprehension. However, I feel that there is enough difference between them to consider critical reading a slightly different aspect. One important element is that of answering critical or evaluative questions from the reading material. This also can be called "reading between the lines." It may help to clarify this level of comprehension by reading the following passage from *Charlotte's Web*:

"Wilbur's heart pounded. He began to squeal. Then he raced in circles, kicking manure into the air. Then he turned a back flip. Then he planted his front feet and came to a stop in front of Charlotte's children."[3]

Question: Do you believe that Wilbur treated Charlotte's babies with great care after they were born? Why do you believe as you do?

In addition, this level of comprehension includes the following subskills:

- discriminating between real and make-believe or between fact and fantasy
- evaluating the accuracy and truthfulness of the reading material
- comparing reading material from several sources
- interpreting figurative language
- sensing the author's biases
- recognizing the various propaganda techniques such as testimonials, the bandwagon effect, card-stacking, and the halo effect

Scriptally Implicit (Schema Implicit, Creative, or Applied) Comprehension

The answers to questions involving script cannot be found in the text and require a response based on relevant prior knowledge gained from experience, perception, and mental scripts. It requires combining prior knowledge with the knowledge gained from reading to develop and use new insights. This is called "reading between the lines." It may help to clarify this level of comprehension by examining the following question:

Question: Why would two such different characters as Charlotte (a spider) and Wilbur (a pig) become such good friends?

In addition, this level of comprehension includes the following subskills:

- application of knowledges gained from reading to one's own life for problem-solving
- cooking and baking activities after reading simplified recipes
- creative writing of prose and poetry
- art activities as a follow-up to reading

---

[3]*Ibid*, p. 177.

- construction activities as a follow-up to reading
- rhythm activities as a follow-up to reading
- creative dramatics and sociodrama
- scientific experiments
- puppetry
- creative book reports
- the reading of materials which appeal to the emotions or the affective domain of reading

A Final Statement

Thus, comprehension can be defined as an active process placing great emphasis on prior knowledge while reconstructing meaning. Although comprehension has been emphasized in reading instruction in the past to some extent, it needs to receive much more stress in the future for it is the purpose of all reading. The next six sections of the *Reading Comprehension Activities Kit* provide countless classroom-tested strategies, activity sheets, and resource lists for assessing and improving your students' reading comprehension.

2

Assessing Comprehension Ability

It is vitally important that teachers of reading learn how to use contemporary, practical ways of assessing children's comprehension ability so they can provide effective corrective or remedial instruction if needed. There are many recent informal and standardized devices to assess comprehension ability that are not commonly used but have great potential for evaluating it in light of the modern view of comprehension detailed in the first section of this resource.

Section 2 of the *Kit* gives the reading teacher many strategies, checklists, and other informal assessment devices that can be reproduced and used in their present form. Most of these materials reflect the contemporary view of comprehension. In addition, the section discusses and provides examples of traditional and modern standardized means of assessing comprehension ability.

This section begins by defining the terms *assessment* and *testing* and then presents several strategies for process-oriented ways of assessing reading comprehension. These are followed by two ready-to-use checklists for assessing all of the elements of comprehension ability—one for the upper primary-grade level and one for the intermediate-grade level. Next the section provides ideas and an activity sheet for assessing a child's prior knowledge before reading a selection and a device for determining if a child monitors his or her comprehension, that can be duplicated and used in its present form. Also included is a comprehension rating scale on the fourth-grade level. All of these ready-to-use devices will help the reading teacher assess a child's competencies in all of the elements of reading comprehension that are currently emphasized.

Next, the section discusses Individual Reading Inventories and group reading inventories and their use in comprehension assessment, and provides an example of the latter type of informal diagnostic device. This is followed by discussions of the traditional cloze procedure and the maze technique with examples of each at the fifth-grade and fourth-grade reading levels, respectively.

The last part of Section 2 describes standardized reading comprehension assessments, including survey reading and achievement tests, criterion-referenced tests, individual and group diagnostic reading tests, and various standardized process-oriented measures of comprehension. Included is one ready-to-use example of a reading assessment test at the third-grade level which evaluates topic familiarity, constructing meaning questions, and use of reading strategies. This type of test is now being used in several states such as Illinois and Michigan and may be much more commonly used in the future.

After reading this section of the *Reading Comprehension Activities Kit*, the reading teacher will have the knowledge, insight, and reproducible materials needed to assess the comprehension ability of the students with whom he or she is working. This comprehension assessment will reflect all of the contemporary and traditional knowledge we now have in the field of reading about the teaching of reading comprehension.

How Can the Assessment and Testing of Reading Skills Be Defined?

At the outset it seems useful to define the terms *assessment* and *testing* in the way in which they are typically used by contemporary reading specialists. *Assessment* can be defined as gathering information to meet the diverse reading needs of a child. *Testing* can be defined as one particular method for obtaining information about learning.

Assessment should be considered a part of instruction, and it should occur continuously. Therefore, assessment obviously is much more informal than is testing. It is often more useful in determining a child's reading strengths and weaknesses, especially if it is done by an experienced teacher of reading. I believe that use of informal, process-oriented assessment of reading competencies is very likely to be more common in the future than use of standardized measures of reading ability. Such informal or internal assessment of reading ability should be done on an individual or small-group basis and should be the basis for subsequent diagnostic-prescriptive teaching of reading for an individual child or a small group of children. This section contains many useful, informal means of reading assessment which should prove useful to the reading teacher as he or she attempts to teach reading more prescriptively.

On the other hand, testing generally means some type of standardized reading device which is given to a group of children or to an individual child. Testing in reading has not changed significantly since the 1920s or the 1930s. For example, *retelling* was the important means of determining comprehension ability in the 1920s and is also used today. The standardized testing of reading has been greatly emphasized recently because of the accountability movement in education. However, as I stated earlier, I believe that informal, process-oriented means of assessment will be emphasized much more in the future with correspondingly less emphasis being placed upon the more traditional standardized testing of reading.

General Strategies for Informal, Process-Oriented Ways of Assessing Reading Comprehension

It is helpful to briefly review here some of the contemporary comprehension strategies that are the focus of this section. While most of the more traditional elements of comprehension are also assessed by the various informal and standardized devices contained in the section, the more recent elements of reading comprehension mentioned in Section 1 are assessed too.

The use of a child's *prior knowledge* as an important determiner of his or her subsequent comprehension of the printed material is the focus of several informal and standardized devices included in this section. Prior knowledge is an extremely important aspect in subsequent good comprehension. *Prequestioning* by both the child and the teacher is also discussed. The child's own purpose or purposes for reading as determined by his or her own questions is extremely important to subsequent reading comprehension. The child's *prediction strategies* also are an aspect of active comprehension and are very important in excellent reading comprehension. Therefore, prediction strategies are assessed as well.

Metacognition, as explained in Section 1, is the child's monitoring of his or her own comprehension skills and the selection of the most useful comprehension strategies. This aspect of successful comprehension is ascertained through both informal and standardized devices presented in this section. The *relating of reading and writing* is another excellent way of improving reading comprehension. *Postquestioning* both by the child and the teacher is also assessed in various informal and standardized devices in this section. Postquestioning by the child can mean testing the hypotheses made during the prediction prior to the reading. It can also mean answering higher-level questions posed by the reading teacher.

INFORMAL COMPREHENSION ASSESSMENT DEVICES

Two Checklists for Assessing Comprehension Ability

The following pages present two ready-to-duplicate checklists for the observation of a child's comprehension ability. Each checklist incorporates both the contemporary and traditional aspects of comprehension in the hope that this combination will best help the reading teacher to determine in which areas of comprehension a child is weak so that appropriate prescriptive instruction can be provided him or her. Each checklist is structured in a way that should be very useful for the reading teacher.

You can reproduce either checklist in its present form or modify it in any way you choose in light of the needs of your own students.

SECOND- THIRD-GRADE CHECKLIST OF TEACHER OBSERVATION OF A CHILD'S COMPREHENSION SKILLS

Name _____ Grade _____ Teacher _____

I. Elements of *Overall* Comprehension Ability

   A. Use of Prior Knowledge

      1. Has adequate prior knowledge (background of experiences) to interpret most narrative material at the instructional and independent reading levels   ____

      2. Has adequate prior knowledge (background of experiences) to comprehend most expository (content) material at the instructional and independent reading levels   ____

      3. Usually activates (uses) the prior knowledge possessed when reading material   ____

      4. Usually contributes useful, accurate information to group or class discussions prior to reading narrative or expository material   ____

   B. Use of Prequestioning Skills

      1. Is able to formulate his or her own textually explicit (literal) comprehension questions prior to reading a narrative or expository passage   ____

      2. Is able to formulate his or her own textually implicit (interpretive or critical) comprehension questions prior to reading narrative or expository material   ____

      3. Is able to set his or her own purposes for reading a narrative selection   ____

      4. Is able to set his or her own purposes for reading an expository selection   ____

   C. Use of Prediction Strategies

      1. Is able to predict the story content of a narrative story from its title   ____

      2. At appropriate stopping points in a narrative story, is able to predict what is going to happen next, such as "What do you think is going to happen now?"   ____

      3. Is able to evaluate if his or her hypotheses prior to reading were accurate upon completion of the reading material   ____

      4. Usually makes predictions (hypotheses) prior to reading which were determined to be accurate following the reading   ____

      5. Has a fairly good understanding of the Directed Reading-Thinking Activity (DRTA)   ____

   D. Use of Metacognitive Skills (Self-Monitoring Skills)

      1. Has a positive attitude toward reading and a good self-perception about his or her reading ability   ____

      2. Is able to understand the purpose of reading   ____

      3. Is able to modify his or her reading strategies for different purposes   ____

      4. Is able to consider how new information relates to what is already known   ____

      5. Is able to evaluate the reading material for clarity, completeness, and consistency   ____

      6. Is able to determine the important information in a passage   ____

      7. Is able to determine after reading how well the material was understood   ____

E. Semantic Networking Skills

   1. Is able to complete a partially completed semantic map or web from narrative material at the appropriate reading level   ———

   2. Is able to complete a partially completed semantic map or web from expository (content) material at the appropriate reading level   ———

F. Use of Visual Imagery

   1. Is able to make useful images while reading narrative material   ———

   2. Is able to illustrate a narrative story which has been read with illustrations not contained in the actual reading material   ———

II. Textually Explicit (Literal or Factual) Comprehension

A. Is able to answer textually explicit (literal, recall, or factual) comprehension questions from narrative material at the appropriate reading level   ———

B. Is able to answer textually explicit (literal, recall, or factual) comprehension questions from expository (content) material at the appropriate reading level   ———

C. Is able to use the retelling or tell-back technique in a fairly competent manner   ———

D. Is able to retell a story written at the appropriate reading level in about the correct sequence   ———

E. Is able to carry out written directions of about 3–5 steps in correct order   ———

F. Is able to locate significant or important details in a story in a fairly rudimentary manner   ———

G. Is able to correctly answer comprehension questions from material which is read aloud to him or her from material at about the fourth- or fifth-grade reading level (listening comprehension)   ———

H. Understands that "Right There" questions are examples of textually explicit, literal, factual, or recall comprehension questions   ———

III. Textually Implicit (Interpretive or Inferential) Comprehension Skills

A. Is able to answer textually implicit (interpretive or inferential) comprehension questions from narrative material at the appropriate reading level. These questions call for interpreting, inferring, drawing conclusions and generalizations, predicting outcomes, and summarizing   ———

B. Is able to answer textually implicit (interpretive or inferential) comprehension questions from expository (content) material at the appropriate reading level   ———

C. Understands that sometimes a question can have multiple acceptable responses which make sense   ———

D. Can orally summarize a tradebook or story in a short paragraph or several sentences   ———

E. Is able to summarize narrative or content material in a written summary of one or several sentences   ———

F. Is able to understand and apply simple cause-effect relationships   ———

(Continued on following page)

G. Is able to understand and orally state an author's purpose for writing a tradebook or story ⎯⎯

H. Understands that "Think and Search" questions are textually implicit (interpretive or inferential) comprehension questions ⎯⎯

IV. Critical (Textually Implicit or Evaluative) Comprehension Skills

A. Is able to answer questions that call for critical (textually implicit or evaluative) responses from narrative material at the appropriate reading level ⎯⎯

B. Is able to answer questions that call for critical (textually implicit or evaluative) responses from expository (content) material at the appropriate reading level ⎯⎯

C. Is able to distinguish between real and make-believe (fact and fantasy) with a fairly high degree of competency ⎯⎯

D. Is able to understand the feelings, actions, and motives of story characters with a rudimentary sense of competence; e.g., "Why do you believe that Joey was so unhappy in this story?" ⎯⎯

E. Understands that "Think and Search" questions are one kind of textually implicit or critical or evaluative question ⎯⎯

V. Scriptually Implicit (Creative) Reading Skills

A. Is able to combine his or her own prior knowledge (experiences or scripts) with the printed material in the understanding and application of what is read ⎯⎯

B. Is able to relate what he or she read or has had read to him or her in some way which contributes to his or her own improvement ⎯⎯

C. Is able to follow up reading in a problem-solving manner such as by cooking or baking activities, art activities, construction activities, dramatic play, creative dramatics, rhythm activities, or creative writing of prose or poetry ⎯⎯

D. Is able to relate reading and writing activities in a creative manner ⎯⎯

E. Understands that "On My Own" questions are examples of scriptually implicit or creative reading ⎯⎯

VI. Several Other Important Elements of Comprehension

A. Observes punctuation marks such as the period and the comma while reading orally ⎯⎯

B. Observes punctuation marks such as the period and comma while reading silently ⎯⎯

C. Has a rudimentary understanding of anaphoric relationships such as: John lost *his* money on the way to school. Then *he* couldn't buy a hot lunch that day. Who could not buy a hot lunch at school because *he* lost *his* money? Answer: John ⎯⎯

D. Is able to complete variations of the cloze procedure such as combining cloze with phonic analysis, cloze with options found at the bottom of the sheet, and traditional cloze at the appropriate reading level ⎯⎯

INTERMEDIATE-GRADE CHECKLIST OF TEACHER OBSERVATION OF A CHILD'S COMPREHENSION SKILLS

Name _____ Grade _____ Teacher _____

●1990 by The Center for Applied Research in Education

I. Elements of Overall Comprehension Skills

   A. Use of Prior Knowledge

      1. Has adequate prior knowledge (background of experiences) to interpret most narrative material at the appropriate reading level _____
      2. Has adequate prior knowledge (background of experiences) to interpret most expository (content) material at the appropriate reading level _____
      3. Usually activates (uses) prior knowledge possessed when reading material _____
      4. Usually contributes useful, accurate information to group or class discussions prior to reading narrative or expository (content) material _____

   B. Use of Prequestioning Skills

      1. Is able to formulate his or her own textually explicit (literal) comprehension questions prior to reading a narrative or expository (content) passage _____
      2. Is able to formulate his or her own textually implicit (interpretive or critical) comprehension questions prior to reading narrative or expository (content) material. _____
      3. Is able to formulate his or her own purposes for reading a narrative selection _____
      4. Is able to formulate his or her own purposes for reading an expository (content) selection _____

   C. Use of Prediction Strategies

      1. Is able to predict the content of narrative or expository (content) material from its title _____
      2. At appropriate stopping points in a narrative story, is able to accurately predict what is going to happen next _____
      3. Is able to evaluate if his or her hypotheses prior to reading were accurate upon completion of the reading material _____
      4. Is able to use the Directed Reading-Thinking Activity (DRTA) successfully in both narrative and expository (content) material _____
      5. Usually formulates hypotheses prior to reading which were determined to be accurate following reading _____

   D. Use of Metacognitive Skills (Self-Monitoring Skills)

      1. Is able to understand the purpose of reading _____
      2. Is able to generate his or her questions while reading _____
      3. Usually self-corrects his or her own word identification errors while reading _____
      4. Is able to modify reading strategies for different purposes _____
      5. Is able to consider how new information relates to what is already known _____
      6. Is able to know which strategies to use when the reading material is not understood well _____
      7. Is able to determine the important information in a passage _____

(Continued on following page)

8. Is able to determine after reading how well the material has been understood ____

9. Has a positive attitude toward reading and a good self-perception about his or her reading ability ____

E. Semantic Networking Skills

    1. Understands the purpose of semantic networking (webbing or mapping) ____

    2. Is able to formulate a semantic map or web from narrative material at the appropriate reading level ____

    3. Is able to formulate a semantic map or web from expository (content) material at the appropriate reading level ____

F. Use of Visual Imagery

    1. Is able to make useful visual images while reading narrative material ____

    2. Is able to use visual imagery as a comprehension strategy while reading expository (content) material

II. Textually Explicit (Literal or Factual) Comprehension Skills

A. Is able to answer textually explicit (literal, recall, or factual) comprehension questions from narrative material at the appropriate reading level ____

B. Is able to answer textually explicit (literal, recall, or factual) comprehension questions from expository (content) material at the appropriate reading level ____

C. Is able to understand the purpose of who, what, when, where, and why questions ____

D. Is able to use the retelling or tell-back technique in a competent manner with or without teacher probes ____

E. Is able to locate the directly stated main idea and/or topic sentence in a paragraph ____

F. Can write a statement of the main idea of a tradebook, basal reader story, or expository (content) selection in an acceptable manner ____

G. Can read and carry out directions at the appropriate reading level effectively ____

H. Is able to locate significant details in a paragraph at the appropriate reading level ____

I. Is able to locate irrelevant details in a paragraph at the appropriate reading level ____

J. Understands the meaning of specialized vocabulary terms in the content areas of social studies, science, and mathematics at the appropriate reading level ____

K. Understands that "Right There" questions are examples of textually explicit, literal, factual, or recall comprehension questions ____

III. Textually Implicit (Interpretive or Inferential) Comprehension Skills

A. Is able to answer textually implicit (interpretive or inferential) comprehension questions from narrative material at the appropriate reading level. These questions call for interpreting, inferring, drawing conclusions and generalizations, predicting outcomes, and summarizing ____

B. Is able to answer textually implicit (interpretive or inferential) comprehension questions from expository (content) material at the appropriate reading level ____

C. Is able to summarize in writing narrative or expository (content) material in a paragraph or a short passage ____

D. Is able to apply comparison-contrast relationships ____

E. Is able to apply cause-effect relationships ____

F. Is able to determine an author's purpose for writing a narrative or expository (content) selection ____

G. Can verify in writing the hypotheses about a selection which were made before reading it

H. Is able to locate the implied main idea in a paragraph ____

I. Understands that "Think and Search" questions are textually implicit (interpretive or inferential) comprehension questions ____

IV. Textually Implicit (Critical or Evaluative) Reading

A. Is able to answer questions which call for critical (textually implicit or evaluative) responses from narrative material at the appropriate reading level ____

B. Is able to answer questions which call for critical (textually implicit or evaluative) responses from expository (content) material at the appropriate reading level ____

C. Is able to distinguish between fact and opinion ____

D. Is able to compare material from several different sources such as a content textbook and an encyclopedia ____

E. Is able to read parts of the newspaper critically such as the editorials, letters to the editor, and the advertisements ____

F. Is able to recognize such common propaganda techniques as testimonials, the halo effect, and the bandwagon technique ____

G. Is able to evaluate the actions of an individual or a group ____

H. Is able to determine an author's biases in writing a selection of any type ____

I. Is able to evaluate the answer to a verbal problem in arithmetic ____

J. Understands that "Think and Search" questions are one kind of textually implicit (critical or evaluative) question ____

V. Scriptally Implicit (Creative) Reading Skills

A. Is able to combine his or her own prior knowledge (experiences or scripts) with the printed material in the understanding and application of what is read ____

B. Is able to relate what he or she has read in some way which contributes to his or her own improvement ____

C. Is able to relate reading and writing activities in a creative manner ____

(Continued on following page)

©1990 by The Center for Applied Research in Education

D. Is able to follow up reading in a problem-solving manner such as by cooking or baking activities, art activities, construction activities, dramatic play, creative dramatics, sociodrama, storytelling, and pantomiming _____

E. Understands that "On My Own" questions are examples of scriptally implicit or creative reading _____

VI. Several Other Important Elements of Comprehension

A. Observes punctuation marks such as a period, comma, exclamation point, semicolon, and colon while reading _____

B. Understands anaphoric relationships such as: The old man and *his* old neighbor woman both had to walk to the grocery store since neither *he* nor *she* owned a car anymore. Who had to walk to the grocery store? Answer: the old man and the old woman _____

C. Is able to complete such different variations of the cloze procedure as traditional cloze, random deletion cloze, and cloze procedures emphasizing omitting nouns, verbs, adjectives, and adverbs at the appropriate reading level _____

D. Is able to understand and apply such elements of *story grammar* as the setting, including characters and location, the basic theme, a few episodes in the plot, and the resolution of the problem that motivated the characters to action _____

E. Is competent in using guide words such as *because, so, if, as, for, when until, meanwhile, before, always, following, finally, during,* and *initially* _____

F. Understands figurative language such as the *metaphor* (She is a bear in her appetite as well as in her personality), the *simile* (She is as hungry as a bear), and *hyperbole* (You're so unpleasant that your own shadow doesn't like you) _____

G. Is able to interpret figurative language such as the following:
Don't put all your eggs in one basket
She is as high as a kite
That boy is as crazy as a loon
He has egg on his face _____

H. Usually employs a study technique while reading expository (content) material such as Survey Q3R, Survey Q4R, PQRST, POINT, or C2R _____

I. Understands such paragraph patterns as enumeration, comparison/contrast, sequence, cause/effect, and question and answer _____

J. Is competent in the use of context clues (semantic clues) as an aid to comprehension _____

K. Is competent in the use of word order (syntactic clues) as an aid to comprehension _____

L. Is able to use such *typographical aids* as bold print, italics, headings, subheadings as an aid to comprehension _____

M. Is able to write a cohesive story using such parts as planning, composing, and revising _____

N. Is able to use a teacher's *prompts* (guidance) after giving the incorrect answer to a comprehension question _____

Assessing Prior Knowledge

As stated in Section 1, a reader's prior knowledge is extremely important in influencing the degree of success he or she has with comprehending a passage effectively. If a student lacks prior knowledge about the topic which he or she is to read, the student will have great difficulty comprehending the material.

One of the more obvious but very effective ways of assessing a child's or a group of children's prior knowledge is simply to note the contributions made to a group or class discussion about a topic prior to reading about it. Sometimes the teacher asks the children to give some ideas which they already have about a topic, and these are listed on the chalkboard or a transparency. Other times these ideas are made into a semantic map or web which is placed on the chalkboard or a transparency. (Semantic maps or webs are explained in detail in Sections 3, 5, and 6 of the *Kit*.)

The *PReP Procedure* can be used to assess and activate a child's prior knowledge before reading a selection. It is probably most effective with an expository (content) selection. Very briefly here is how it can be used to assess prior knowledge:

1. The teacher chooses three major concepts from a 700- to 800-word content textbook passage. As an example, from a passage about the Soviet Union, the teacher might select the concepts: *Communism, glasnost*, and *atheism*.

2. The teacher then tells the children that they will be using what they already know about the important ideas that will appear in the passage they are going to read. The children are told that this prereading discussion will help the teacher to determine if any additional background discussion is needed before they read the story. They are also told that this discussion will help them activate their own prior knowledge of the material because readers comprehend new information by relating it to what they already know.

3. The children are to make associations with the first important concept. "Tell anything that comes to your mind when you hear the term *communism*." The teacher then writes down the children's responses in the form of a semantic map as illustrated:

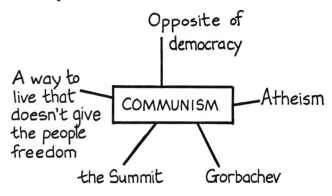

4. The next step is for the teacher to ask the children to think about their initial associations. "What made you think about _____?" This helps the children to better develop their associations with the concept being talked about.

5. The final step is to ask the children to rethink their knowledge about the concepts being discussed. The teacher can say: "Considering our discussion, do you have any new ideas about _____?" This step helps the children to understand any new or modified associations formulated from the discussion. The procedure is repeated for each major concept.[4]

This prereading discussion helps the teacher learn how much prior knowledge the child or children have about the topic to be read. If they have much prior knowledge, the responses will be in the form of a superordinate concept. (Communism is a form of government in which the state is more important than the interests of the individual people in it.) If the children lack prior knowledge in the topic, the responses are normally in the form of examples. (Communism is used in Russia.)

Another similar procedure was recently described by Zalulak, Samuels, and Taylor.[5] In this way of assessing children's prior knowledge, the teacher has them free-associate orally or in writing with several key concepts about the material which they are to read (normally from a content textbook). For example, free associations for Arizona might be as follows:

Arizona—state

Arizona—Southwest

Arizona—desert

Arizona—cactus

Arizona—gila monsters

Arizona—scorpions

On the other hand, free associations for Phoenix might be the following:

Phoenix—large city

Phoenix—United States

From these two examples it can be seen that this group of children knew quite a bit about Arizona but very little about Phoenix. Thus, much more prior knowledge would have to be presented to this group of children before reading about Phoenix than before reading about Arizona.

---

[4]Adapted from Judith A. Langer, "From Theory to Practice: A Prereading Plan," *Journal of Reading*, Volume 25 (November, 1981), pp. 152–156.

[5]Adapted from Beverly L. Zalulak, S. Jay Samuels, and Barbara M. Taylor, "A Simple Technique for Estimating Prior Knowledge: Word Association," *Journal of Reading*, Volume 30 (October, 1986), pp. 56–60.

Assessing Prior Knowledge Activity Sheet

As another way of assessing a child's prior knowledge about a topic, the reading teacher can put a list of terms on an activity sheet. Some of the terms should be related to the content material to be read, while others should be unrelated. Have the child then place a check-mark next to all of the words on the list which are related to the topic about which they are going to read. For example, this section provides a sample prior knowledge assessment activity sheet at the intermediate-grade reading level which follows this format. You may duplicate this sheet, revise it in any way you wish, or use it as a model for your own assessment of prior knowledge activity sheets which your students use before they read a content assignment.

ASSESSMENT OF PRIOR KNOWLEDGE ACTIVITY SHEET
(Intermediate-grade level)

Name _____ Grade _____ Teacher _____

You are going to read a passage later about the Sonoran Desert in the South-western part of the United States. Place a check-mark in front of each term which you believe probably will be included in the passage which you will read.

_____ Atlantic Ocean

_____ gila monster

_____ roadrunner

_____ saguaro cactus

_____ lobster

_____ balsam evergreen

_____ tarantula

_____ scorpion

_____ arid

_____ desert

_____ rain forest

_____ snowfall

_____ coyote

_____ prickly pear

_____ barrel cactus

_____ hippopotamus

_____ mesquite tree

_____ Tucson

_____ arroyo

_____ Minneapolis

_____ Phoenix

_____ lake

_____ heat

```
┌─────────────────────────────────────────┐
│              Answer Key                   │
│                                           │
│  gila monster       coyote                │
│  roadrunner         prickly pear          │
│  saguaro cactus     barrel cactus         │
│  tarantula          mesquite tree         │
│  scorpion           Tucson                │
│  arid               arroyo                │
│  desert             Phoenix               │
│                     heat                  │
└─────────────────────────────────────────┘
```

A Self-Monitoring Checklist of Reading Comprehension

As stated in Section 1, one of the contemporary research emphases in reading comprehension is that of *metacognition* or the child's monitoring of his or her own comprehension ability. It is very important that the child be cognizant of his or her own competencies and weaknesses in comprehension so that appropriate correction strategies can be selected and used to improve reading comprehension.

The following page presents a self-monitoring checklist of reading comprehension which can be duplicated and used in its present form if the reading teacher wishes. It also can be modified or used as a model for other checklists.

SELF-MONITORING CHECKLIST OF READING COMPREHENSION
(Upper-primary or intermediate-grade level)

Name _____ Grade _____ Teacher _____

	Yes	No
1. Do I already know something about what this material is going to be about?	___	___
2. Do I need to read every word of this material carefully?	___	___
3. Do I need to read the *first sentence* of each paragraph in this material more than once?	___	___
4. Do I need to read *all* of the material *more than once* to understand it?	___	___
5. Do I need to ask myself some questions about what the material may be about before I begin to read it?	___	___
6. Do I need to predict what the material will be about even before I begin to read it?	___	___
7. Do I understand just why I am going to read this material?	___	___
8. Do I know just how fast I should probably read this material?	___	___
9. Do I know what to do when I meet a word in the material that I don't understand?	___	___
10. Do I know what to do if I don't understand the material at all after I have finished reading it?	___	___
11. Am I able to answer most of my teacher's questions after I have read the material?	___	___
12. Am I able to remember what I have read well enough to do well on a test about the material?	___	___
13. Do I know how to decide which is the important information in the material I have read and which information in the material is not very important?	___	___
14. Do I look up the meaning of unknown words in the dictionary?	___	___
15. If I don't understand just one part of the story, do I usually *reread just that one part*?	___	___
16. Can I state the main idea of the material after I have finished reading it?	___	___

A Self-Monitoring Comprehension Rating Sheet

As stated a number of times before, it is very important that children learn to monitor or assess their own comprehension ability. They should know when they do and do not understand what they are reading. They also should be able to find the sources of their comprehension difficulty when they do not understand what they are reading. In addition, they should know how to correct the comprehension difficulties which they are experiencing.

One technique for assessing a child's self-monitoring skills of reading comprehension is to ask him or her to rate a number of paragraphs in a reading selection in terms of his or her ability to comprehend it. The child can use a three-point rating system. In this system the child can rate each paragraph of a longer selection in terms of whether he or she understands it very well, fairly well, or not very well at all. The reading material should be copied with blanks placed at the end of each paragraph and at the end of the selection for the child's rating. Then a number of different types of vocabulary, explicit, and implicit comprehension questions should be provided which assess the child's actual comprehension of the material. Obviously, the child's own assessment of his or her comprehension ability should closely match his or her actual performance following the selection. If they do not, the child needs to have instruction in the concept and application of self-monitoring of reading comprehension.[6]

An example of a self-monitoring comprehension rating sheet follows. You can duplicate and use it with your own students if it is applicable. More importantly, it can serve as a model for you in developing your own self-monitoring comprehension rating sheet based upon narrative or expository (content) material which the child needs to know how to comprehend.

---

[6]Adapted from Beth Davey, and Sarah M. Porter, "Comprehension Rating: A Procedure to Assist Poor Comprehenders." *Journal of Reading*, Volume 26 (December, 1982), pp. 197–202.

SELF-MONITORING COMPREHENSION RATING SHEET
(Approximately fifth-grade reading level)

Name _____   Grade _____   Teacher _____

In each blank line at the end of each paragraph, put a *1* if you understood the passage very well, a *2* if you understood the paragraph pretty well, and a *3* if you did not understand that paragraph very well at all. You can also put a *1*, *2*, or *3* to show your understanding of the entire passage in the box at the end of the passage. Then you should answer the comprehension questions found at the end of the passage.

Jacqueline Jackson—Influential Wife

1. Jacqueline (Jackie) Jackson, wife of prominent black leader Jesse Jackson, is an interesting, influential person in her own right. Her friends say that she has had more influence on the career and life of her husband than anyone else. However, she is mainly a private person who has so far put the interests of her husband and children ahead of any of her own personal interests. She has been described as elusive, private, and mainly unknown to the public—a direct contrast to her outgoing, forceful husband.   _____

2. Jacqueline Lavinia Davis Brown Jackson was born 47 years ago to a 15-year-old mother who was a migrant worker who then earned 15 cents an hour picking beans in a field. She had no father for awhile until her mother eventually married Julius Brown, a civilian employee of the Navy who later worked in the post office. Her mother worked outside the home while raising her children in a pleasant, two-story house in a quiet neighborhood in Newport News, Virginia. Jackie was raised very well. For example, a typical meal might be pork chops, corn, and green beans, and the children usually were in bed by about 8:30 p.m.   _____

3. Neighbors who lived next door to the Browns said that Jackie was always the different child in the family. She always was the girl who wanted to get ahead and amount to something. She had a great drive to excel. Jackie went to college in North Carolina where she met and later married Jesse Jackson, a top athlete and a popular young man on the campus. She did not finish her college education, instead concentrating on having and raising her family of five children. However, Jackie wants to finish her college education after all of her children have completed college.   _____

4. Jackie and Jesse Jackson used to live in a two-story, fifteen-room house on the South Side of Chicago, but recently have established residency in Washington, D.C. They have five children—three boys and two girls. Their children are all very political because they have traveled with their father many times. They also always were included in the family parties where they met many famous people. Therefore, all of the Jackson's children have always been interested in political issues.   _____

©1990 by The Center for Applied Research in Education

5. Jackie Jackson always has been mainly interested in the women's and children's issues. She is concerned about the fact that so many women and children are living in poverty and is interested in helping them. She is a very religious person and is a forceful public speaker on the issues that concern her. She often gives advice to her husband, Jesse Jackson, and says that sometimes he takes her advice and sometimes he doesn't. However, she says that she has never taken advantage of her relationship with her husband. _____

Comprehension Questions

1. Jackie Jackson probably can best be described as a person who is
   a. private   b. outgoing   c. selfish   d. flamboyant
2. Although the story does not tell you directly, it makes you believe that
   a. Jackie's mother probably was from a very poor family
   b. Jackie's mother probably was from a very wealthy family
   c. Jackie's mother probably was not a very good mother
3. The word in paragraph *1* that means *hard to define* is

   _____.

4. Jackie Jackson probably did not finish her college education because
   a. she did not do well in college
   b. she wanted to get married to Jesse Jackson and have children
   c. she probably could not afford to keep on going to college
5. The word in paragraph *3* which means *to succeed* is

   _____.

6. One of the issues in which Jackie Jackson's children probably are interested may be
   a. civil rights
   b. Europe
   c. the Eskimos of Alaska
7. Jackie Jackson wants to finish her college education some day.
        Yes   No   It doesn't say
8. Jackie Jackson is mainly interested today in
   a. women's issues
   b. the issues of Central America
   c. the banking industry
9. Jesse Jackson always takes his wife's advice on political issues.
        Yes   No   It doesn't say
10. The word in paragraph *5* that means *poor* is _____.

```
┌─────────────────────────────────────┐
│              Answer Key              │
│                                      │
│      1. a            6. a            │
│      2. a            7. yes          │
│      3. elusive      8. a            │
│      4. b            9. no           │
│      5. excel       10. poverty      │
│                                      │
└─────────────────────────────────────┘
```

Using a Comprehension Rating Scale

Another informal, process-oriented means of assessing comprehension ability is a type of *comprehension rating scale*. This is a way to strengthen the diagnostic value of typical multiple-choice questions so that children must rate each alternative answer as to the probability of correctness rather than having them select only the one best answer. This should enable students to judge the correctness of all of the four options to a multiple-choice question rather than to select just one correct answer.[7]

Children can use a rating scale of *1* through *4* with *1* indicating the most likely correct answer and *4* indicating the least likely correct answer.

Here is an example of this type of activity:

The reason that John Wilkes Booth assassinated Abraham Lincoln probably was that

    __3__   John Wilkes Booth was a Southerner.

    __4__   John Wilkes Booth wanted to die.

    __1__   John Wilkes Booth wanted to punish Lincoln because the South had been defeated in the Civil War.

    __2__   John Wilkes Booth could not accept the fact that the South had lost the Civil War.

Notice that the first alternative is an example of a literal, low-level although accurate response. On the other hand, the second alternative is unknown to the student—merely a speculation that is not supported in the text either explicitly or implicitly. The third alternative requires an implicit response or an inference

---

[7]Sandra McCormick, *Remedial and Clinical Reading Instruction.* (Columbus, Ohio: Merrill Publishing Company, 1987), pp. 148–149.

from the student and is probably the correct motivation for Booth's action. Finally, the last alternative is also an implicit and probably accurate response, but not, in my opinion, as accurate as is the third alternative. However, an argument could be made about this fact. This is at the essence of responding at the higher levels of comprehension. There often is more than one correct, logical answer to a textually or scriptally implicit question.

Sample Comprehension Assessment Scale

The following page presents a sample comprehension rating scale which you can duplicate and use in your classroom in its present form or modify in any way you wish. It should serve as a model for this type of comprehension assessment.

COMPREHENSION ASSESSMENT SCALE
(Approximately fourth-grade level)

Name ——————————————— Grade ——— Teacher ———————————

FLORIDA

Florida is an exceedingly unusual state in many ways. It is found in the Southeastern part of the United States.

The northwestern part of Florida is called the "Panhandle." This part of Florida has lovely beaches located on the Gulf of Mexico. It also is where the Pensacola Naval Air Station is located.

Surprisingly, Florida also is the home of a number of cattle ranches. They are located in the north central part of the state. How many of you knew that Florida has cowboys?

The central part of the state is best known for the fantastic amusement park Disneyworld. Many thousands of adults and children from all over the world have visited Disneyworld since it has opened. Epcot Center is another popular tourist attraction located in the center of the state near the city of Orlando. It contains many examples of future inventions that are very interesting. The area around Orlando is now very busy due to both Disneyworld and Epcot Center.

Both the southeast and southwest coasts of Florida are the home of beautiful, sun-filled beaches which are the attraction for many visitors from the northern part of the country. The east coast in particular is the home of many new high-rise hotels and luxurious resorts.

One of the most interesting parts of Florida are the Florida Keys, a chain of lovely islands that stretch south of Miami. These islands are connected by a series of bridges, with the bright blue Atlantic Ocean on the east and the equally bright blue Gulf of Mexico on the west. At the end of Highway 1 through the Keys is found the city of Key West, the city that is located the farthest south of any city in the country.

If you have the opportunity to do so, visit Florida. You'll be glad you did.

Now answer each of these questions by placing a 1 by the best answer, a 2 by the next best answer, a 3 by the next best answer, and a 4 by the poorest answer.

1. The reason that Florida is considered to be an unusual state is

——— it has beautiful beaches

——— it contains many different types of areas

——— Disneyworld and Epcot Center are two very different types of tourist attractions

——— it is able to attract many different types of tourists

2. The reason that most people don't know that Florida is a cattle state is that

——— it is much better known as a tourist state

——— it has fewer cowboys than Texas

——— Florida is surrounded by water

——— the movies have never shown Florida cowboys

3. Orlando is a rapidly growing city mainly because

_____ it is in the central part of the state

_____ so many tourist attractions are located near it

_____ it is not on a body of water

_____ it is the home of Disneyworld

4. Most of the resorts on the southeastern coast of Florida are the most expensive to rent in

_____ winter

_____ summer

_____ fall

_____ spring

Answer Key

The following answers are my view of the best answers. Children who can defend other answers should have them considered correct.

1. 4	2. 1	3. 3	4. 1
1	4	1	4
3	3	4	3
2	2	2	2

Quick Assessment Procedure for Instructional Reading Level

Albert J. Harris and Edward R. Sipay have formulated a quick assessment on reading comprehension which may be useful to the teacher of reading. This informal device should only be used for preliminary screening of reading comprehension and should be followed up by a more in-depth, informal, or standardized assessment procedure. As Harris and Sipay state in their textbook:

> "For a quick check on comprehension, one can choose a short selection (four or five pages) from near the beginning of the book and ask the children to read it silently. As each child finishes, he or she closes the book and looks up; in this way, the slowest readers are spotted quickly. When all have finished, the teacher can read a list of questions to which the pupils write their answers. The children who score below *60%* are likely to have difficulty understanding the book; the *60%* scorers are marginal.[8]"

It is obvious from reading Section 1 of this book that the questions should include textually explicit, textually implicit, and scriptally implicit types. Especially at the intermediate-grade level, the higher-level questions should be much more emphasized. Of course, they should also receive emphasis in the primary grades.

---

[8]From *How to Increase Reading Ability* by Albert J. Harris and Edward R. Sipay. Copyright © 1980 by Longman Inc. Reprinted by permission of Longman Inc.

The Individual Reading Inventory

The Individual Reading Inventory (IRI—also called the Informal Reading Inventory) is one way of assessing a child's comprehension ability in an informal manner. Although it has been used for a long time and certainly does not assess comprehension ability completely accurately, it still may be very useful in assessing comprehension ability especially if the questions which accompany each oral or silent reading passage contain some textually implicit (interpretive or critical) and scriptally implicit (creative) comprehension questions.

As you may know, the Individual Reading Inventory is an informal device which is designed to attempt to determine a child's *approximate* independent, high instructional, instructional, low instructional, and frustration reading levels. It also can be used to determine a child's specific reading skill strengths in such areas as sight word recognition, phonic analysis, structural analysis, contextual analysis, and the various elements of comprehension. Although it could usefully be given to all students in an elementary classroom, it usually is given only to disabled readers in special reading programs due to the time which is involved in giving and scoring it. It most typically is given by Chapter I reading teachers and teachers in any other type of reading clinic to the disabled readers with whom they are going to work near the beginning of tutoring sessions. In tutoring sessions that I have supervised, my college students give an interest inventory at the first session during which time rapport with the child is established, and the IRI is given during the second and third tutoring sessions.

As stated before, the Individual Reading Inventory is not well-accepted by all reading specialists and may be considered somewhat traditional today. However, if it is structured properly to include enough implicit comprehension question, I think that it can be very useful in determining a child's *tentative* reading levels and reading strengths and weaknesses. However, I always emphasize that any IRI should be considered as only a *very tentative indicator* of a child's independent, instructional, frustration, and capacity levels. It certainly is *not* a standardized device nor was it designed to be one.

The IRI as it is known today originated with Emmett A. Betts and his doctoral student Patsy K. Kilgallon. Kilgallon established criteria for accuracy in word identification and comprehension which then were tested with 41 students. However, in this informal reading test the children read each passage silently and then orally, which is a very different procedure than that normally used when giving the IRI today. Today the child reads many of the passages orally first. Betts then spelled out his definitions of the independent, instructional, and frustration reading levels in a textbook which was published in 1946.[9] In my two IRIs which have been published by The Center for Applied Research in

---

[9]Emmett A. Betts, *Foundation of Reading Instruction.* (New York: American Book Company, 1946), pp. 448–481.

Education and which are listed shortly, I use somewhat different criteria as the result of trying these criteria with hundreds of children for many years in various types of tutoring situations.

The Individual Reading Inventory varies somewhat in format depending on different reading specialists. The components of the IRI which are outlined here represent one version of this useful informal diagnostic technique. It is the one which we use in tutoring. This version can be given successfully by any elementary reading teacher, Chapter I reading teacher, or a reading teacher in any other type of reading clinic.

Establishing Rapport with the Student

The reading teacher first asks the child informal questions about his or her interests, his or her hobbies, his or her after-school and weekend activities, his or her view of his or her reading ability, and his or her strengths and weaknesses in reading. We normally attempt to do this in a creative manner such as by tape recording it, placing the questions in a puzzle format, placing the questions in a game format, or some other interesting manner so that the child does not have to write or dictate the answers in a more formal way.

Giving the Sight Word Test

The reading teacher can give the child a sight word test such as the *Dolch Basic Sight Word Test, Fry's Instant Words*, the *Kucera-Francis Corpus (Dale Johnson List)*, or *Hillerich's 240 Starter Words*. A copy of *Fry's Instant Words* can be found in one of the following sources:

The NEW Reading Teacher's Book of Lists, by Edward B. Fry *et al* (Englewood Cliffs, NJ: Prentice-Hall, 1985), pp. 27–36.

Reading Teacher's Complete Diagnosis & Correction Manual, by Wilma H. Miller (West Nyack, NY: The Center for Applied Research in Education, 1988), pp. 97–99.

This type of test usually is given only to a child who is severely or moderately disabled in reading and who has evidenced weakness in sight word recognition by teacher observation. Otherwise, it overlaps to a great extent with the graded word lists on an IRI.

Giving the Graded Word Lists

The graded word lists in an IRI usually are lists of words which begin at the preprimer or primer level and end at the twelfth-grade reading level. There usually are 20 or 25 words in each list. The child is to read each word aloud, and continues until he or she reaches the obvious frustration reading level. The main purpose of giving the sight word lists is to determine how well the child is able to pronounce words in isolation in comparison to pronouncing words in context and to determine at about which level to begin having the child read the oral reading paragraphs.

Giving the Graded Oral Reading Paragraphs

The graded oral reading paragraphs are a series of passages which begin at the preprimer or primer level and usually continue through the twelfth-grade reading level. Some of the passages can be used for a silent reading measure or for a listening comprehension test. Obviously all children do not read all of the paragraphs either silently or orally. A child usually begins reading a paragraph orally which is about two or more grade levels below his or her estimated instructional reading level. This estimation can be made from teacher observation or from the word lists as mentioned earlier. Each IRI has its own directions on how to evaluate the graded oral reading paragraphs of that IRI. There are considerable differences in this evaluation.

Giving Inventories in the Word Identification Techniques

The last part of an IRI sometimes is the giving of an informal inventory in the word identification techniques of phonic analysis, structural analysis, and contextual analysis. These inventories normally are given only to those students who evidence a clear weakness in the particular word identification technique by the use of teacher observation or some other standardized means.

General Directions for Giving and Evaluating the Graded Word Lists and Graded Oral Reading Paragraphs of an Individual Reading Inventory

Since all of the Individual Reading Inventories vary somewhat in format, the directions for giving and evaluating an IRI which are contained in this section are necessarily very general. You will have to study the directions of the IRI which you are going to give in detail to learn how to give it.

I believe that it is essential for the reading teacher to tape-record the entire administration of an IRI since it is so difficult to mark the miscues (errors) as the child reads, and it also makes him or her anxious when he or she sees the teacher marking miscues (errors) of various kinds as he or she is reading. I recommend that all of the marking be done later when the tape recording is played back. This has proven to be the most successful procedure in the tutoring situations which I have supervised.

When using the graded word lists, have the child begin pronouncing the words aloud on a word list that is at least two reading levels below his or her estimated instructional reading level. Have the child continue pronouncing the words on the graded word lists until he or she reaches the point when he or she can pronounce less than *80% to 90%* of the words on a list correctly. This could be called his *ceiling or frustration level*. Later when the reading teacher evaluates the performance on the graded word lists, a + can be placed by each word pronounced correctly, while a − or a 0 can be placed by each word pronounced incorrectly. The child's mispronunciation of a word can also be written on the teacher's copy of the graded word lists. The percentages contained on the word lists found later in this section can be used in determining a child's performance in pronouncing the word lists in terms of his or her independent, instructional, or frustration reading levels.

Then the reading teacher should have the child begin reading aloud the oral reading paragraph which corresponds to the level at which at least *80%-90%* of the words on a list were recognized. It is *very* important to have a child begin reading aloud at a low enough level so that he or she will experience success at the beginning and not become discouraged. Have the child continue reading succeeding paragraphs aloud until he or she reaches the frustration reading level, the point at which obvious signs of frustration and nervousness are reached. After the child has finished reading each paragraph orally, ask the comprehension questions which accompany that paragraph. They should be of both the explicit (literal) and implicit (interpretive, critical, and creative) levels.

NOTE: It is very important to prepare the child for reading each of the paragraphs by activating his or her prior knowledge before the material is read aloud.

If you wish, you also can read aloud the next more difficult paragraph to the child and ask him or her the comprehension questions which accompany it in an attempt to establish a *potential or capacity level* (the level to which he or she may learn to read with excellent prescriptive reading instruction).

As you will see from examining any of the IRIs included in the list in this section, there are a number of ways in which the word lists and the paragraphs can be used in any reading program. They can be given in such ways as oral-silent-oral, silent-oral, oral-silent, and silent-oral-oral. Normally, each IRI contains at least two parallel forms though some of them contain even more than that.

Later the reading teacher can mark the child's oral reading miscues (errors) by playing back the tape recording. Although each IRI has its own system for marking oral reading miscues, I have included the marking system which I used in the two publications which I have written that are cited later. Here is that marking system:

Omissions	Circle the entire word or letter sound	(of)
Additions	Insert with a caret	prętty
Draw a line through a substitution or mispronunciation and write in the correct word		than ~~then~~
Reversals	Use the transposition symbol	⌐from ⌐out⌐

| Repetitions | Use a wavy line to indicate a repetition of *two* or more words | old man |
| Words Aided | If the child says nothing after about five seconds, give him or her the word and then cross it out | ~~elephant~~ |

There are two major purposes for giving the graded oral reading paragraphs of an IRI. They are to determine the child's *approximate* reading levels and to determine the *pattern* of the reading miscues which he or she has made. All of the commonly used IRI's vary somewhat in how they determine the child's reading levels in that they score the oral reading miscues somewhat differently. To help you understand approximately how the oral reading miscues are evaluated, I include the following concepts which are applicable *only* to the IRIs that I have written. After each statement, I have indicated how the other major IRI's deal with this issue.

1. Count as a *major* oral reading miscue and deduct one point for any error which interferes significantly with comprehension. Some examples are *horse for house, stop for spot, was for saw, then for than,* and *but for bet.* Notice that this takes into account the *primary importance of comprehension* over mere word identification. While a few other IRIs also consider this issue, most of them count all of the word identification miscues as the same.

2. Count as a *minor* oral reading miscue and deduct one-half point for any deviation from the printed text which does not seem to interfere significantly with comprehension. Some examples are *joyful for happy, sad for unhappy, large for big,* and *lady for woman.* Although a few IRIs mark the oral reading miscues in this manner, most of them give the same weight to oral reading miscues which do not interfere with comprehension as they do to those that do interfere with comprehension.

3. Count an addition as half an oral reading miscue if it does not change the meaning of the material significantly. Usually an addition is a *minor* oral reading miscue since it does not interfere with comprehension significantly. Most other IRIs count an addition as one oral reading miscue and do not consider whether or not it interferes with comprehension.

4. Do *not* count a self-correction as an error if it occurs within a short period of time such as five seconds. A self-correction often indicates that the child is attempting to correct the error himself or herself and thus is *reading for meaning,* obviously the most important aspect of reading. Some IRIs count self-corrections as errors, while some do not.

5. Count a repetition as half an oral reading miscue if it occurs on *two or more words.* A repetition of a single word may indicate that the child is

trying to correct the word. The repetition may give the child some "thinking time" in figuring out the word. Some IRIs count a repetition of a single word as an error, while a few count a repetition of two or more words as an error. There is considerable difference in this area.

6. Do *not* count more than one oral reading miscue on the same word in any one paragraph or passage. For example, if the child mispronounces the same word more than once while reading an oral reading paragraph, count it as an error only once. To count it each time would unduly penalize the child. I believe that most IRIs count the errors in this way.

7. Do not count an oral reading miscue on any *proper noun* which is found in any paragraph. I believe that this is standard practice in the way in which IRIs are evaluated.

8. Deduct one point for any word which a child cannot pronounce after about five seconds if that word *interferes with comprehension*. Deduct one-half point for any word which a child cannot pronounce after about five seconds if that word *does not seem to interfere with comprehension*. Thus, comprehension is seen to be the primary purpose of reading in scoring the IRI in this manner. There is considerable variation among IRIs in this regard. A number of them count each word which is not pronounced as an oral reading error whether or not it interferes with comprehension.

9. Do *not* count as an oral reading miscue that which exemplifies the child's cultural and regional dialect. To do this, you must be quite familiar with the basic characteristics of the child's dialect. Although not all IRIs consider this principle, many more of them currently are doing so than was the case in the past.

When the reading teacher has marked all of the oral reading miscues from any series of graded oral reading paragraphs, he or she can use the information to attempt to determine the child's *approximate* independent, instructional, and frustration reading levels. Here are the basic characteristics of the three major reading levels which are used in IRIs although there is some variation depending upon the IRI:

Independent reading level—The point at which the child is *about 99%* accurate in word identification and has *95%* or better comprehension

Instructional reading level—The point at which the child is about *90%-95%* accurate in word identification and has *75%* or better comprehension

Frustration reading level—The point at which the child is less than about *90%-95%* accurate in word identification and has less than about *50%* accuracy in comprehension

However, I believe from using the graded oral reading paragraphs with hundreds of children over many years that the addition of several other reading levels in addition to the three basic reading levels can be very helpful in determining the child's actual reading level. I do this in the two publications which I wrote that are cited later in this section. Here are the additional reading levels which I use:

Low independent reading level

High instructional reading level

Low instructional reading level

You must use your judgment in arriving at these additional reading levels, and you take into account the child's word identification and comprehension skills *together*. I usually weight the child's performance *on comprehension more highly* than I weight his or her performance on word identification since comprehension is so much more important, as was emphasized in Section 1. I think that use of the three additional reading levels is justified since the graded oral reading paragraphs are *informal devices* and *cannot* be thought of as infallible indicators of a child's accurate reading levels.

The following is a fairly comprehensive list of the commercially available Individual Reading Inventories which the reader may wish to consult:

Advanced Reading Inventory—William C. Brown.
This inventory is designed for use in grades 7 through college. It can be given in a group situation.

Analytical Reading Inventory—Charles E. Merrill.
This inventory is designed to analyze the reading performance of children in grades 2-9. It consists of three forms, 21 graded word lists, and 30 graded reading selections.

Bader Reading and Language Inventory—Macmillan, Inc.
This inventory consists of 36 graded reading passages and is available in three forms. It is designed for grades preprimer through grade 12.

Basic Reading Inventory—Kendall/Hunt Publishing Company.
This inventory is available in three forms and consists of 30 graded word lists and 30 graded reading passages. It is designed for use in grades preprimer through 8.

Burns/Roe Informal Reading Inventory—Houghton Mifflin.
This inventory contains two forms of graded word lists and four forms of graded passages. It is designed for use in grades preprimer through 12.

Classroom Reading Inventory—William C. Brown.
This inventory has four forms of the graded oral reading paragraphs. Forms A and B are for the primary grades; Form C is for the Junior High/Middle School level; and Form D is for high school through the adult level. There also are graded word lists for each form and level.

Contemporary Classroom Reading Inventory—Gorsuch Scarisbrick.
This inventory is designed for use in grades primer through 9. It contains graded word lists, selections for oral reading, and cloze selections.

Ekwall Reading Inventory—Allyn & Bacon.
This inventory is designed for use in grades preprimer through 9. It consists of four forms of graded word lists and silent reading passages. It also contains a number of additional tests such as the Quick Survey Word List and the El Paso Phonics Survey.

Reading Diagnosis Kit*—The Center for Applied Research in Education.
This inventory is designed for use in grades preprimer through 12. It consists of two forms of graded word lists and oral reading passages. It also contains many other informal diagnostic devices such as cloze procedures, the maze technique, and projective devices.

Reading Miscue Inventory—Richard C. Owen.
This inventory is mainly based upon the contemporary view of reading comprehension. Its purpose is to emphasize that the purpose of reading is to gain meaning and that some miscues are "better" than others. No reading level is obtained from this inventory, but rather it provides information about strengths and weaknesses in reading strategies.

Reading Teacher's Complete Diagnosis & Correction Manual*—The Center for Applied Research in Education.
This reading resource for teachers contains one individual reading inventory for use in grades preprimer through 12. It also contains many diagnostic and corrective reading strategies.

Using Group Reading Inventories

Many children in the intermediate grades and secondary school have some or great difficulty in comprehending and studying their selected social studies, science, or arithmetic textbooks. You can use a variation of a *group reading inventory* to determine if your students have the abilities to comprehend a content textbook effectively. Although lower-level content textbooks in these areas need to be provided if possible for moderately and severely disabled readers, many of the other children should be taught the unique reading-study skills which are needed for successful comprehension in these content areas. A variation of a group reading inventory can help you to determine the special reading-study skills that should be presented in the content areas.

There are several somewhat different variations of group reading inventories. One such variation tries to determine if a group of children can use the various aids which are included in the chosen content textbook. This informal inventory usually is given at the beginning of a course or semester. To formulate such an inventory, construct about 20 to 25 questions on the use of textbook aids such as the table of contents, the glossary, the maps, the index, the italicized words, the diagrams, the pictures, the tables, and the graphs. The students then try to complete the inventory by using their textbook to answer the questions.

---

*These sources were authored by Wilma H. Miller.

Another version of a group reading inventory is designed to ascertain if students can successfully comprehend and study a chosen content textbook. To make this type of inventory, the reading teacher selects a passage of about 1,000 to 2,000 words near the middle of the content textbook. Each child then answers an open-ended question such as the following: "What was this passage about?" Notice that this question is an example of the retelling or tell-back technique for assessing comprehension which was discussed in Section 1. Each child also should answer some objective questions about the passage. These questions should evaluate the child's competency in such reading skills as textually explicit (literal), textually implicit (interpretive or critical) comprehension, specialized vocabulary, the directly stated main idea, significant details, irrelevant details, and the implied main idea.

The third version of the group reading inventory is based on one specific chapter of the selected content textbook. This also is an open-book test that is given near the beginning of the class or the semester. It is designed to determine if the child possesses the unique reading skills which are required to comprehend the selected content textbook successfully. This type of informal reading inventory includes a matching vocabulary exercise containing some of the specialized vocabulary terms included in the chapter. It also can consist of textually explicit (literal), textually implicit (interpretive or critical), and creative comprehension questions as well as questions about the main ideas and important details from the chapter.

Models of each of these variations of the group reading inventories are found in the following source:

Wilma H. Miller, *Reading Diagnosis Kit*, Third Edition. West Nyack, New York: The Center for Applied Research in Education, Inc., 1986, pp. 307–310.

A Sample Group Reading Inventory

The following page presents an example of the third type of group reading inventory which was designed as a model for you. You can duplicate and use it in its present form or revise it in any way you like.

EXAMPLE OF A GROUP READING INVENTORY
BASED ON A SPECIFIC CHAPTER*
(Intermediate-grade level)

Name _____   Grade _____   Teacher _____

A. *Matching Vocabulary Exercise*

_____ 1. globe
_____ 2. map projection
_____ 3. Mercator's projection
_____ 4. interrupted projection
_____ 5. equal area map
_____ 6. map
_____ 7. parallels
_____ 8. meridians
_____ 9. Mercator map
_____ 10. longitude lines
_____ 11. latitude lines

a. a drawing of part of the earth's surface
b. the device that gives the best picture of the earth
c. distance north or south of the Equator measured in lines
d. the device which the map-maker uses to show the round earth on a flat piece of paper
e. this map is made by cutting the pictures of the earth's surface in the middle of the oceans and then flattening it out
f. distance east or west on the earth's surface measured in degrees from a certain meridian
g. a map which is good for ocean travel because it makes it easy to find directions and distances for long ocean trips
h. in this map within each four-sided section an area of the earth's surface is pictured
i. a map in which all of the areas of the world have the same shape on the map that they do on the earth
j. the circles passing through the North Pole and the South Pole of the earth
k. the circles around the earth making degrees of latitude

©1990 by The Center for Applied Research in Education

B. Put an X in front of the following statements that are true:

_____ 1. The map maker cannot make a true likeness of the round earth on a flat piece of paper.
_____ 2. On a Mercator map, the reader can get a true idea of the size of certain areas.
_____ 3. A map is a better representation of the earth than is a globe.

C. Put an X in front of the following generalizations that are true.

_____ 1. A projection is used by a map-maker in an attempt to make the map as representative as possible of the actual earth's surface.
_____ 2. An interrupted projection map shows the relationships between earth and water in an entirely accurate manner.
_____ 3. All types of maps are equally useful for the same purpose, such as studying land areas.

_____

*Formulated as a model of this type of group reading inventory.

```
┌─────────────────────────────────┐
│          Answer Key             │
│                                 │
│  A.                             │
│  1. b      8. j                 │
│  2. d      9. i                 │
│  3. g     10. f                 │
│  4. e     11. c                 │
│  5. h     B.                    │
│  6. a        ___X___  1.        │
│  7. k     C.                    │
│              ___X___  2.        │
│                                 │
└─────────────────────────────────┘
```

Using the Cloze Procedure to Assess Comprehension Ability

The *traditional cloze procedure* can be used as one informal means of assessing a child's comprehension ability. The cloze procedure was developed in 1953 by Wilson L. Taylor and is based upon the psychological theory of *closure* which states that a person wants to finish any pattern which is incomplete. The cloze procedure also is based on prediction in reading, a concept that was described in Section 1. Predicting in reading means that the reader wishes to predict the unknown words that he or she may meet in a passage. The cloze procedure makes use of both semantic (word meaning) and syntactic (word order) clues to help a person deduce the unknown words which are met in reading.

The cloze procedure has been researched in a number of different ways for many years. It has been researched in relation to its potential validity as a way of ascertaining a child's various reading levels. In addition, it has been researched as a way of improving the child's ability in comprehension and in contextual analysis.

Research has determined that the *traditional cloze procedure* may be used as an alternative or supplemental way of determining a child's independent, instructional, or frustration reading levels. However, I believe that the traditional cloze procedure probably provides a *rough estimate* of these levels. Therefore, with most disabled readers it probably is best to use the results as *only a supplement* to the reading levels established by an IRI. The cloze procedure also has many different variations which I have found in tutoring to be extremely useful in improving a child's ability in both comprehension and contextual analysis. Examples of these variations which the reading teacher can duplicate and use are found in Sections 2 and 5 of this resource. However, only *traditional cloze* can be used as an assessment procedure of comprehension ability.

To assess comprehension ability, the reading teacher can construct a traditional cloze procedure from a basal reader story, supplementary reading materials, a tradebook, or a content textbook. To construct a traditional cloze procedure, the teacher should select a passage of about 250 words at what he or she believes to be the appropriate reading level. The first and last sentences of the passage then are typed with no deletions on a ditto, stencil, or word processor. Every *fifth* word must be omitted if the traditional cloze procedure is to be used in assessment of comprehension ability.

When traditional cloze is used to determine a child's *approximate* reading levels, the reading teacher must count as correct only those completed blanks which are the same as in the original passage although incorrect spelling is not held against the child. In evaluating only the traditional cloze procedure, the reading teacher first must count the number of blanks in the passage. Next count the number of blanks which were completed with the exact deleted word. Then the reading teacher should divide the total number of blanks into the number of blanks completed with the exact omitted word to get a percentage. As an example, if a traditional cloze procedure contained 50 blanks and the student completed 25 of the blanks with the exact omitted word (even if spelled incorrectly), divide 50 into 25 to get a percentage. The child obtained *50%* of the blanks correct. Then the following percentages can be used to gain a *rough estimate* of the child's different reading levels:

independent reading level—60% or more of the blanks completed with the exact omitted word

instructional reading level—40%-60% of the blanks completed with the exact omitted word

*frustration reading level—*less than about *40%* of the blanks completed with the exact omitted word

Other reading specialists use slightly different criteria for determining approximate reading levels by the use of the cloze procedure. None of the percentages have been verified by research sufficiently to state they are entirely accurate. However, I think that the percentages given here have been verified the best by objective research. This is one of the reasons why, however, the reading levels and comprehension ability as ascertained by the traditional cloze procedure always must be considered to be only *very tentative indicators* of a child's actual instructional reading level.

Sample Cloze Exercise at the Fifth-Grade Reading Level

The following pages present one sample traditional cloze exercise at the fifth-grade reading level. You can duplicate this cloze procedure in its present form and use it to determine a child's approximate reading level and ability to comprehend the passage. It can also serve as a model for constructing a traditional cloze procedure.

TRADITIONAL CLOZE PROCEDURE*
(Approximately fifth-grade level)

Name _____ **Grade** _____ **Teacher** _____

Read this passage about Matt Henson, a black hero of the ice, silently. Write a word in each blank which makes sense. When you have completed the passage, reread it to be sure that it is correct.

MATT HENSON, BLACK HERO OF THE ICE

Most people know that Admiral Robert E. Peary and his men discovered the North

Pole in April, 1909. However, almost no one _____ that a black man

_____ Matthew "Matt" Henson went _____ the expedi-

tion with Peary _____ probably was the first _____ to

stand at the _____ of the North Pole _____ addition to

native Eskimos.

_____ was an extremely cold _____ on the gloomy

April _____ in 1909 when Matt Henson _____ his

Eskimo guides reached _____ "top of the World" _____

is the North Pole. Henson _____ the Eskimos built an

_____, a snow house made _____ blocks of ice, and

_____ waited eagerly for Peary _____ arrive and verify

whether _____ calculations were correct. Less _____

one hour later, Peary _____ and exclaimed that they

_____ were at the North Pole.

Matt Henson _____ the United States flag _____

the ice at the North Pole. _____ the news reached the United States,

_____ was very thrilling to _____ who read of it.

_____ time later Matt wrote _____ his experiences and

described _____ exciting moment: "Three cheers _____

_____

*Every fifth word was omitted from the cloze procedure except when it was a proper noun or would be unduly difficult.

(Continued on following page)

out in the still, _____ air. Our husky dogs _____ on in puzzled surprise."

_____ took Admiral Peary twenty-three _____ to reach his goal _____ being the first man _____ the North Pole. Matt Henson _____ met Peary while he _____ employed as a clerk _____ a clothing store in Washington, D.C., Peary _____ him to be his _____, and Matt accepted. Since _____ time Matt had been _____ of Peary's dream to _____ the North Pole.

To _____ for the challenge, Matt _____ learned to speak Eskimo, _____ an easy task since _____ was no written language. _____ had to learn it _____ listening, by speaking, and _____ by remembering accurately. Henson _____ to become skilled in _____ of surviving in sub-zero _____. One other member of _____ Peary expedition has stated _____ Matt that he was _____ most popular man aboard _____ with the Eskimos. He _____ talk their language like _____ native. He made all _____ sleds that went to _____ North Pole, and he _____ all the stoves.

In 1945 Congress _____ Matt Henson with a _____ for outstanding service to _____ government of the United States _____ to the field of _____. Ten years later, President Eisenhower _____ him at the White House. _____ 1965 the state of Maryland _____ a memorial plaque in _____ State House for him.

Matt Henson _____ received his recognition from

©1990 by The Center for Applied Research in Education

_____ government because of the _____ of another black explorer _____ Herbert Frisby. He spent _____ during trips to the North Pole _____ to gather evidence that Matt Henson _____ discovered the North Pole _____ Admiral Peary. After that, Frisby _____ more years bringing that _____ to the attention of _____ people who could honor _____. However, most history books _____ do not include Matt Henson's _____ along with that of Peary's? Before you read this story, had you ever heard of him?

Answer Key

knows	planted	reach	the
named	in	prepare	and
on	When	had	science
and	it	not	honored
man	everyone	there	In
site	Some	He	placed
in	about	by	its
It	the	then	mainly
day	rang	had	the
back	frosty	methods	efforts
and	looked	temperatures	named
the	It	the	years
which	years	about	attempting
and	of	the	actually
igloo	on	ship	with
of	first	could	spent
then	was	a	evidence
to	in	the	the
their	asked	the	him
than	assistant	made	still
arrived	that	presented	name
indeed	part	medal	

*There were *87* blank spaces in this cloze procedure.

Using the Maze Technique for Assessing Comprehension Ability

The *maze technique* is a fairly interesting informal way of learning more about a child's comprehension ability. However, as explained in Section 6 of the *Kit*, perhaps more importantly, it can be used to improve a child's comprehension ability. Most children whom we have tutored have enjoyed the maze technique very much and have found it much easier than the traditional cloze procedure. In any case, as a diagnostic device, the maze technique can be used as a supplement to the graded oral reading paragraphs of an IRI or a traditional cloze as an informal device for assessing a child's comprehension ability.

To construct a maze technique, choose a passage of about *120-150 words* from a basal reader story, other supplementary reading materials, a content textbook, or a tradebook on the child's approximate high-instructional or instructional level. Then modify the passage by separating it into sentences. In place of about every *fifth* word, provide three alternative words. One alternative should be the correct word, another alternative should be an incorrect word which is the same part of speech, and the third alternative should be an incorrect word which is another part of speech. Then type or print the maze technique so that it can be duplicated.

The maze technique can be given either on an individual or group untimed basis. Since the research on the maze techniques is very limited, the findings from the use of this procedure should be interpreted very cautiously. That is why I recommend that the maze technique only be used as *another way* of studying the child's comprehension ability. This is a very tentative way of interpreting the results of a maze technique:

> *independent reading level—80%* or more of the words correct
>
> *instructional reading level—60%-80%* of the words correct
>
> *frustration reading level—*less than *60%* of the words correct

However, some of the children with whom we have worked are able to obtain *100%* correct responses on the maze technique partially because they have found it to be very interesting to complete.

Sample Maze Technique at the Fourth-Grade Reading Level

The following pages present a sample maze technique at about the fourth-grade reading level which you can duplicate and use in your reading program. You also can use it as a model for making your own maze technique. Such a device is quite easy to make and very simple to score.

MAZE TECHNIQUE
(Approximately fourth-grade level)

Name _____ Grade _____ Teacher _____

Read each sentence silently. Then circle the one word in each sentence which makes that sentence correct.

JOHN BUTTERFIELD, STAGECOACH KING

In 1801 when John Butterfield was found / born in rural
(found / was / happy) born in rural

New York, (stagecoaches / rockets / made) were expanding through the eastern (unhappy / eastern / quickly)

part of the United States.

(Jumped / Flowery / Young) Johnny liked to sit (up / on / beautiful) his farmyard

fence and (watch / made / pretty) the colorful procession of (books / stagecoaches, / angrily)

freight wagons, and covered (wagons / marshes / quickly) go by on the (sky / turnpike. / put)

He especially admired the (rapidly / dry / stagecoach) driver who sat

(those / on the / mother) box like a king (up / on / made) a throne.

Since Johnny (have / always / father) wanted to be a (famous / tiny / fly) stagecoach

driver, when he (fast / is / was) nineteen he left the (sky / farm / fast)

```
                at                      lake
and went to Albany to    find work at a stageline. Since
                fell                    angrily


              tree                take
he had no experience, he first had to pull      a job at the
              lovely              quickly


ugly                            heads
bakery     cleaning out the horses' stalls.
stageline                       fall


                          such
    Later, however, he became  much   a valuable employee
                          money


      play                         an
that it    learned how to become a   conductor on the
      he                           is


            So                          kite
stagecoaches. As conductor he collected fares, played
            It                          looked


                        look
after the passengers, and took charge of the mail.
                        toy


    Finally,                     then
    Before, Johnny realized his dream when he was told he
    Boy,                         went


cow
has    become a stagedriver.
could


        it               go                      of
    Now he    was John's turn to be   "king of the road," jumped
        girl             nice                    admired


                    so
and cheered by boys as   he drove along the highway.
                    see


                      house              and
    He wore a beautiful costume of a beaver hat but  silver buttons
                      can                sold


      feet
on his coat.
      run
```

Answer Key	
was	stageline
stagecoaches	stalls
eastern	such
Young	he
on	a
watch	As
stagecoaches	looked
wagons	took
turnpike	Finally
stagecoach	when
the	could
on	it
always	be
famous	admired
was	as
farm	highway
to	costume
stageline	and
experience	coat
take	

STANDARDIZED COMPREHENSION ASSESSMENT DEVICES

There are a number of standardized devices which can be used to assess a child's comprehension ability. As stated earlier in this section, at the present time informal devices seem to be gaining in popularity while standardized devices seem to be less popular in assessing comprehension ability. It remains to be seen whether this trend will continue in the future, but in my opinion standardized devices of several types still have some relevance for this purpose. There also are both traditional and innovative standardized devices which can be used for assessing comprehension by the reading teacher. The following discusses both the traditional and contemporary standardized devices and also provides a model of the newest standardized device for assessing comprehension ability.

Standardized Survey Reading or Achievement Tests

Nearly every child with whom the reading teacher will be working in any reading program has been given a number of standardized survey reading or achievement tests during his or her school years. Although such tests can be given alone, they are most often given as part of an achievement test battery which also includes tests in other curricular areas such as language usage, social studies, science, and arithmetic. Often the survey reading test can be purchased separately from the rest of the achievement test battery.

A standardized survey reading test or the reading subtests of an achievement test battery try to evaluate the child's general or overall reading ability in the word identification skills (mainly in the primary grades), word meaning (vocabulary), sentence or paragraph comprehension, rate of reading, and sometimes reading-study skills.

A standardized survey reading test is a group-administered, norm-referenced test which indicates that the reading teacher can compare the results achieved by a similar group of students in the standardization sample. Usually these are students of the same grade level, sex, geographic location, or socioeconomic group.

Norms can be reported in grade equivalent scores, percentile ranks, stanine scores, or standard scores. Although they are not very valid and are *not* recommended by the International Reading Association, grade equivalent scores still are very commonly used to report the scores on a survey reading test. The *grade equivalent score* is the grade level for which a raw score is the median score. Such scores often overestimate the child's actual instructional reading level due to the guessing factor possible on such a test. The *percentile rank* indicates how a student compares in performance with other students of his or her own age or grade. *Stanines* are normalized standard scores which range from a low of *1* through a high of *9* with *5* being the average performance. A *standard score* is a normalized score which enables the teacher to compare a child's performance on a number of different tests.

A standardized survey reading test should be reliable and valid, and most of them are. *Reliability* refers to the degree to which a test provides consistent results. *Validity* indicates the degree of accuracy with which a test evaluates what it is supposed to measure.

A standardized survey reading test or the reading subtests of an achievement test have these *advantages* in assessing comprehension ability:

— They are easy to administer.
— They are easy to evaluate, and the evaluation can be done by a computer.
— They were formulated by test experts.

— They are reliable and valid.
— They are useful to serve as a screening device to determine which children need additional testing.

However, such tests generally have these *limitations*:

— They should be passage dependent (the child should have to read the material to be able to answer the comprehension questions).
— All of the comprehension questions on such a test have only one right answer according to the scoring system.
— They are not culture-free and may penalize a child from a minority group.
— They may *overestimate* the child's actual instructional reading level due to the guessing factor inherent in such a test.
— They have difficulty in evaluating the child's competency in textually implicit (interpretive and critical) and scriptally implicit (creative) comprehension due to the format of the test.

Here is a brief listing and description of some of the more commonly used traditional standardized survey reading tests which also serve as tests of reading comprehension:

California Achievement Tests—CTB/McGraw-Hill.
This test is available in two forms, and the various levels are designed for use in grades K-12. It evaluates ability in vocabulary and comprehension.

Comprehensive Tests of Basic Skills, S&T—CTB/McGraw-Hill.
This test is available in two forms, and the various levels are designed for use in grades K-12. It evaluates ability in vocabulary and comprehension.

Comprehensive Tests of Basic Skills, U & V—CTB/McGraw-Hill.
This test is available in two forms, and the various levels are designed for use in grades K-12. It evaluates ability in word attack, vocabulary, and comprehension.

Gates-MacGinitie Reading Tests, Revised Edition—Riverside Publishing Company.
This test is available in seven levels for grades 1.0-12. It evaluates ability in vocabulary and comprehension.

Iowa Silent Reading Tests—Psychological Corporation.
This test is available in three levels for use in grades 6-12. It evaluates ability in vocabulary, comprehension, study skills, and speed of reading.

Iowa Tests of Basic Skills—Riverside Publishing Company.
This is available in three levels for use in grades K-8. It evaluates performance in vocabulary, comprehension, word attack, listening, and various reading-study skills.

Metropolitan Achievement Tests—Reading—Psychological Corporation.
This test is available in various levels for use in grades K-12. It evaluates performance mainly in comprehension ability.

Nelson Reading Skills Test—Houghton Mifflin.
This test is designed for use in grades 3-9. It evaluates performance in word meaning and comprehension ability.

SRA Achievement Series—Science Research Associates.
This test is available in a number of levels designed for use in grades K-12. It evaluates performance in such areas as vocabulary, comprehension, word attack, listening, and language arts.

Stanford Achievement Test—Psychological Corporation.
This test is available in two forms and various levels are designed for use in grades 1.5-9.9. It evaluates performance in such areas as vocabulary, comprehension, word attack, listening, and spelling.

Test of Reading Comprehension: A Method for Assessing the Understanding of Written Language (TORC)—Pro-Ed.
This test is designed for grades 2-12. It evaluates paragraph comprehension, sequencing sentences, and determining whether sentences are similar.

Criterion-Referenced Tests

Another more traditional group of standardized reading tests of which the reading teacher should be aware are *criterion-referenced* or *mastery tests*. Usually these are not extensively used in a contemporary reading improvement program. However, a number of state and local school districts have devised some type of mastery or performance-based reading testing during the past 10 or 15 years. Although such tests still are in use at the present, it is my belief that they will become less popular in the near future because they view reading as a composite of separate skills rather than as a global, language-based process which is the new research emphasis as explained in Section 1.

In any case, criterion-referenced or mastery tests deal with one or several of the reading subskills and specify the point at which the child has achieved mastery of that subskill or those subskills. They differ from norm-referenced tests which compare a child's performance with the performance of other children who possess similar characteristics.

Criterion-referenced tests can be constructed to assess competency in many different reading skills such as the various elements of phonic analysis, structural analysis, contextual analysis, and reading comprehension. The major purpose of using criterion-referenced tests is to enable a teacher to individualize reading instruction effectively. They are designed to help the reading teacher ascertain the reading skills in which a student is competent and those in which additional instruction and/or reinforcement is necessary. As stated earlier, they subdivide the reading process into small, discrete segments.

Very briefly, here are some of the *advantages* of using criterion-referenced tests:

— Theoretically, they ensure that the student receives instruction and/or reinforcement in only those reading skills in which he or she lacks competence.
— They may help the reading teacher to be sure that a child has mastery of any of the reading skills which he or she has been taught.

Here are several *limitations* of using such tests of which the reading teacher should be aware:

— They fragment the reading process, dividing it into many different reading skills. That is not consistent with contemporary research about the reading process. The *80%* criterion level is an arbitrary cut-off point.
— It is difficult for such a test to assess ability in the higher level reading skills such as implicit comprehension (interpretive comprehension or critical reading).

Here is a very brief list of some currently-available criterion-referenced tests:

Assessment of Basic Competencies—Scholastic Testing Service.
This is an individual test designed for ages 3-15. It must be given over three or four sessions.

Corrective Reading Mastery Tests—Science Research Associates.
This is a group test designed for use in grades 4-adult.

Prescriptive Reading Performance Test—Western Psychological Services
This is an individual test for grades 1-12.

PRI Reading Systems—CTB/McGraw-Hill.
This is a group test designed for use in grades K-9.

Task Assessment for Prescriptive Teaching—Scholastic Testing Service.
This is an individual and group test for ages 6 and up.

Wisconsin Tests of Reading Skill Development: Comprehension—NCS Interpretive Scoring Systems.
This is a group test for grades K-6.

Wisconsin Tests of Reading Skill Development: Study Skills—NCS Interpretive Scoring Systems.
This is a group test for grades K-6.

Standardized Individual and Group Diagnostic Reading Tests

A number of reading teachers can use either an *individual* or a *group diagnostic reading test*, usually with children who are enrolled in a corrective or remedial reading program, to assess their comprehension ability as well as their word identification skills. They may use such a test instead of an Individual Reading Inventory or as a supplement to an IRI. In any case, such a test normally is used with a child who has not performed well on a standardized survey reading or achievement test. Such a child usually has scored one or more years below grade level in the primary grades and two or more years below grade level in the intermediate grades.

A standardized diagnostic reading test is an individually administered or group-administered reading test which attempts to determine the child's specific reading skill strengths and weaknesses in the various word identification and comprehension skills. It sometimes also tries to determine a child's approximate instructional reading level. It can evaluate any element of sight word recognition, phonic analysis, structural analysis, contextual analysis, vocabulary knowledge, textually explicit (literal) comprehension, and textually implicit (interpretive or critical) comprehension.

Normally an individual diagnostic reading test is given to a moderately or severely disabled reader. Such a test takes quite a bit of time to give and evaluate. On the other hand, a group diagnostic reading test usually is given to a mildly disabled reader because this kind of test takes less time to give and evaluate. However, a group diagnostic reading test can be given either to a small group of students or to an individual student *even though* it is called a group diagnostic reading test. Most diagnostic reading tests evaluate a child's reading strengths and weaknesses through the seventh-grade or the eighth-grade reading level. However, such a test cannot help you to determine the causes of a child's reading difficulties, but instead attempt to determine his or her exact reading strengths and weaknesses so that appropriate corrective or remedial reading instruction can be given to him or her.

Both individual and group diagnostic reading tests are very effective in locating a child's exact reading weaknesses in the various comprehension and word identification skills and are also quite effective in determining the instructional reading level. Thus, the corrective or remedial reading program can focus on the child's diagnosed reading weaknesses. This is probably the most important *advantage* of the use of such a test. Such a test also is standardized, which means that it normally is more valid and reliable than is the typical IRI. Most such tests also include norms which the reading teacher can use to compare one child or group of children with children who possess similar characteristics.

However, any diagnostic reading test contains several *limitations* of which you should be aware. Usually an individual diagnostic reading test takes quite a bit of time to give and score. It often takes practice and experience to become adept in administering and evaluating such a test. This is especially true of individual diagnostic reading tests. Group diagnostic reading tests take much less time to give, score, and interpret. Standardized diagnostic reading tests may discriminate at least to some extent against children from minority groups and those who speak the nonstandard dialect.

In summary, group and individual diagnostic reading tests are a traditional way of evaluating the comprehension ability of mainly disabled readers. Although they may have some value for this purpose, you should determine if the test considers reading comprehension in the contemporary global, language-based process which was described in Section 1 of this resource.

Here is a brief listing of some of the more useful group and individual diagnostic reading tests:

Botel Reading Inventory—Follett Publishing Company.
This is both a group and an individual test for use in grades 1-high school. It measures general comprehension and oral reading fluency.

Diagnostic Reading Scales—McGraw-Hill.
This is an individual test for use in grades 1-7. It contains 17 tests and assesses oral and silent reading abilities and phonic knowledge.

Durrell Analysis of Reading Difficulty—Psychological Corporation.
This is an individual test for use in grades preprimer through sixth grade. It measures many reading skills such as oral reading, silent reading, listening comprehension, word recognition, sounds in isolation, phonic spelling, and visual memory.

Gates-McKillop-Horowitz Reading Diagnostic Tests—Teachers College Press.
This is an individual test designed for use in grades 1-6. It evaluates such reading skills as oral reading, reading sentences, flash and untimed words, word attack, and auditory abilities.

Roswell-Chall Diagnostic Reading Test—Essay Press.
This is an individual test designed for use in grades 1-4. It evaluates such areas as the various elements of word attack.

The Test of Language Development—Pro-Ed.
This is an individual test designed for above six years of age. It evaluates semantics, syntax, and phonology.

Wide Range Achievement Tests (WRAT)—Jastak Associates.
This is an individual or small group test in two levels designed for ages 5.5 through the adult level. It evaluates word recognition, spelling, and arithmetic.

Woodcock Reading Mastery Tests—American Guidance Association.
This is an individual test designed for kindergarten through grade 12. It evaluates letter identification, word identification, word attack, word comprehension, and passage comprehension.

Standardized Process-Oriented Measures of Comprehension

As stated earlier in this section, the newest standardized testing thrust in reading comprehension seems to be some variation of a process-oriented measure of comprehension. Although I am the most familiar with the *Illinois Goal Assess-*

ment Program since I teach at Illinois State University, a number of other states also are attempting to assess reading instruction in this more contemporary manner. Here, I will attempt to explain some of the basic characteristics of this type of standardized testing of reading and will provide one ready-to-duplicate model which you can use if it seems applicable for you. In any case, it should serve as a model of this kind of testing on which you can base your own type of test if you wish. It should help you understand what the standardized testing of reading *may* be like in the future.

These new types of standardized reading tests attempt to reflect contemporary comprehension research. As stated in Section 1, this research has found that reading is an active process involving the use of a combination of reading skills which include knowledge about how to read and the reader's existing knowledge of the material being read about. Thus, reading always involves the combination of the reader, the text, and the context of the reading material. The *reader element* includes such aspects as these: prior knowledge, attitudes about reading and the topic, ability to read the text, and knowledge of strategies to use to facilitate comprehension. The *text elements* includes such aspects as the following: the genre, how the author has structured the information about the topic, the difficulty of the text, and the organization of the text. Finally, some *common contexts* include the following: the reader's purpose for reading, the setting where the reading is being done, and how the reader has to demonstrate comprehension of the material.

The *Illinois Goal Assessment Program* differs from traditional standardized testing of reading in several important ways. For example, the typical standardized survey reading test or diagnostic reading test includes only a short passage for each assessment of comprehension. It normally presents a number of such short passages, each followed by comprehension questions. In the new type of testing, an entire narrative or expository passage is included in the text. This passage often is copied directly from an appropriate basal reader or content textbook and is several pages long. The rationale behind this concept is that a longer passage is more like the actual reading which a child does at school and at home.

Prior to reading the passage the children complete a *topic familiarity section* which contains a very brief summary of the selection followed by a number of questions to assess the child's prior knowledge of this type of material. Each of the questions then is followed by the three options: *Yes, Maybe, No*. This section then attempts to assess prior knowledge, with the ultimate outcome being to show how effective a class of children is with this important aspect of reading.

Next the test contains a very brief practice section on constructing meaning questions. This is designed to help the child become at least somewhat adept at answering questions with multiple acceptable responses.

The test next contains the complete narrative or expository passage. Pictures, graphs, diagrams, tables, charts, and all other such information are printed directly onto the test booklet as they were in the original basal reader or content textbook.

Next the *Illinois Goal Assessment Test* contains a number of constructing meaning items (comprehension questions). Each question may have *one, two,* or *three* correct answers, and the child is not told how many correct answers there are to any one question. Both textually explicit (literal) and textually implicit (interpretive, critical, and creative) questions are included in the constructing meaning section of the test.

The next part of the test is a reading strategies section in which the child is to determine what reading strategies would be the most helpful in comprehending the passage. This part of the test is designed to ascertain if a child knows how to use different strategies such as rereading the entire story, rereading only part of the story, skimming through the material, looking up unknown words in the dictionary, and others. The child is to determine if each of these strategies would help a great deal, somewhat, or very little.

The final part of the *Illinois Goal Assessment Program* is a very brief survey of literacy experiences in which the child is to indicate how often he or she reads just for enjoyment, shares his or her writing, tells a friend about a favorite book, and reads something for homework.

Sample Process-Oriented Test of Comprehension

This section dealing with the assessment of comprehension closes with a process-oriented test of comprehension which is partially based on the model of the *Illinois Goal Assessment Program.* However, it also exemplifies these types of measures now being used or studied in many other states. You can duplicate and use it in its present form if it is applicable. However, you also may wish to use it as a model of such a test which you construct from your own basal reader or content materials.

PROCESS-ORIENTED MEASURE OF COMPREHENSION ABILITY
(Third-grade reading level)

Name _____ Grade _____ Teacher _____

Topic Familiarity (Prior Knowledge) Section

This section is read aloud to the children. The children are to answer each question after the teacher has read it aloud.

You are going to read a story today about a town in northern Minnesota named Hibbing. This story describes how the entire town had to be moved because iron ore had been discovered right under it. This move was begun in 1912 and was not completed until 1954.

Here are some statements. For each idea, decide whether or not you might find it in a story like this. Then underline the answer which says what you think for each idea.

YES—I think the idea probably would be in a story like this.
MAYBE—The idea might be in a story like this.
NO—I don't think the idea would be in a story like this.

1. Iron ore was discovered in northern Minnesota.   Yes   Maybe   No
2. The miners help build a space shuttle.   Yes   Maybe   No
3. Iron ore was discovered under the roots of trees.   Yes   Maybe   No
4. Iron was needed to build streets.   Yes   Maybe   No
5. There were schools in Hibbing.   Yes   Maybe   No
6. All of the iron miners had no food to eat.   Yes   Maybe   No
7. Many of the people of Hibbing had pets that they loved.   Yes   Maybe   No
8. Trees could be used in moving the buildings of Hibbing to
   their new locations.   Yes   Maybe   No
9. Wolves also were moved to the new location.   Yes   Maybe   No
10. The winters in Minnesota were quite warm in 1891.   Yes   Maybe   No
11. Iron was needed around 1900 to build railroad tracks and
    trains.   Yes   Maybe   No
12. Some of the people in Hibbing lived in log cabins.   Yes   Maybe   No
13. A doctor helped people who were ill with smallpox.   Yes   Maybe   No
14. A horse can move a big building.   Yes   Maybe   No
15. Logs for moving buildings were easy to find in Minnesota.   Yes   Maybe   No

Now read the story "The Town That Moved" to yourself. Then answer the questions that follow the story.

THE TOWN THAT MOVED*

by Mary Jane Finsand

Many towns grew up in the United States during the 1700s and 1800s. Towns grew in different places for different reasons. Read to find out how a small town in northern Minnesota grew and became famous.

———————————— ● ————————————

Once upon a time, when the United States was still a young nation, much of the country was wilderness.

And so it was in northern Minnesota.

What was there? Forests and lakes. Bears and deer and wolves.

Some men thought there might even be gold and silver. They were not sure, but they were curious. So they went to the wilderness to seek their fortunes.

Some of these men came to hunt the animals. Then they sold the furs to people in cities far away. Others came to cut down trees and sell the lumber.

Still other men came to look for silver or gold. They did not find much of either in northern Minnesota. They did not have an easy life either!

There were no towns. There were no roads. The winters were long and cold. It was no place to bring a family. The men had to come by themselves.

Then, in August of 1891, a cyclone blew over the wilderness. The winds were fast and strong. They blew down many great trees.

Underneath, on the roots of the trees and in the holes they left behind, men discovered iron ore! There may not have been gold in northern Minnesota, but in the 1800s iron ore was almost as exciting.

Iron ore is the rock from which we get iron. In the 1800s iron was badly needed to build railroad trains and tracks.

It wasn't long before news of the iron ore in Minnesota had spread all around the country. Men began to pour into Minnesota. They came to start iron ore mines.

One of those men was named Frank Hibbing. Frank Hibbing knew that if he started an iron ore mine he would need many men to work in it. The men would want to bring their families. So Hibbing decided to build a town.

First he bought land. Then he hired men to build roads. He hired other men to build log cabins for the families.

Soon people were coming from all over the country to work in Hibbing's mine and live in his town. People even came from coun-

The Town That Moved by Mary Jane Finsand, copyright 1983 by Carolrhoda Books, Inc., 241 First Avenue North, Minneapolis, MN 55401. Reprinted by permission of the publisher.

tries far away like Ireland, Sweden, and Germany. Many came to work in the mine, but others came to open stores. Soon there were schools and churches and banks, too.

On August 15, 1893, the people voted to become the town of Hibbing, Minnesota. Hibbing became famous for its rich iron ore. The town grew and grew. Everyone who lived there was very proud of Hibbing. They wanted to make it a beautiful city.

They built fancy theaters and lovely parks and fine houses. They started excellent schools for their children, and they took wonderful care of their town.

Then one day the mine owners made a discovery: THE VERY BEST IRON ORE WAS RIGHT BENEATH THE TOWN OF HIB-BING!

The people of Hibbing would have to move. If they didn't, the mines would have to shut down. The miners would be out of work. Soon the other businesses would have to close down, too.

The people of Hibbing were very upset. They had worked so hard to build their beautiful town. How could they leave it? How could they watch it be torn down to make way for new mines?

"Where will we go?" they asked.

"We will build you a new town," said the mine owners.

"But what about our fine homes and our fancy theaters and our beautiful hotels?" the people asked.

The mine owners thought and thought, and finally they came up with a solution. "We will move your homes!" they said. "We will move the whole town!"

It sounded like a wonderful idea. But how on earth would they do it?

The mine owners and the people sat down together to think and talk.

"We have horses and tractors," said one man. "Maybe we could pull the buildings."

"But we can't pull big buildings along the ground," said the mayor. "They will break into pieces. We need wheels or something."

"Wheels are a problem," said the mine owners. "Most of our wheels are just not large or strong enough to move a building."

"Well," said someone else, "we certainly have lots of trees. We could cut them down, then make them smooth, and roll our houses on them."

"That's it!" everyone cried.

So the mine owners and the people began to get ready for moving day. They separated all the buildings from their basements. Then they dug new basements for all those buildings. They chopped down trees. Then they cut away the branches. They made the logs smooth.

People all over the world heard about Hibbing's plan to move. "Impossible!" they said.

One big city newspaper wrote: "HIBBING GONE CRAZY!"

Continued on following page

No one believed that the people of Hibbing could move their whole town.

Finally moving day arrived. The Hibbing Hotel would be the first building moved. The miners attached large chains and ropes to cranes from the mine. The cranes would be powered by steam engines. Then the chains were wrapped over and under the Hibbing Hotel. Slowly the cranes lifted the hotel. Then they swung it over and lowered it gently onto a log roller.

Next ropes and straps were wrapped around the hotel, then attached to horses up front. "Giddap! Giddap!" shouted the drivers. The horses started forward. Slowly the Hibbing Hotel rolled down the street.

As soon as the back log rolled out from under the building, people grabbed it. They strapped it to a horse and pulled it up to the front. Then then slid it underneath again.

Down the street the buildings rolled to their new locations. Day in and day out the people of Hibbing worked to save their beautiful town.

At last all the business buildings had been moved. Next would come the houses.

"What should we do with our furniture?" the women asked.

"And our toys and clothes," said the children.

"Leave everything in the houses," they were told. "And you can ride in your houses, too."

The very next day the first house was lifted onto logs. Down the street it came. A log was placed up front. Then a log rolled out back. That log was placed up front, and another log rolled out back.

And so it went until, one after another, 186 houses had been moved. The people of Hibbing had done it! They had moved their whole town!

Hibbing's move began in the year 1912, but the major push didn't come until 1921, and most of the buildings were moved in the 1920s. It wasn't until the fall of 1953 or the spring of 1954, though, that the very last building was finally moved.

The people of Hibbing moved their town because they loved it. It wasn't until many years later that they found they had made history. Today if you go to Hibbing you can see many buildings that were rolled on logs to where they now stand. And people are still proud to say, "We are from Hibbing, the town that moved!"

CONSTRUCTING MEANING QUESTIONS

Name _____ **Grade** _____ **Teacher** _____

Now read each question to yourself and put an *X* in front of each answer that is correct.

REMEMBER THAT THERE MAY BE *1, 2,* or *3* CORRECT ANSWERS TO EACH QUESTION.

16. In northern Minnesota in 1891, what kind of wild animals were fairly common?

_____ lions

_____ wolves

_____ bears

_____ hippopotamuses

_____ deer

17. Why did it take a cyclone for men to discover iron ore in this story?

_____ The iron ore had been hidden under the roots of the trees.

_____ Men had never looked for iron ore before anywhere.

_____ The men were looking only for silver and gold.

_____ There were no miners in Minnesota then.

_____ The men were too lazy to look for iron ore before.

18. What was iron ore used for around 1900?

_____ railroad tracks

_____ log cabins

_____ horseshoes

_____ parks

_____ rope

19. Why did Frank Hibbing decide to build a town?

_____ The iron ore miners had to have somewhere to live.

_____ He wanted to make money for himself from the iron ore mines.

_____ He wanted to move to California.

_____ He wanted to live in Sweden.

_____ He wanted to live in a very large city.

20. Why did the town of Hibbing have to move to another place?

_____ The people didn't like the present location of the town.

_____ The best iron ore was discovered right below the town.

_____ If it didn't move, the miners would lose their jobs.

_____ It was too cold in Minnesota in the winter.

_____ If it didn't move, the businesses would have to shut down.

21. How were the buildings in the town moved?

_____ They were rolled on smooth logs.

_____ Tractors were used to pull them.

Continued on following page

_____ They were torn down and then rebuilt.

_____ A cyclone destroyed them.

_____ The miners pushed and pulled them.

22. How may the people have gotten to the new location of Hibbing?

_____ They rode in their houses.

_____ They walked.

_____ They rode in a space shuttle.

_____ They flew in an airplane.

_____ They didn't go at all.

23. What was the first building to be moved?

_____ a theater   _____ a school

_____ a hotel   _____ a park

_____ a house

24. How many houses were moved altogether?

_____ 540   _____ 1,000

_____ 186   _____ 10,000

_____ 17

25. Why did it take so long for the entire town of Hibbing to move?

_____ there were so many buildings to move

_____ some of the buildings were very large

_____ they could not move any of the buildings in the winter

_____ it is easy to move a theater

_____ miners are not good at moving buildings

READING STRATEGIES SECTION

Read this section aloud to the students. They can look back to the story if they want while answering the questions.

CHECK ONLY ONE ANSWER PER QUESTION IN THIS PART. These questions are about helpful things you do while you read. Think about how helpful each of the activities would be and *check off* the one right answer per question.

You have just read the story "The Town That Moved," but pretend that one of your friends has not read it. Pretend that you are asked to tell him or her what the story is mainly about.

How much would it help them understand what the story is mainly about if you said:	*Won't Help Help at All*	*Will Help a Little Bit*	*Will Help Quite a Bit*	*Will Help a Lot*
26. "It is about iron ore mining around the year 1900."	——	——	——	——
27. "It is about a town that had to move because it was located above iron."	——	——	——	——
28. "It is about life in northern Minnesota around the year 1900."	——	——	——	——
29. "It is about how a town was moved during the years 1912–1954."	——	——	——	——
30. "It is about a man named Frank Hibbing who lived in northern Minnesota."	——	——	——	——

You have just read "The Town That Moved." Pretend that one of the questions you have to answer is:

Under what was the iron ore first discovered?

How much would if help if you were to:	*Won't Help Help at All*	*Will Help a Little Bit*	*Will Help Quite a Lot*	*Will Help a Lot*
31. reread the whole story	——	——	——	——
32. reread the part of the story that happened right after the cyclone	——	——	——	——
33. look quickly through the paragraphs	——	——	——	——
34. look up the meaning of the word "ore" in the dictionary	——	——	——	——
35. reread the part of the story about moving the hotel	——	——	——	——

Answer Key

Topic Familiarity (Prior Knowledge)

(I am including the answers which I believe are the most appropriate. I believe any answer that the child can defend should be considered correct in this section.)

1. Yes	4. No	7. Maybe	10. No	13. Maybe
2. No	5. Yes	8. Maybe	11. Yes	14. No
3. Maybe	6. No	9. No	12. Yes	15. Yes

Constructing Meaning Questions

(I am including the answers which I believe are the most appropriate. I believe any answer that the child can defend as logical should be considered correct in this section.)

16. __X__ wolves
    __X__ bears
    __X__ deer
17. __X__ the iron ore had been hidden under the roots of the trees
18. __X__ railroad tracks
    __X__ horseshoes
19. __X__ the iron ore miners had to have somewhere to live
    __X__ he wanted to make money for himself from the iron ore mines
20. __X__ the best iron ore was discovered right under the town
    __X__ if it didn't move, the miners would lose their jobs
    __X__ if it didn't move, the businesses would have to shut down
21. __X__ they were rolled on smooth logs
22. __X__ they rode in their houses
    __X__ they walked
23. __X__ a hotel
24. __X__ 186
25. __X__ there were so many buildings to move
    __X__ some of the buildings were very large
    __X__ they could not move any of the buildings in the winter

Reading Strategies Section

(I am including the answers which I believe are the most appropriate. I believe any answer that the child can defend as logical should be considered correct in the section.)

26. Will help quite a bit	31. Won't help at all
27. Will help a lot	32. Will help a lot
28. Will help quite a bit	33. Will help quite a bit
29. Will help quite a bit	34. Will help a little bit
30. Will help a little bit	35. Won't help at all

3

Vocabulary Knowledge
and Comprehension

Do you think a person is less likely to understand what he or she is reading if that person has a limited meaning vocabulary? The conventional wisdom is that a reader must possess a large, varied vocabulary to be able to comprehend what is being read. It is also obvious that an extensive vocabulary generally is viewed as the mark of an intelligent, well-educated person. We consider a person such as William F. Buckley, Jr., to be highly intelligent since he has such a good command of the English language even though many of us cannot always understand just what he is saying. However, it is because of the high positive relationship between the possession of vocabulary knowledge and understanding what is read that the assessment and improvement of vocabulary knowledge is the focus of this section.

Section 3 opens by summarizing the various types of meaning vocabularies and providing examples of the relationships between meaning vocabulary and efficiency of reading comprehension. Next it summarizes some of the contemporary aspects of vocabulary development which reflect the modern view of reading comprehension as described in Section 1, and discusses using elements of prior knowledge such as the vocabulary overview guide as a very effective way of improving meaning vocabulary.

The section then briefly explains some of the standardized and informal means of assessing meaning vocabulary development. Included are two ready-to-duplicate context assessment sheets at the sixth- and third-grade levels for using context as a means of vocabulary improvement.

The major part of the section contains many strategies and ready-to-duplicate activity sheets that can be used in the primary grades and/or at the middle-upper level for improving meaning vocabulary. Some of these strategies are direct strategies for vocabulary development, while others transfer to independent learning of vocabulary. Also included are brief lists of some materials and games and some computer software that can be used for vocabulary development.

69

RELATION OF MEANING VOCABULARY AND READING COMPREHENSION

It seems important at the outset to define *meaning vocabulary*. This can be defined as the number of words to which an individual can attach one or more meanings. The reading teacher also should understand that there are several different types of meaning vocabularies which the child must acquire. The *listening vocabulary* is the first type of vocabulary which the child learns. It is learned in the home by hearing parents and other family members speak. Obviously, if the very young child is placed in a day care center, the adults there also are important in the acquisition of the child's listening vocabulary. The child next learns the *speaking vocabulary* from the imitation and modeling of family members and the other adults with whom he or she comes in contact. That is why it is important for the child's speech models to use correct grammar and an interesting, precise vocabulary. It also is why the child may acquire a nonstandard dialect such as the black dialect or an Hispanic dialect.

Next the child learns the *reading vocabulary*. This is learned primarily at school unless the child is an early reader, in which case it could be learned in the home or in a child-care facility. By the time the child is in the intermediate grades, his or her reading vocabulary usually exceeds the speaking vocabulary unless the child is a disabled reader. The fourth type of meaning vocabulary is the *writing vocabulary*, which also is primarily learned in school although its beginning may be made outside of school. Normally the writing vocabulary is the smallest since a person normally would not use many words in his or her writing which would be used in speaking or met in reading.

The fifth type of meaning vocabulary is the *potential* or *marginal vocabulary*. This type of meaning vocabulary is made up of all the words which the child can determine the meaning of on a specific occasion while reading by using context clues, the meaning of prefixes, suffixes, or word roots, or by understanding derivatives. It is impossible to determine the size of this vocabulary since the context in which a word is located may determine whether or not it will be known. As stated later, it is important that the reader have a very good understanding of the use of context and know the meaning of many word parts so that he or she will have a large and useful potential or marginal vocabulary.

Vocabulary knowledge has been found by significant research studies to be very highly related to reading comprehension. In a classic study conducted in 1944 which was replicated in 1968, Frederick B. Davis researched the reading process and by factor analysis of reading comprehension subskills found that comprehension was composed of two primary skills—knowledge of word meanings (vocabulary) and reasoning ability which probably can be equated with reading comprehension.[1,2]

---

[1]Frederick B. Davis, "Fundamental Factors in Comprehension in Reading," *Psychometrika*, Volume 9 (September, 1944), pp. 185–197.

[2]Frederick B. Davis, "Research in Comprehension in Reading," *Reading Research Quarterly*, Volume 3 (Summer, 1968), pp. 449–545.

In another research study R. L. Thorndike discovered correlations between vocabulary knowledge and reading comprehension that ranged from .66 to .75 for 10-, 14-, and 17-year-old students in 15 countries. These are fairly high correlations indicating that vocabulary knowledge indeed is important to effective reading comprehension.[3]

John D. McNeil has offered three hypotheses or reasons why he believes that there is a powerful relationship between vocabulary knowledge and reading comprehension. The *aptitude hypotheses* state that individuals with large vocabularies comprehend better mainly because they have better innate verbal ability. The *instrumental hypotheses* state specific vocabulary knowledge contributes to comprehension mainly because the prospective reader knows more words. On the other hand, the *knowledge hypotheses* state that the more knowledge in the form of concepts or schematas which a reader has about a topic, the more words he or she knows which are related to that topic.[4] Undoubtedly none of these hypotheses is truly an adequate explanation for the relationship between vocabulary and reading comprehension. Any single one or more of these hypotheses may apply in any given situation.

The traditional view of meaning vocabulary states that words are of primary importance in reading comprehension, and without adequate comprehension of individual words there can be no adequate comprehension. Although this seems logical and still is accepted by many reading specialists, there is more to the comprehension of printed material than the meaning of the individual words taken together. Some contemporary reading specialists believe that because of the redundancy in language, cues within written material provide the information needed for comprehension, and that knowledge of individual word meanings really is not that important. While it is accurate that the redundancy (word order clues) in language provides important clues to word meanings, the following example may show you that the reader also must know the meanings of the individual words to insure comprehension of what is read.

> The talkative old man has made me very angry since he talks so much that no one else has a chance to talk. He always becomes a nuisance when he talks to anyone.

> The loquacious elderly gentlemen has rendered me exceedingly agitated since he converses so extensively that no one else has an opportunity to participate in the conversation. He consistently becomes obnoxious whenever he converses with another person.

It is obvious that although the sentence structure and content of the second passage is essentially the same as that of the first one, the vocabulary in the

---

[3]R. L. Thorndike, *Reading Comprehension Education in Fifteen Countries*. (New York: Wiley and Company, 1973).

[4]John D. McNeil, *Reading Comprehension: New Directions for Classroom Practice* (Glenview, IL: Scott, Foresman and Company, 1984), pp. 96–97.

second passage makes it much more difficult for an elementary-school child to comprehend.

Another research study conducted by P. L. Roelke found that the most important aspects of vocabulary knowledge affecting comprehension are the following, which are listed in order of importance:

1. The number of words a student knows the meaning for.

2. The knowledge of multiple meanings of words; for example, knowing that the word *run* may mean: moving the legs quickly, blood flowing as from a cut, extending as the shelves stretched around the walls of a room, getting past as run a blockade, being a candidate for an election, and giving free use as having the run of the house among many other meanings.

3. Ability to select the correct meaning of a word having multiple meanings in order to fit a specific context.[5]

It is obvious that content areas such as social studies, science, and arithmetic have many specialized vocabulary terms that the student must be able to understand in order to effectively comprehend content textbooks and other reference materials in the area. Since a number of these content textbooks also are written at a level which is higher than the reading level of many of the children who are to read them, in addition to containing the specialized vocabulary terms, they can indeed present a very different challenge to children's comprehension. Some of these specialized vocabulary terms have a different meaning in a content area than they do in narrative reading, such as the term "cabinet" in social studies, while others are simply very difficult, such as the terms *capillary, embolism,* and *platelet* in science. In any case, these specialized vocabulary terms must be dealt with in some manner by the reading teacher if the comprehension of the material is to be successful. This section suggests some ways of presenting and/or reinforcing such specialized vocabulary terms as by semantic mapping or webbing, semantic feature analysis, vocabulary overview guides, use of structural analysis, and semantic associations.

SOME ASPECTS OF CONTEMPORARY TEACHING OF VOCABULARY

Several issues in the contemporary teaching of vocabulary can be mentioned briefly at this point in the hope of clarifying the most effective means of improving meaning vocabulary.

It is important to realize that in the past and also at present little time has been devoted in elementary classrooms and special reading programs to the teaching of vocabulary knowledge. Much more time has been spent on lower level, but important, skills such as sight word recognition and phonic analysis.

---

[5]P. L. Roelke, "Reading Comprehension as a Function of Three Dimensions of Word Meaning," *Dissertation Abstracts International,* 30 5300A-5301A. (University Microfilms No. 70-10, 275).

Much more time should be spent on meaningful vocabulary instruction in the future.

First it must be determined which words should be taught, and then the method(s) of teaching and/or reinforcing them must be decided upon. The teacher also must consider whether or not the meaning of the word can be determined from context, how thoroughly the word needs to be taught, and how much the child already knows about that term and related terms. All reading specialists agree that vocabulary instruction should provide for active student involvement.

Although specific strategies for vocabulary development are presented later in this section of the *Kit*, very briefly the following five steps can be used as a *general guide* to vocabulary independence:

1. Trigger background knowledge. Have the child ask himself or herself: "What do I already know about these words?"

2. Preview the reading material for clues as to what the words might mean.

3. Read the material.

4. Refine and reformulate predicted meanings of the vocabulary based upon information gained from reading the material.

5. To make the new word permanent, the child must read it and use it. Have him or her use new vocabulary in writing and be alert to the word in future reading.

Another aspect of contemporary vocabulary instruction is determining whether it should be explicit (direct) or incidental. Although most reading specialists believe that both kinds of vocabulary instruction are helpful for students, many of them believe that explicit (direct) vocabulary instruction is the most useful and will result in the best achievement by children.

Direct instruction in vocabulary is needed for good vocabulary growth since the process of learning new words incidentally through repeated exposures is slow. Direct strategies that include active student involvement are needed for optimum vocabulary development. The typical child needs many repeated exposures to new vocabulary in different contexts before they are truly part of his or her meaning vocabulary. For good vocabulary development students also need many opportunities to relate target words to known concepts or prior knowledge.

At the present time target vocabulary words often are *wrongly* presented by the teacher in isolation or in sentences before a selection is read, the words decoded by the students, and their meanings determined either from the sentence context or by looking them up in the glossary or the dictionary. Sometimes students are asked to use the target words in sentences of their own after reading the selection in which the words are found. Sometimes the words are not discussed at all or are only listed on the chalkboard, pronounced, and their meanings briefly discussed. Vocabulary instruction traditionally has focused on drill and memorization instead of on activities requiring active student involvement and the opportunity to relate the new terms to their own concepts and prior knowledge. Students have not been asked to apply their own skills in contextual analysis, structural analysis, and prior knowledge effectively in vocabulary development.

In summary, the best contemporary vocabulary instruction *combines passage-specific (content-oriented) direct instruction* with active student involvement and extensive use of prior knowledge with *incidental vocabulary instruction* stressing the use of sentence context, use of structural analysis such as the meanings of prefixes, suffixes, and word roots, and especially wide reading of fairly easy, high-interest material.

USING PRIOR KNOWLEDGE FOR VOCABULARY DEVELOPMENT

As stated in Section 1, *prior knowledge* (background of experiences) is crucial to comprehension of the reading material. *It is equally important to the learning of new vocabulary terms.* The child always should learn to incorporate existing word knowledge with the new target words for optimum vocabulary growth. There are a number of strategies and concepts which can be used successfully for this purpose.

For example, Mary Ann Jiganti and Mary Ann Tindall have discovered that a new word is learned more easily if *it is incorporated into existing cognitive schemes* and that methods which *excite student interest* are the most effective. Jiganti and Tindall conducted a study in which they used a set of categorization exercises to help students tie words into existing schemata of knowledge. They also used drama techniques to enhance student interest. These techniques were compared with a traditional method in which students were asked to find the meanings of words in the dictionary and then write a sentence indicating their knowledge of the word. Jiganti and Tindall found that the categorization and drama exercises had superior results over the traditional approach on multiple choice tests and on sentence tests of word usage for both immediate and long-range recall.[6]

In using prior knowledge for vocabulary development, it is important that the child have well-developed schemata to lend preciseness and elaboration to each schema. For example, if the child knows the meaning of the word, *dog,* his or her schema for the word might include *fur, colors, four legs, tongue,* and *barking.* However, the child who has a large schema may also know such vocabulary terms as *temperament, bassett hound, collie, and cocker spaniel,* and also may have a schema for each of the dogs about size, color, and running characteristics. Then when the child reads a story about a particular kind of dog, the child who has the more precise or extensive vocabulary related to that dog can interpret the story at a much higher level than can a child who has a more limited schema about that kind of dog. Schema *cannot* best be expanded by having the child look up and memorize the definition of a number of vocabulary terms, but it can be

---

[6]Mary Ann Jiganti and Mary Ann Tindall, "An Interactive Approach to Teaching Vocabulary," *The Reading Teacher,* Vol. 39 (Jan.,1986), pp. 444–448.

done much more effectively by trying to incorporate existing word knowledge with the new vocabulary terms.

Semantic maps and *vocabulary overview guides* also can be used in the effort to incorporate existing prior knowledge or schema with new vocabulary to enhance vocabulary development. Semantic maps or webs are explained and illustrated later in this section. However, the vocabulary overview guide is presented at this time as a means for using prior knowledge for vocabulary development, and a sample vocabulary guide is included later in the section.

Using the Vocabulary Overview Guide

Eileen M. Carr has developed a useful metacognitive vocabulary strategy which teaches children to locate unfamiliar words as they are reading independently, to define these words, and then to relate them to their own personal experiences.

What, Why, and *How*—The teacher explains to the children that they are going to be learning how to find and define unfamiliar words while they are reading and then to relate these words to their own experiences. This procedure should help them better understand what they are reading and improve their vocabulary knowledge. The teacher then models the procedures as he or she reads a selection and writes unfamiliar words and their page numbers on the board or on a sheet of paper. The teacher always uses context clues first and then the glossary or dictionary to determine and write down the meanings of the unknown words.

The teacher next shows the children how to complete the vocabulary overview guide. The title of the reading selection is written at the top of a sheet of paper. Category titles, reflecting the topics of unfamiliar words, are listed under that title of the reading selection. The unfamiliar words may describe or be associated with these category titles. As an example, a section from the children's social studies textbook entitled "The Corn Belt of the United States" might contain such unknown terms as *contour farming* and *strip farming* which are associated with the category title *methods of farming.* In addition, the unknown terms such as *detassling* and *hybrid seed corn* might be associated with the category *growing corn.*

The unknown terms are then listed under the appropriate category titles. Next definition or synonyms as determined from the context, the glossary, or the dictionary are written under the unfamiliar words. Lastly, *personal clues which connect the unfamiliar words to personal experiences are written in boxes under the unfamiliar words.*

When—In addition to teaching the above procedure to children, the reading teacher should explain to them when to use this kind of vocabulary overview guide as they are reading on their own. The reading teacher should tell them that whenever they are reading on their own, they should use context clues to determine an approximate word meaning. However, they should look the word up in the glossary of their textbook or in the dictionary if they feel that a more precise definition is needed. After finishing their content reading assignment, they should prepare a vocabulary overview guide which includes the unknown words which they met.[7]

The accompanying brief illustration of a vocabulary overview guide should show you how a completed one might look.

Sample Vocabulary Overview Guide

Page 78 provides a sample vocabulary overview guide at about the sixth-grade reading level from the content area of science. You can duplicate it and have your students complete it in its present form if you wish. However, more importantly, you can use it for a model in having children in your reading class construct vocabulary overview guides of their own from expository (content) textbooks.

---

[7]Eileen M. Carr, "The Vocabulary Overview Guide: A Metacognitive Strategy to Improve Vocabulary Comprehension and Retention," *Journal of Reading,* Vol. 28 (May, 1985), pp. 684–689.

The Corn Belt of the United States

Methods of Farming

Contour Farming

- farming in curves
- way to save
- land from
- running away

Strip Farming

- strips of crops and grass
- way to save
- land from
- running away

Growing Corn

Detassling

- pulling tassels out
- way to grow
- seed corn

- way to stop pollination

Hybrid seed corn

- good for planting
- drought - resistant
- often yields
- more than 100
- bushels per acre

Types of Blood Cells
(Upper grade level)

Red Blood Cells

Blood Platelets

White Blood Cells

Answer Key

(The answers are only for illustrative purposes. They will vary because of students' prior knowledge.)

Red Blood Cells
    red corpuscles
    disk-shaped, resembling coins
    erythrocytes
    made of protein and iron
    made from bone marrow
    they are always wearing out
    5,000,000 in a cubic millimeter of blood

Blood Platelets
    thrombocytes
    300,000 in a cubic millimeter of blood
    they produce thromboplastin if they are damaged
    dry thromboplastin may form a scab
    clot formed in vessels is called a thrombosis

White Blood Cells
    leukocytes
    white corpuscles
    5,000 to 9,000 per cubic millimeter of blood
    neutrophils form in the bone marrow
    they can change their shape
    they engulf bacteria or foreign particles, destroying them
    they form pus
    leukemia occurs when there are 6,000 to 200,000 per cubic millimeter
      of blood

ASSESSING MEANING VOCABULARY ABILITY

There are a number of standardized and informal devices which can be used to effectively assess a child's meaning vocabulary. As stated in Section 2, although it seems that informal assessment is the wave of the future in reading diagnosis, there probably remains some role for formal assessment. Following are an overview of the most useful standardized means of vocabulary assessment and strategies and ready-to-duplicate sheets which the reading teacher can use for the assessment of meaning vocabulary.

Standardized Devices

As stated in Section 2, *group standardized survey reading or achievement tests* normally have a subtest devoted to the assessment of vocabulary or word meaning. Since examples of this type of test were listed in Section 2, they are not relisted here. However, for vocabulary assessment, they have the following general purposes:

- To evaluate the overall vocabulary development of a group of children
- To compare the group's vocabulary achievement with its comprehension ability
- To locate, if possible, specific areas of strengths and weaknesses such as in social studies, science, and mathematics vocabulary
- To establish a starting point in evaluating a child's vocabulary development
- To measure a number of classes' overall improvement in vocabulary over a period of time

However, the reading teacher should be aware of the following factors when using this type of test in evaluating vocabulary development:

- Assessment of general vocabulary knowledge is difficult because of the problems associated with developing an appropriate sample of words. For example, random sampling of words from the dictionary does not consider word frequency.

- Most of the tests evaluate vocabulary in isolation, not a similar situation to that used in reading when context clues can be used.

- The child may not have the word attack skills to decode a word even though its meaning might be known if he or she could do so.

- The child may know only one meaning of the vocabulary word but not the one required by the test. Such a test should not be used to determine the grade placement of disabled readers.

Individual diagnostic reading tests, such as the *Durrell Analysis of Reading Difficulty, Revised Edition* (see Section 2), also contain subtests which attempt to assess an individual child's oral vocabulary knowledge. In the Durrell, this subtest is called "Listening Vocabulary." This diagnostic reading test does not evaluate reading word meaning but rather knowledge of word meanings when children hear the words read to them. The authors of the test state that oral vocabulary can be thought of as a good predictor of reading capacity. I agree to some extent if *great caution* is used in making this determination.

In taking this subtest, the child looks at three pictures (examples). The teacher then explains that the first picture is for words about time (a picture of a clock), the second picture is for words that mean big (a picture of an elephant), and the third picture is for words about color (a picture of a rainbow). The teacher then reads a number of words, and the child points to the correct picture. The Durrell Analysis of Reading Difficulty also ascertains the child's ability to read these same words in another subtest so that the teacher may make a determination if word identification weaknesses are a function of vocabulary difficulties. This may be the case as was explained earlier. The tests were constructed to minimize learning transfer between the two subtests.

The vocabulary section of some individual intelligence tests such as the *Wechsler Intelligence Scale for Children—Revised Edition (WISC-R)*, the *Wechsler Adult Intelligence Scale—Revised (WAIS-R)*, and the *Stanford-Binet Intelligence Scale (1972)* may be useful in assessing a child's oral vocabularies. The WISC-R and the WAIS-R both contain a vocabulary subtest from which a raw score is obtained. This score is then converted to a scaled score from which interpretations can be made in terms of IQ, percentile rating, and grade equivalents. The Stanford-Binet also contains a subtest for oral vocabulary from which it is possible to derive a mental age and thus a grade equivalent. The real value of tests of oral vocabulary is to determine whether there is a difference between a child's oral and reading vocabularies. When the test results indicate a normal reading vocabulary, very little was gained from giving the test. On the other hand, when the child achieves a low reading and vocabulary score, the information obtained form the oral vocabulary test can be useful in determining whether the difficulty lies in a low oral or overall vocabulary.

> NOTE: All three of these individual intelligence tests must be given and interpreted by a psychologist. Here are the addresses of the publishers:

WISC-R and WAIS-R
The Psychological Corporation
555 Academic Court
San Antonio, Texas 78204

Stanford Binet
Houghton-Mifflin
1 Beacon Street
Boston, Massachusetts 02108

The *Peabody Picture Vocabulary Test—Revised (PPVT)* can be used from the ages of two through the adult level to make a fairly useful estimate of the child's oral vocabulary knowledge. It involves having the subject identify a series of plates (pictures) as they are shown. The administration time may run from only 15 to 20 minutes. It can be somewhat useful to the reading teacher in determining the range of the child's experiences and vocabulary as reflected by the child's knowledge of the pictures. However, although its results *must be interpreted very cautiously* as a measure of intelligence, it may be somewhat useful in determining the child's understanding and use of vocabulary terms. Here is the publisher's address:

Peabody Picture Vocabulary Test (PPVT)—Revised Edition
American Guidance Service
Publisher's Building
Circle Pines, Minnesota 55014

Informal Devices

Individual Reading Inventories, as explained and listed in Section 2 of the *Kit,* may provide the reading teacher with a little information about a child's word meaning knowledge. Most of the IRIs contain at least one vocabulary question per passage. However, it is obvious that this source must necessarily provide only a very cursory look at the child's vocabulary knowledge since the opportunities to demonstrate knowledge of vocabulary are so limited.

One of the best informal means of evaluating a child's vocabulary knowledge is simply by *teacher observation and careful questioning.* For example, during or after reading a story, the child can simply be asked: "What did the word _____ mean in this story?" (selection). In informal questioning, the reading teacher has the opportunity to probe into questionable answers, which enables him or her to have some confidence in the validity of the assessment of the child's vocabulary knowledge. However, since there are no standards with which to compare the child's answers to informal questions about vocabulary, it is obvious that the more experienced the teacher is, the more likely it is that an accurate assessment will take place.

One of the more important informal means of assessing meaning vocabulary knowledge is through *contextual analysis inventories of various types.* Contextual analysis to determine word meanings is a skill which becomes very important at about the third-grade reading level. One of the useful ways of assessing a child's ability to use context clues is to present the child with a list of eight or ten frequently encountered vocabulary words from his or her basal reader or expository (content) material at the instructional reading level. Have the child write down the meanings for any words which are known. Initially, the words should be presented in sentences with minimal context clues to determine if the child knows the words without the help of good context clues. Next the teacher presents the same eight or ten words in sentences containing good context clues and asks the child to give meanings for the words. When the child is to complete this type of assessment sheet independently, the sentences should not contain words which would cause decoding problems. For each child the teacher can arrive at a score indicating the number of words defined correctly from context out of the total number of words which originally were not known. Answers should be scored on this kind of inventory leniently since different meanings based on context may be possible and should be considered correct.

Sample of an Informal Context Assessment Sheet

The following pages present a sample of the type of informal context assessment sheet which was just described. Although the sample is designed for about the sixth-grade reading level and can be duplicated and used by the reading teacher if it seems appropriate, more importantly, it should serve as a model in constructing this kind of assessment.

INFORMAL CONTEXT ASSESSMENT SHEET
(Approximately sixth-grade reading level)

NOTE TO THE READING TEACHER: *Place Parts 1 and 2 on separate sheets of paper.*

Name _____ **Grade** _____ **Teacher** _____

Part 1: Directions

Write as many definitions or synonyms as you know for the following underlined words.

1. The wealthy man owned a *chalet.* _____
2. My mother wishes that she had a new *comforter.* _____
3. The *hangar* was destroyed by a tornado. _____
4. That animal seems to be very *cumbersome.* _____
5. My older sister made a *soufflé.* _____
6. My doctor is never *punctual.* _____
7. The gentleman had a white *goateé.* _____
8. Unfortunately, the *plankton* seemed to be dead. _____
9. The hot-air balloon's *descent* was not very successful. _____
10. Jenny read about *extraterrestrial* beings. _____
11. He *jettisoned* some heavy baggage. _____
12. In the accident the car *plummeted.* _____

Part 2: Directions

Write a *meaning* for each underlined word.

1. The wealthy man in Switzerland owned a beautiful *chalet* with four bedrooms. _____

2. My mother wishes that she had a new *comforter* to put on the bed to keep it warm. _____

3. The *hangar* in which four airplanes were stored was destroyed by a tornado. _____

4. That large, clumsy animal seems to be very *cumbersome*. _____
   _____

5. My older sister made a light, airy *soufflé* for lunch today. _____
   _____

6. My doctor is never *punctual* since he is always late due to emergencies.
   _____

7. The old gentleman wore a white *goateé* since he liked wearing a beard. _____

8. Unfortunately, the *plankton* which was growing in the ocean seemed to have died. _____

9. The hot-air balloon's *descent* to the earth was not very successful. _____
   _____

10. Jenny read about *extraterrestrial* beings from outer space. _____
    _____

11. He *jettisoned* some heavy baggage from his hot-air balloon so it wouldn't fall. _____

12. In the accident the car *plummeted* down the mountain. _____

Total number not known in Part 1 _____

Number correct in Part 2
out of number not known in Part 1 _____

Answer Key

(Score leniently since any approximation of a correct answer should be scored as accurate, as was explained earlier in this section).

1. a cottage or house in the style of a Swiss cottage
2. a stuffed or quilted cover for a bed
3. a shelter for housing airplanes
4. clumsy, awkward
5. a spongy hot dish, omelette
6. on time, prompt
7. a man's beard on his chin which is trimmed somewhat
8. plant life in a body of water
9. dropping, falling
10. from outer space
11. threw overboard
12. fell down, fell over

Sample of Another Informal Context Assessment Sheet

Another approach for assessing a child's ability in vocabulary knowledge by using context clues which may be useful for the reading teacher *involves using the multiple-choice format*. The child is asked to provide meanings for about 10 vocabulary words presented in sentences with minimal context clues. Then the child is given a group of 10 sentences, each one containing an underlined vocabulary term followed by three or four synonyms or definitions. The child is to use the context of the sentences to select that synonym or definition which best fits the underlined word. The reading teacher should use vocabulary terms from the child's own basal reader or expository (content) material at the instructional reading level. The use of the multiple-choice approach for assessing the use of context has several advantages. The activity is fairly easy for the child to complete because he or she does not have to devise his or her own responses. The context assessment sheet also can be scored more objectively than the assessment sheet just illustrated which required some subjective analysis.

The following pages present a sample of the kind of informal context assessment sheet which was just explained. Although it is designed to be used at about the third-grade reading level and can be duplicated and used by the reading teacher if this is appropriate, it also may serve as a model for the reading teacher in constructing this type of assessment sheet for his or her children on the use of context clues for vocabulary improvement.

INFORMAL CONTEXT ASSESSMENT SHEET
(Approximately third-grade reading level)

NOTE TO THE READING TEACHER: *Place Parts 1 and 2 on separate sheets of paper.*

Name _____ **Grade** _____ **Teacher** _____

Part 1: Directions

Write as many *definitions or synonyms* as you know for the following underlined words.

1. There was a large *boulder* in the way. _____

2. Paul's father was a *lumberjack*. _____

3. I don't like *flapjacks*. _____

4. My mother has a new *griddle*. _____

5. Pa has a very large *ox*. _____

6. Mr. Jensen owns a *sawmill*. _____

7. A *stork* is usually white. _____

8. The *bunkhouse* was very old. _____

9. My father is a *mighty* man. _____

10. There is a large *stump* in our yard. _____

Part 2: Directions

Circle the word after each sentence which is the best *definition or synonym* for the underlined word in the sentence.

1. The farmer's field had many rocks and one large *boulder* in it.
   rock, tree, fence

2. Paul's father was a *lumberjack* who cut down trees for a living.
   farmer, logger, trucker

3. I don't like *flapjacks* with syrup on them for breakfast.
   pancakes, toast, waffles

4. My mother has a new *griddle* for making pancakes.
   toaster, pail, thin frying pan

5. Pa had a very large *ox* pulling our covered wagon.
   cow, horse, mule

6. Mr. Jensen had a *sawmill* where lumber was cut.
   building for cutting timber
   building for selling groceries
   building for making horseshoes

7. A *stork* has a long neck, long legs, and a long bill and is usually white.
   fish, animal, bird

8. The *bunkhouse* in Texas was very old.
   house where the cowboys sleep
   house where the owners live
   house where the cowboys work

9. My father is a *mighty*, powerful man.
   strong, small, weak

10. There is a large *stump* among the trees in our yard.
    branch, end and roots of a tree, bush

Total number not known in Part 1 _____

Number correct in Part 2
out of number not known in Part 1 _____

Answer Key

(Score leniently in Part 1 since any approximation of a correct answer should be scored as accurate as was explained earlier in this section.)

1. rock
2. logger
3. pancakes
4. thin frying pan
5. cow
6. building for cutting timber
7. bird
8. house where the cowboys sleep
9. strong
10. end and roots of a tree

It is important to assess a child's use of *structural analysis as an aid to word meanings* from about the third-grade reading level on up. Usually a child's use and knowledge of prefixes, suffixes, and word roots is best assessed along with his or her skill in using context clues since roots and affixes seldom have only one meaning. The child may need to know the context in which the affix or root occurs to determine the appropriate meaning of the element. The child has to provide meanings for the underlined words and for each prefix, suffix, or root as it is used in a particular sentence. Therefore, only several affixes or roots should be included in a single test. An example of one variation of such an informal test is the following:

> Read each sentence below and write down what you think is the meaning of each word (which has one line under it) and each prefix (which has two lines under it).
> The submarine is an interesting ship since so much of it travels under water.
> My mother has always wanted to go on a transatlantic voyage.
> He is a very abnormal man.

STRATEGIES FOR IMPROVING VOCABULARY KNOWLEDGE

There are many strategies, activity sheets, materials, and computer software which can be used in both the primary and intermediate grades for the improvement of meaning vocabulary. This section summarizes many of the most useful strategies and provides some ready-to-use activity sheets for improving meaning vocabulary knowledge as well as listing some materials, games, and computer software. The strategies are not divided into primary- and intermediate-level activities since it was thought that occasionally they are appropriate for either level. However, an approximate grade level designation is provided when it seems useful. The reading teacher should find these materials very useful in helping him or her improve the vocabulary knowledge of his or her students.

There are both *incidental and preplanned activities* which should be used for vocabulary development in the primary and intermediate grades. Although both types of activities can be useful, neither one should be used solely. *Incidental activities for vocabulary development* involve a good classroom environment, use of contextual analysis, use of wide reading, use of structural analysis, dictionary use by the child while reading, and interpreting ambiguous words such as homographs and figurative language.

Direct activities for vocabulary development can involve vocabulary expansion as a result of direct experiences and vicarious experiences, use of vocabulary overview guides, semantic maps, semantic feature analysis, lessons on the use of structural elements such as prefixes, suffixes, and word roots for vocabulary development, vocabulary presentation prior to reading, motor imagery, activity sheets, games, computer software, and commercial materials. Although both preplanned and incidental activities should be used for vocabulary development, in most classrooms vocabulary development is predominately left to incidental development, and more time and effort should be made in direct, preplanned lessons.

The *single most effective way of improving vocabulary knowledge is through wide reading of narrative and content material if there are not too many unknown words in the material for context to be a useful clue to word identification.* Most reading specialists think that there should not be more than *1 unknown word in 50 running words* if context is to be used effectively. When vocabulary knowledge is improved in this manner, an *approximate word meaning* is all that is required for effective comprehension and the correct pronunciation of the word is *not* of primary importance. It is simply necessary that the child make an approximation of the word's meaning so that effective comprehension can take place. Of course it is very difficult to motivate disabled readers to read very much at all, and it is even more difficult to get them to generate an approximate word meaning for an unknown word. Instead, they often merely skip over the unknown word without paying much attention to its approximate or actual meaning. However, if it can be motivated, wide reading is extremely effective in improving word meaning knowledge at both the primary and intermediate levels.

Although Barbara Taylor, Larry A. Harris, and P. David Pearson have stated that contextual analysis is very effective in developing reading vocabulary, they have also stated that children are not very skilled in the use of this strategy.[8]

Sometimes distinct context clues for unfamiliar words are not provided in naturally occurring text. However, even when context clues do occur, elementary children have been found to have difficulty. For example, several researchers found that sixth-grade students were able to determine the meanings of unfamiliar words through the use of context clues about *40%* of the time. Children had the greatest difficulty when contextual information was separated from unfamiliar words. However, they also stated that elementary children can be taught to improve their skill in using context clues to determine word meanings. A modification of the instructional technique which they developed is as follows:

What, Why, and When—First the teacher explains to children what they will be working on and why this is important. They should learn how to look for meaning clues for unfamiliar words which will help them better understand what they are reading. Contextual analysis is useful because if children are able to generate an approximate meaning for an unfamiliar word, they will not be forced to stop and use the dictionary.

How—Next the teacher models contextual analysis using the reading material which the children currently are using themselves. The teacher may read a paragraph aloud containing an unfamiliar word (such as loquacious) and discuss how other words in the same sentence or in nearby sentences provide clues to word meanings. The teacher then helps the children to come up with an approximate meaning for the word. After modeling the process a few times, the teacher and children together locate clue words and derive approximate meanings for unfamiliar words. The child then continues to read independently and stops to write down clue words and approximate meanings for unfamiliar words which have been targeted by the teacher.[9]

Types of Context Clues

Although it is not important for children to label context clues, you may wish to be able to differentiate between the following types of context clues:

---

[8]Barbara Taylor, Larry A. Harris, and P. David Pearson, *Reading Difficulties: Instruction and Assessment* (New York: Random House, 1988), p. 257.

[9]Adapted from Douglas Carnine, Edward J. Kameenui, and Gayle Coyle, "Utilization of Contextual Information in Determining the Meaning of Unfamiliar Words," *Reading Research Quarterly*, Volume 19 (Winter, 1984), pp. 188–204.

Experience Clues—The reader uses his or her own background of experiences to determine the meaning of the unknown word.

Association Clues—The reader tries to associate the unknown word with a word that he or she knows. *Example*: He felt as *ravenous* as a bear.

Synonym Clues—There is a synonym to the unknown word in the sentence to explain it; e.g., My grandfather seems to be a very *frugal*, stingy man.

Summary Clues—Several sentences are used which summarize the meaning of the unknown word.

Comparison or Contrast Clues—There is a comparison or contrast to the unknown word in the sentence or paragraph which gives it its meaning.

Previous Contact Clues—The reader can determine the meaning of an unknown word from a previous contact which he or she has had with a similar word.[10]

A Sample Activity Sheet Using the Context Method

The *context method for vocabulary development* requires children to read a paragraph in which the target word appears in each of three sentences which provide context to help define the word. The children then are asked to write something which would relate the word to their own experiences. The following pages present an activity sheet on approximately the fifth-grade reading level which uses the context method. You can duplicate and use this activity in its present form if it seems appropriate for you. However, it mainly should serve as a model for you of this type of activity.

---

[10]Harold L. Herber, *Teaching Reading in Content Areas.* (Englewood Cliffs, NJ: Prentice-Hall, Inc., 1967), p. 163.

ACTIVITY SHEET USING THE CONTEXT METHOD
(Approximately fifth-grade reading level)

Name _____ **Grade** _____ **Teacher** _____

Read each set of sentences to yourself. Try to determine the meaning of the *target word* in each set of sentences. Then answer the question following each set of sentences.

1. A bullet is an example of a *projectile*.
   A *projectile* is anything that is thrown forward at a high rate of speed.
   A paper airplane may be a child's *projectile*.

   Write down what you could make a *projectile* out of.

   _____

2. My mother was *hospitable* toward her new neighbor.
   An *hospitable* person is a friendly person.
   At the open house my teacher was *hospitable* toward the parents.

   Write down how you could be *hospitable* toward a new child in your classroom.

   _____

3. My older sister had a *rendezvous* with her boy friend last evening.
   My father and mother had a *rendezvous* at the movie theater last night.
   A *rendezvous* is a place to meet.

   Who would you like to have a *rendezvous* with?

   _____

4. A *souvenir* is an object to remind a person of something.
   I brought a *souvenir* back from a trip to Mexico.
   It is fun to get a *souvenir* when someone comes back from a trip.

   What would you like to receive as a *souvenir*?

   _____

5. The *thermostat* in our furnace does not work very well.
   A *thermostat* is a device for keeping temperature even.
   The *thermostat* at our house is on the living room wall.

   Write at what temperature you believe a *thermostat* should be set in the winter.

   _____

6. A rattlesnake has a very dangerous *venom*.
Some snakes give off a very poisonous *venom*.
The female black widow spider has a poisonous *venom* also.

Write down what you should do if a person is afflicted by poisonous *venom* from a snake bite.

_____

7. Amy often *exasperates* me when she is late.
Exasperates means to make angry or annoy.
It *exasperates* me to have to do my homework.

Write down what *exasperates* you.

_____

8. My friend was *flabbergasted* when she won the lottery.
Flabbergasted means very surprised.
I was *flabbergasted* by the amount of my electric bill.

Write down when you are *flabbergasted*.

_____

9. Jess was *indignant* that he was not chosen captain of the football team.
Indignant means angry at something unfair.
I was *indignant* that he didn't keep his word.

Write down what makes you *indignant*.

_____

10. A *contraption* is something made to do a special job.
My father made a *contraption* for getting our car out of a snowbank.
That is a *contraption* for draining antifreeze from an automobile.

Write down what you would like your *contraption* to do.

_____

Answer Key

(The answers included here are only for illustrative purposes. Obviously, any logical answer to a question should be considered correct. Creativity in responses should be encouraged in this activity sheet.)

1. a paper cup
2. I could show him around the school building after school and invite him to my house later to watch television.
3. the cute boy who sits right behind me.
4. A shell from Florida from my grandmother who lives there
5. about 72°
6. run and get help as fast as possible.
7. when my brother hits me for no good reason
8. when I get an A on a history test
9. when somebody doesn't tell me the truth
10. I would like a robot who makes dinner.

In general the most effective way of encouraging vocabulary expansion after that of wide reading probably is the use of *direct experience,* especially in the primary grades where this type of experience normally is the most feasible. For direct experience to be most effective, new vocabulary terms have to be emphasized *prior to the experience,* and even more importantly, *have to be featured after the experience.* Both before and after the direct experience, the important, new vocabulary terms should be written on the chalkboard or a transparency, pronounced, and defined with the children's help using the context in which they are going to occur or have occurred. For example, prior to a second-grade field trip to a local radio station such vocabulary words as *satellite dish, transmitter, microphone, frequency, program, schedule, announcer, weather-man,* and *tower* might be featured. These words should be discussed while at the radio station and then again emphasized after returning to the classroom by using them in written stories.

Examples of some direct experiences include such activities as school trips, cooking and baking activities, discussing out-of-school activities such as a soccer game, science experiments, classroom visitors of various types, food-tasting experiences, rhythm activities, or demonstrations of various types.

> NOTE: The most important fact is that the new vocabulary terms have to be used in follow-up writing and reading for them to be learned effectively.

Vicarious or second-hand experiences also are a useful way of enhancing vocabulary growth. Although not as effective on the whole as are direct experiences, they often are more feasible and still are quite useful in vocabulary expansion. Obviously, a child cannot take a trip into space but can learn many new vocabulary terms such as *rocket, launching pad, eject, rocket fuel, astronaut,* and *space suit* from viewing a film, filmstrip, or videotape about space travel. Some examples of vicarious experiences are viewing a film, filmstrip, or videotape, watching a television program, using computer software, especially simulations such as *The Oregon Trail* (MEEC), listening to cassette recordings or records, looking at pictures, and watching a scientific experiment. However, as was the case with direct experiences, vocabulary terms must be stressed *prior to the experience and after it* for the optimum in vocabulary development.

Daniel R. Hittleman has stated that successful programs for vocabulary development must focus on *specific exercises (direct instruction)* as the major means to vocabulary development. According to Hittleman, such a program must include the following elements:

1. A few words should be taught in-depth rather than many words being presented in a more cursory fashion.
2. Any technique which is employed should call attention to the meanings of word parts such as prefixes, suffixes, and word roots.
3. Context, the dictionary, and the derivations of words should be studied to obtain word meanings.
4. The instruction should be systematic and continuous.
5. Students must be exposed to the same word in many different contexts.
6. Game-like activities are incorporated into the schedule to stimulate children to study vocabulary.[11]

Another example of *direct practice* which has proven to be effective was described by a number of other researchers. This instructional strategy involves presenting words and their meanings written on index cards to children and conducting the following procedure:

1. Teacher says the word (*loquacious*).
2. Child says the word.

---

[11]Daniel R. Hittleman, *Developmental Reading, K-8.* (Boston: Houghton Mifflin Company, 1983), p. 242.

3. Child is asked to read the word's meaning(s) from the card (talkative).

4. Teacher asks questions related to the word such as: "Do you know anyone who is very loquacious?" "Can a dog be loquacious?"

5. Teacher asks child to say the meaning of the word again.

6. Teacher presents a second card, and instruction on the second word begins employing the same five steps.

7. Instruction on the third word is conducted using the same steps.

8. After instruction on the third word, a review is conducted: The child is asked questions about each of the three words to determine if the meanings are known. If not, the appropriate card is shown again, and the child is asked to respond to questions while looking at the card.

9. Following the cumulative review, all of the above steps are carried out with three additional words.[12]

Although the preceding strategy was found to be extremely useful in vocabulary development, children who were exposed to this technique made even more progress when the following aspect was added to it:

Technique Number Two consisted of all of the steps just described but also children were taught to *integrate their meanings of the words during passage reading*.

Integration means that their reading was halted whenever they encountered one of the target words in a passage, and they were required to say its meanings as well as to answer a question asked by the teacher, which also required knowledge of the meaning of the word.

Semantic Maps (Webs)

Semantic maps (webs) can be used as a very important strategy for improving vocabulary knowledge, especially in content areas, as well as for improving comprehension ability as is described in Sections 5, 6, and 7 of the *Reading Comprehension Activities Kit*. Semantic mapping is based on the principle that children learn by relating the new to the known; that is, by relating new concepts to existing concepts (prior knowledge). Recently it has been found that vocabulary instruction which helps children relate unfamiliar words and their meanings to known concepts is more effective than conventional approaches which focus on learning definitions or using context to determine the meanings of unfamiliar words.

Semantic mapping or webbing involves linking vocabulary words to as many related words as possible. It is particularly useful in vocabulary development in the expository (content) areas. For example, pretend that a class of children has

---

[12]Adapted from Edward L. Kameenui, Douglas W. Carnine, and Roger Freschi, "Effects of Text Instruction and Instructional Procedures for Teaching Word Meanings on Comprehension and Recall," *Reading Research Quarterly*. Vol. 17 (Winter, 1982), pp. 367–388.

just read a passage in their social studies book about the *Dust Bowl of the 1930s*. The teacher might help the children construct a semantic map about the concept Dust Bowl on the chalkboard while the children attempt to construct their own map on sheets of paper. Free associations with the various concepts help in the making of the semantic map.

The major head of the semantic map would be *Dust Bowl*. Some of the categories under this concept may be definition, where it occurred, reasons for it, and the results of it. The following is an example of such a semantic map:

definition   *where it occurred*
lack of significant rainfall   Kansas
topsoil blown away by strong winds   Midwest
                                                Nebraska
                                                South Dakota
                                                North Dakota

                        DUST BOWL

reasons for it   *results of it*
drought   crops such as corn, wheat, oats, and barley not
high winds   being grown
low humidity   high heat
wind erosion   topsoil blowing away
                        farmers going bankrupt
                        farmers leaving the area

Another strategy for vocabulary development involving the technique of semantic mapping (webbing) involves taking a familiar concept about a reading selection which the children are going to read and having them generate ideas related to this concept. *After reading, new concepts gained from the reading can be added to the map.* For example, before reading a science chapter on the *process of digestion* children might generate these vocabulary terms relating to the process: *mouth, teeth, tongue, stomach, small intestine, large intestine, colon*, and *liver*. After reading the chapter, such vocabulary terms as these may be added to the map: *primary or deciduous teeth, permanent teeth, orthodontist, pharynx, esophagus, fundus, pyloric end, duodenum, jejunum, ileum, gall bladder, ascending colon, transverse colon, descending colon, pancreas*, and *bile*.

This is called a *pre-/post-semantic map* and is illustrated now using these vocabulary terms. Words on this map which the children knew before the reading are written in regular type, while new words which were added after the reading are placed in capital letters.

The Mouth   *ESOPHAGUS*   *Stomach*
PRIMARY OR DECIDUOUS teeth   FUNDUS
PERMANENT teeth   PYLORIC END
ORTHODONTIST
tongue
PHARYNX

PROCESS OF DIGESTION

Small Intestine	*Large Intestine (Colon)*	PANCREAS	*Liver*
DUODENUM	*ASCENDING COLON*		*BILE*
JEJUNUM	*TRANSVERSE COLON*		
ILEUM	*DESCENDING COLON*		

Semantic Feature Analysis

Another strategy which helps children learn the meanings of unfamiliar words by relating them to known words is called *semantic feature analysis*. This technique involves looking at the similarities and differences of related concepts. Semantic feature analysis has proven very useful as a technique for improving children's vocabulary.

Semantic feature analysis involves the reading teacher's selecting a category such as *vegetables* and listing in the left-hand column some members of this category such as *carrot, asparagus, turnip, spinach, potatoes,* and *broccoli.* Features which may be common to the category such as *skin, green color, roots,* and *peel* may be listed in a row across the top of the semantic feature analysis grid. The teacher and children can use a system of pluses and minuses to determine which members of the category under investigation have which features. A plus in a semantic feature analysis grid means *yes* (that the category members have this feature), a minus means *no* it does not have the feature, and a question mark means perhaps or maybe it has this feature. If one of the category members is a new vocabulary word, children will be able to see how this new vocabulary term is similar to, yet different from, the other words which the child already knows.

For example, the teacher puts the new vocabulary terms at the top of the column of category members and asks the children to add other examples of category members to the grid. The children then are asked to add features of the category members to the grid. The children then complete the grid by using pluses and minuses to match members and features as explained earlier.

Sample Feature Analysis Grid at Approximately the Sixth-Grade Level

The following page presents a sample feature analysis grid at the upper intermediate-grade reading level based on the content area of science. You may copy and use this semantic feature analysis grid if it seems applicable for you. However, it is designed primarily to serve as a model of this type of technique which you can construct from your own children's material especially in the expository (content) areas.

SAMPLE FEATURE ANALYSIS GRID
(Approximately sixth-grade level)

Name —————— Grade —————— Teacher ——————

CATEGORY-REPTILES

Place an X in the proper spaces of this grid.

Category Members	Beak with Sharp Cutting Edge	Exoskeleton or Shell	Lung Breathing	Rows of Sharp, Pointed Teeth	Reproduction with Eggs on Land	Body Covered with Horny Scales and Tough Skin	Poisonous	Eggs Have a Protective Shell That Prevents Evaporation	Restricted to Tropical and Subtropical Climates
Turtle									
Alligator									
Crocodile									
Lizard									
Snake									

Answer Key

Turtle—beak with sharp, cutting edge
        exoskeleton or shell
        lung breathing
        reproduction with eggs on land
        eggs have a protective shell that prevents evaporation

Alligator—lung breathing
          rows of sharp, pointed teeth
          reproduction with eggs on land
          body covered with horny scales and tough skin
          eggs have a protective shell that prevents evaporation
          restricted to tropical and subtropical climates

Crocodile—lung breathing
          rows of sharp, pointed teeth
          reproduction with eggs on land
          body covered with horny scales and tough skin
          eggs have a protective shell that prevents evaporation
          restricted to tropical and subtropical climates

Lizard—lung breathing
        reproduction with eggs on land (sometimes)
        poisonous (only the gila monster)
        eggs have a protective shell that prevents evaporation

Snake—lung breathing
        reproduction with eggs on land (sometimes)
        poisonous (some of them)
        eggs have a protective shell that prevents evaporation

---

Semantic Association

Another strategy that can be used for vocabulary expansion especially from the lower intermediate grades on up is *semantic association*. The purpose of semantic association is to extend vocabulary by involving children with words that share some common feature. Although this can be begun as a group or independent activity, it must end in group discussion to be useful. The following are the basic steps in this procedure. They can be varied if you want to do so.

1. Select any word or words of interest to the class or to you. They can be words from a basal reader story or a social studies or science lesson.

2. Write the word(s) on the chalkboard. For example, the reading teacher might write the words *fly* and *eggs* before reading a chapter in a science textbook about *birds*.

3. Have half the class write as many things as they can think of related to flying. Have the other half write as many words as they can think of related to eggs. Have the children think and write independently or in small groups.

4. Compile lists on the chalkboard of all the words the children thought of. For example:

Fly

space shuttle	wings	wind surfing	eagle	kite
airplane	soar	hang gliding	insects	rocket
jet	hot-air balloon	Canada	vulture	hummingbird
sky	glide	geese		
		airliner		

Eggs

yolk	reproduction	poach	green	mottled	hen
whites	boil	albumen	brown	chicken	scrambled
shell	fry	speckled	blue	oval	soufflé
nest	incubation	bird	whip	hatch	goose

5. If you wish, you may have the children use several of the words in sentences.

6. Lead a discussion on the meanings and uses of any of the words that were unknown to the children. For example, although they may know the meaning of the words *yolk, shell, boil,* and *fry,* they may not know the meanings of the words *incubation, albumen, mottled,* and *soufflé.* The new words can be learned by classifying them with words already known. Besides learning new words, new meanings or connotations for known words probably will develop. *Discussion is crucial to the expansion of vocabulary because it helps children to expand categories.*

Motor Imagery

Motor imagery has been found by Ula Price Casale to be useful for vocabulary development. Casale discovered that when children attempted to remember word meanings, they made slight hand gestures similar to the ones she used in teaching these same words. Her other observations confirmed the theory that most people use subtle hand or body gestures when they search for a word in memory. From her observations Casale developed the following six-step procedure for teaching a word through *motor imagery*:

1. The teacher writes a word on the chalkboard or overhead projector, pronounces it, and then tells the class its meaning.
2. The teacher tells the children to imagine how they might pantomime the word to show its meaning.
3. The teacher has the class pantomime the word. Upon being given a specific cue, all of the children begin.
4. The teacher watches the children to determine the most common pantomime, and then explains it to the class. The children pantomime the word while saying it.
5. The teacher repeats each new word and has the class pantomime it and say a brief meaning or synonym.
6. The children then read the selection which contains the new words.

Casale has stated that fairly abstract words can be defined for children in language which translates easily into motor imagery. For example, the word *abode* can be defined as a "place where you live." Several examples of the language meaning and motor meaning for this and several other words are as follows:

New Word	Language Meaning	Motor Meaning
abode	place where you live	hands meeting above the head in a triangular roof shape
appropriate	right or fit for a certain purpose	both palms together matching perfectly
woe	great sadness or trouble	one or both hands over the eyes, head slanted forward[13]

Dale Johnson has stated the following about vocabulary development which also should prove useful for the reading teacher:

All words, like all real-word objects and events, can be placed in categories. In fact, the ability of the human mind to categorize, to examine the similarities and differences between two or more concepts, to draw relationships, is what

---

[13]Adapted from Ula Price Casale, "Motor Imagery: A Reading-Vocabulary Strategy," *Journal of Reading*, Vol. 28 (April, 1985), pp. 619–621.

enables humans to learn. Nothing can be learned in isolation. Try to think of anything you have ever learned and how you learned it and you will quickly recollect that you learned it in relation to something you already knew. You categorized it. You might have learned the meaning of *lavender* in relation to your knowledge of blue or red or purple or pink. *Spindle* might have been learned in relation to bend, fold, and mutilate and your experience with computer-card mentality. A child may not know the meaning of *mammoth* but can be helped to relate it to big, large, huge, and gigantic. The meaning of *Albasa* will remain a mystery unless you are able to relate it to things already known—that is, to categorize it.[14]

Association Method

Direct practice with words and their synonyms is an effective way to enhance vocabulary knowledge. Joan Gipe calls this the *association method.* There are a number of activities that can be used to improve ability in the use of *synonyms*,[15] as well as both teacher-made and commercially available games and activity sheets which can be used for this purpose. The following page provides an activity sheet at about the fourth-grade reading level which can be used for the purpose of improving ability in the knowledge and use of synonyms. You can duplicate and use this activity sheet in its present form if it is applicable, or use it as a model for constructing your own activity sheets.

---

[14]From *Three Sound Strategies for Vocabulary Development* by Dale D. Johnson, Number 3 of the GINN OCCASIONAL PAPERS, © Copyright 1983 by Ginn and Company. Used by permission of Silver, Burdett & Ginn Inc.

[15]Joan Gipe, "Investigating Techniques for Teaching Word Meanings," *Reading Research Quarterly*, Vol. 14 (1978–1979), pp. 624–644.

ACTIVITY SHEET FOR IMPROVING COMPETENCY IN THE USE OF SYNONYMS FOR VOCABULARY DEVELOPMENT
(Approximately fourth-grade reading level)

Name _____ Grade _____ Teacher _____

Put an *X* in front of the word which would best substitute for the underlined word.

1. Jamie found the *carcass* of a deer when he went walking in the woods last summer.

    ____ body ____ antlers ____ feet

2. My older brother is hoping to *conquer* his drug addiction very soon.

    ____ continue ____ defeat ____ complete

3. Ashley happend to see an *enormous* bear when she went with her family to the garbage dump.

    ____ frightening ____ huge ____ small

4. The *gallant* policeman helped my little sister find her way home when she was lost.

    ____ polite ____ rude ____ young

5. We saw a mother red fox and her three baby foxes when they came out of their *lair* yesterday.

    ____ hole ____ woods ____ den

6. The old man used to have a traveling *managerie* which children were interested in seeing.

    ____ group of wild animals ____ circus ____ carnival

7. *Myths* are often a good way to learn about the history of a country.

    ____ old stories ____ textbooks ____ films

8. All living things need a certain amount of *oxygen*.

    ____ a gas ____ food ____ water

Use a *thesaurus or your own mind* to choose a more effective *synomym* for the underlined word. Then write it on the blank line.

9. Jeff *said* that he was very angry when his best friend was late for the birthday party. _____

10. That *cute* girl is my older sister. _____

11. Mrs. Jackson is always very *nice*. _____

12. The man was *happy* when he won the state lottery. _____

13. The prizes in that contest are always *great*. _____

14. Mrs. Lopez made a *swell* meal for us last night. _____

15. My father is *sad* today because he lost his job. _____

Answer Key

1. _X_ body   5. _X_ den

2. _X_ defeat   6. _X_ group of wild animals

3. _X_ huge   7. _X_ old stories

4. _X_ polite   8. _X_ a gas

(Any acceptable answer should be considered correct in this part. The answers given are only for illustrative purposes).

9. yelled   13. wonderful

10. adorable   14. delicious

11. pleasant   15. depressed

12. jubilant

The Predict-O-Gram

Camille Blanchowicz recently described the *predict-o-gram* as a strategy that combines vocabulary development and story structure awareness. Children are encouraged to make predictions about how the author will use vocabulary to tell about the setting, characters, the problem or goal, the actions, resolution, or feelings of a character in a story.[16]

Given the following vocabulary for a short version of the narrative story *Charlotte's Web* by E. B. White, the children would be asked to classify the words according to how they predict the author might use them in the story. Children can learn to use this strategy independently when they meet vocabulary lists by predicting how the words relate to the elements of story structure. The following illustrates how this strategy might be used:

---

[16]Camille Blanchowicz, "Making Connections: Alternatives to the Vocabulary Notebook," *Journal of Reading*, Vol. 29 (April, 1986), pp. 643–649.

Charlotte's Web

twilight
spider
killing
goslings
weaving
pig
sign
barn
swallows
death
message
cutting

Charlotte's Web

The Setting	*The Characters*	*The Goal or Problem*
twilight	spider	killing
barn	goslings	death
	pig	
	swallows	

The Actions	*The Resolution*	
weaving	sign	
cutting	message	

Semantic Categories

Another strategy for vocabulary development that attempts to relate the known (prior knowledge) to the unknown is that of *semantic categories*. This strategy involves introducing new words through the use of semantic categories. New words are introduced in a word list which deals with a specific semantic category. Joan Gipe has suggested that each word list contain one unknown word and three unfamiliar words. Children are told to study the list and add words to the list from their personal background.[17] For example, the category heading of *Famous People* may be used to introduce the new word *eminent*. Three known words such as *famous, well-known,* and *prominent* can be used in the word list to provide clues to the meaning of the unknown word. Here is an example of children's words added to the category of *Famous People*:

---

[17] Joan Gipe, "Use of Relevant Context Helps Kids Learn New Word Meanings," *The Reading Teacher*, Vol. 33 (January, 1980), pp. 398–402.

Famous People

famous
eminent
talented
well-known
prominent
celebrities

The following page presents an activity sheet on approximately the sixth-grade reading level which uses semantic categories as a strategy for vocabulary expansion. You can duplicate and use this activity sheet if it seems applicable, but it is meant primarily as a model of this kind of activity sheet that you can construct on your own for vocabulary development.

ACTIVITY SHEET USING SEMANTIC CATEGORIES FOR VOCABULARY DEVELOPMENT
(Approximately sixth-grade reading level)

Name _____ Grade _____ Teacher _____

Read each group of words silently. Then write two more words between the ruled lines which belong to that category.

Ways to Ask

beseech
beg
plead
please

_____

_____

Types of Diseases

tuberculosis
cancer
measles
pneumonia

_____

_____

Types of Metal

gold
bronze
tin
iron

_____

_____

Types of Wild Cats

panther
leopard
wildcat
mountain lion

_____

_____

Types of Criminals

arsonist
thief
murderer
rapist

_____

_____

Types of Jewels

amethyst
diamond
emerald
pearls

_____

_____

Types of Trees

eucalyptus
birch
maple
basswood

_____

_____

Types of Profession

architect
doctor
lawyer
minister

_____

_____

Types of Scientists

biologist
chemist
botanist
geologist

_____

_____

Types of Color

indigo
lilac
pink
yellow

_____

_____

©1990 by The Center for Applied Research in Education

Answer Key

(The answers included here are only illustrative of possible answers to this activity sheet. Other acceptable answers also should be considered correct.)

implore	diabetes
ask	heart disease
	flu
silver	tiger
platinum	lion
aluminum	jaguar
robber	ruby
burglar	sapphire
forger	topaz
oak	teacher
elm	nurse
zoologist	green
meteorologist	orange
oceanographer	brown
paleontologist	

Word Connection Procedure

Camille Blanchowicz also has described another interesting strategy for vocabulary expansion called *word connections*. Given a word list from a basal story or content textbook, she suggests that children should use the *word connection procedure* to broaden word meaning knowledge.[18] Children can pick any two

---

[18]Blanchowicz, *op. cit.*, pp. 643–649.

words from the instructional word list and tell how they might be related. For example, an instructional word list for a chapter on *leaves* and their functions from an upper grade science textbook might be the following:

chlorophyll   *deciduous*
evaporation   *water*

A child might be able to connect evaporation and water since much of the water in a plant evaporates when it receives a high amount of direct sunlight. A child might possibly be able to relate chlorophyll and deciduous since the plant does not manufacture chlorophyll when a deciduous tree is free of leaves in the winter. Word connection is simply a form of *classification*. It is important to note that only through group discussion with children of how the words relate to each other can this strategy be used in a most optimum way for vocabulary expansion. Children always should be encouraged to develop independence in the use of word connections by having them make connections between and among vocabulary words which are presented in basal reader stories and in content (expository) units.

Very Brief List of Materials, Games, and Computer Software that Can be Used for Vocabulary Development

Materials

Vocabulary Drills—Jamestown Press

Vocabulary Building—Zaner-Bloser

Word Power—Developmental Learning Materials

Words Are Important—Hammond Publishing Company

SRA: Structural Analysis—Science Research Associates

Prefix Puzzles—Developmental Learning Materials

Suffix Puzzles—Developmental Learning Materials

Developing Structural Analysis Skills—Educational Record Sales

The Vocabulary Development Series—Macmillan Publishing Company

Reading Reinforcement Skilltext Series—Charles E. Merrill Publishing Company

Reading for the Real World—Charles E. Merrill Publishing Company

Verbal Classifications—Midwest Publications

Vocabulary Building Exercises for Young People—Dormac Publishing Company

Vocabulary Fluency: Book A and Book B—Curriculum Associates, Inc.

Wordly Wise Reading Series—Educators Publishing Service, Inc.

Vocabulary Skills—Scholastic, Inc.

Idioms—Dormac Publishing Company

Many Meanings—Dormac Publishing Company

Schoolhouse Series: Vocabulary—Science Research Associates, Inc.

Words in Context—Opportunties for Learning

Games

Concentration—Make pairs from vocabulary words and synonyms or antonyms for these words. New vocabulary words also can be matched with their definitions.

Scrabble

Spill-and-Spell

Crossword Puzzles—The teacher can make crossword puzzles using new vocabulary words. Computer software also can be employed in the preparation of these crossword puzzles if the reading teacher wishes.

77 Games for Reading Groups—Fearon Publishing Company

Reading Skills: Simple Games, Aids, and Devices to Stimulate Reading Skills in the Classroom—Fearon Publishing Company

The Reading Box: 150 Reading Games and Activities—Educational Insights, Inc.

Vocabulary Development—Barnell-Loft. Ltd.

The following publishers sell commercially available games for the improvement of vocabulary:

Creative Publications
DLM Teaching Resources
Garrard Publishing Company
Kenworthy Educational Service, Inc.
Milton Bradley Company
Trend Enterprises, Inc.
(The addresses of these publishers are listed in Section 7 of this resource.)

Computer Software for Vocabulary Development

The Game Show—Computer Advanced Ideas

Stickybear Opposites—Weekly Reader Family Software

Dictionary—Microcomputers and Education

Vocabulary Builders—Orange Cherry Media

Vocabulary Builder and Vocabulary Expander—Micrograms, Inc.

Antonyms/Synonyms—Scholastic, Inc.

Homonyms—Scholastic Inc.

PAL—Universal Systems for Education, Inc.

Language Arts Elementary Volume 5—Scholastic Inc.

Word Master—Scholastic Inc.

Homonyms in Context—Random House, Inc.

Word Focus II Prefixes and Suffixes—Random House, Inc.

Create—Vocabulary—Hartley Courseware, Inc.

4

Using
Questioning Techniques
to Improve
Comprehension Ability

Perhaps an effective way to begin this section is to relate the words of a first-grade child who was reported to have said the following about a question his teacher asked him about a basal reader story: "My teacher asked me what color Jerry's shirt was in the story. Who cares what color his shirt was anyway? What does that have to do with the story?" Section 4 is designed to help the reading teacher understand the importance of truly meaningful comprehension questions and provides many classroom-tested strategies for using questioning techniques to improve students' comprehension ability.

The section opens by describing the various levels or types of comprehension and providing examples of comprehension questions of the different types or levels. Next it explains the importance of using questions for *teaching* comprehension skills instead of for merely assessing or evaluating it. The section discusses in detail how to use pre-reading questions to activate prior knowledge before reading a selection and also to set purposes for reading the selection. It also describes how to use prediction and questioning strategies to enhance a child's higher-level comprehension skills such as textually implicit and scriptally implicit skills. Next, it explains how to use post-reading questions to enhance a child's comprehension and to better enable the child to retain what has been comprehended.

This section also presents some practical strategies which should be considered for improving comprehension ability at both the primary-grade and the middle-upper grade levels. After reading it, the teacher of reading should better understand how questioning skills can play a crucial part in the development of effective comprehension ability at both the beginning and middle school levels.

THE LEVELS OF COMPREHENSION AND EXAMPLES OF COMPREHENSION QUESTIONS OF VARIOUS TYPES OR LEVELS

At the outset it is important for the reading teacher to have some understanding of the various levels or types of comprehension questions that can be posed before, during or after reading a passage. For the sake of clarification, they are called levels of comprehension questions even though they can be called types of questions. To call them levels of comprehension questions may give the reading teacher the idea that lower-level questions should be used with beginning readers, while higher-level questions should be used with children in the middle grades. In reality, all of the three main types of comprehension questions should be used with children at every reading level.

In any case, here is a brief description of the three major levels or types of comprehension questions:

Textually Explicit Questions (Literal, Factual, or Recall Questions)
These are also called questions in which the answer is found *"Right There."*

In this type of question the response is found directly in the reading selection and no interpretation is required. These questions are simple to formulate and easy to evaluate since there normally is only one correct answer to each question.

Textually Implicit Questions (Interpretive, Inferential, or Critical Questions)
These are also called *"Think and Search Questions."*

These are questions which require the reader to interpret, infer, draw conclusions and generalizations, predict outcomes, sense the author's mood and purpose, and critically analyze what is read. Examples of such critical analysis are discriminating between fact and fantasy, comparing material from several sources, and analyzing propaganda techniques. Although in the past most reading specialists differentiated between interpretive questions and critical questions, at the present time both of these types of questions normally are called *textually implicit comprehension questions.*

Scriptally Implicit Questions (Creative, Applied, Script Implicit, Schema Implicit, Integrative, or Assimilative Questions)
These are also called *"On My Own Questions."*

These are questions which require the reader to use his or her own prior knowledge or scripts in combination with the printed material to answer the comprehension questions. The term script comes from computer scientists who have stated that any information processor (whether human or computer) brings the mundane knowledge possessed to bear to a real-life situation. Then whenever the computer encounters a story dealing with an instance such as going to the zoo, it calls up or comes up with an appropriate *script.* This procedure makes for much more efficient computer programs, especially in programs which attempt to answer questions. An analogy can be made with the human information processor or reader. The reader who calls up the proper script or prior knowledge will be able to comprehend the material much more effectively and will be able to answer high-level comprehension questions about the material.

Scriptally implicit comprehension also can take other forms besides that of questioning. It can be any way in which reading is followed up, such as by creative writing of prose and poetry, expository writing as a follow-up to reading, creative dramatics, rhythm activities, music activities, construction activities, and art activities as a follow-up to reading.

Types of Comprehension Questions

The types of comprehension questions may become clearer by examining the following questions which were constructed from a fifth-grade basal reader story:

Jean Fritz, "The Cabin Faced West," *Landmarks, The HBJ Reading Program*, Orlando, Florida: Harcourt Brace Jovanovich, Publishers, 1987, pp. 432–447.

This is a basal reader story taken from the award-winning children's historical fiction tradebook *The Cabin Faced West* by Jean Fritz.

The story is set just after the Revolutionary War in the era when pioneers headed west across the Allegheny Mountains to homestead and turn the wilderness into farmland. The story focuses on the next-to-the youngest child in the family named Ann Hamilton and some of her experiences on the frontier, such as how upset she was when she let the fire in the fireplace burn out.

Some of Ann Hamilton's memories of growing up at that time were recorded by her great-great-granddaughter Jean Fritz in this story.

Textually Explicit (Literal) Comprehension Questions
What was to happen to the first brother who criticized the West?
What type of vegetable did Ann pick?
What did Ann put on her braids to make herself look special for the dinner?

Textually Implicit (Interpretive) Comprehension Questions
Why do you believe that Ann kept her few treasured possessions hidden so carefully?
Why do you think that it would be hard to kill a wild turkey with a slingshot?
Why do you think that Ann was afraid to start a fire from the beginning?

Textually Implicit (Critical) Comprehension Questions
Do you think that Ann was justified in complaining about life in the West? Why or why not?
Do you think that Ann should have felt bad when the fire went out? Why or why not?
Do you think that Ann was justified in not telling her family that she let the fire go out? Why or why not?

Scriptally Implicit (Creative) Comprehension Questions
Would you like to have lived in the same time and place as Ann? Why or why not?
Would you have told your family that you had allowed the fire to go out, or would you not have told them the truth? Why?
Would you have invited Arthur Scott to dinner if you had been Ann? Why or why not?

What Is a Question?

It may be helpful at this point to consider what constitutes a question? Most people believe that *wh-type* interrogative sentences are questions: *Who, What, Which, What did, When, Where, Why,* and *How.* Linguists normally would add *yes—no* questions, and *tag questions* such as "My mother made a good apple, pie, didn't she?" They also often add *intonation questions* such as "Sally went to school?" and *cleft questions* such as "where was it that Sally went?" to the list of various types of questions.

The reading teacher also should be concerned with some types of instructional directions that do not meet the grammatical test of being described as true questions. These can be called *pseudoquestions.* Pseudoquestions may be called "questions" in disguise. Pseudoquestions may use such words as *name, enumerate, discuss, describe,* or *give a reason.* Pseudoquestions will become clearer by examining the following true question and related pseudoquestion:
What were the causes of the Revolutionary War?
Describe the causes of the Revolutionary War. It is obvious that both can really be called questions although the second does not meet the grammatical test for a question.

The Importance of Using Questioning for Teaching Comprehension Instead of for Merely Assessing It

It is obvious that questions during and following reading traditionally have been the most important way of assessing a child's comprehension of the narrative and content material which he or she has read. They have been used for this purpose for many, many years. Unfortunately most of these questions have been of the explicit or literal (lower-level) type. In fact, a study by Frank J. Guszak recorded about 2,000 questions in second-grade, fourth-grade, and sixth-grade classrooms. Guszak found that teachers mainly asked explicit (literal) comprehension questions although the percentage of such questions decreased from about *67%* in second grade to about *48%* in both fourth and sixth grades. He found that even the critical questions which were asked often required only a *yes* or *no response* instead of a rationale for the response.[1] I believe that approximately the same results could be discovered today in a similar research study.

---

[1]Frank J. Guszak, "Teacher Questioning and Reading," *The Reading Teacher,* Volume 21 (Dec., 1967), pp. 227–234.

Some reading teachers also tend to rephrase the questions in the basal reader manuals so that a number of them are of the lower-level type which are easier to evaluate than are the interpretive or implicit type which often have more than one logical answer.

Dolores Durkin of the University of Illinois did a research study a number of years ago which found that elementary teachers of reading did little in the way of the teaching of comprehension, instead focusing primarily on the assessment of comprehension by the use of comprehension questions.[2] I believe that her results were somewhat overstated in that questioning along with many other elements of comprehension such as following directions, placing a number of items in correct sequence, and locating the main idea and important details among others can be considered *both* the teaching and the assessment of comprehension. However, I agree with her findings to the extent that more emphasis should be placed on the teaching of comprehension, obviously the most important element of reading instruction. I further believe that reading teachers today are placing much more emphasis on the teaching of comprehension skills than they did in the past as they better understand its great importance and effective techniques for doing so.

Therefore, effective questioning is perhaps the *single most effective and simple way* of improving a child's comprehension ability if it is used judiciously. Pre-questioning can help the child set purposes and make predictions for reading a selection and thus enable him or her to comprehend it much more effectively. The child will comprehend most effectively if the pre-questioning involves the extensive use of student-made questions of various types which he or she will then read to answer. The child only can learn to pose questions of various types which he or she will read to answer if these types are modeled for him or her. This is especially true in the case of textually implicit (interpretive and critical) and scriptally implicit (creative) questions.

Effective questioning and prediction *during* the reading of a narrative or content selection also can greatly add to the child's comprehension of the material. Questioning during reading can mainly involve prediction of what is going to happen later in the material. It can consist of such questions as these while reading a narrative selection:

What do you think is going to happen next in the story?
How is _____ going to solve his problem?
How do you think this story is going to end?
How would you like this story to end?

It also is important both during and after reading a selection to ask mainly *important* or *relevant questions*. For example, the following explicit or literal question is not really very relevant to the comprehension of the story: What color was Sue's dress? A child who was asked this question may have a right to think: "I don't know and I don't care. What difference does it make in the story

---

[2]Dolores Durkin, "What Classroom Observation Reveals About Reading Comprehension." *Reading Research Quarterly*, 14 (Summer, 1978–79), pp. 481–533.

anyway?" This is another reason why it is important to pose as many implicit or interpretive comprehension questions as possible. They normally are more crucial to the true understanding of the selection.

Questioning both during and after the reading of a selection should follow naturally from the initial question. For example, examine the following several questions:

Question: What is going to happen in this story?
Response: She is going to lose her glasses.
Question: What makes you think that this will happen in the story?
Response: She never knows where she puts them when she takes them off. You know, she is supposed to wear them all of the time.

It is important at the beginning of reading a selection to *activate* (use) prior knowledge in a way that will not be too distracting for the children who are to read the selection. For example, if the children are to read a basal reader story about the zoo, it may be more helpful to ask them *What kind of animals do you think live in the zoo?* rather than to ask them *Have you ever been to a zoo?* The latter questions may take the children too far from the actual comprehension of the story. The former question is likely to be somewhat less *diversionary* than is the former.

It also is important to avoid *diversionary questions* while the child is reading a selection. A diversionary question may detract from the comprehension of the actual story by allowing the child to go off on a tangent relating his or her own experiences. For example, in the middle of the story, the reading teacher normally should not ask: "What would you do in this situation?" or "Have you ever had this kind of problem?" Although this may be an attempt to relate prior knowledge to the reading material, it may be a distraction both to the child and to other children in the comprehension of the material. Therefore, while these types of questions may often be found in teacher's manuals, they can act as a distraction during the reading of a story.

It also is important to ask *predictive questions* during reading which explore more than a single possibility. For example, after a child's first prediction, it can be important to encourage divergent thinking by asking "What's another possibility?" "Who has a different idea?" "What else may be going to happen?"

In summary, if teachers of reading modeled and used excellent questioning techniques before, during, and after a reading selection, the child's comprehension would improve greatly with very little additional effort expended by either the teacher or the child.

Effective Questioning Before and During Reading

Pre-reading questioning traditionally has not been used as often or extensively as post-reading questions in the improvement of comprehension. Pre-reading questioning helps children set purposes of reading a selection, and the questions can be formulated either by the child or the reading teacher. Generally the questions are more effective if they are child-formulated questions which activate prior knowledge and set purposes for reading although they can be of either type. Student-formulated questions generally will help the child read the material more purposefully.

In either case, the child's *prior knowledge must be activated (used)* in order to enable him or her to experience the greatest amount of success possible with the reading selection. An interesting concept which should be considered in this area has been called by Pearson and Johnson the *Charlie Brown syndrome:*

> Recall what Charlie Brown does whenever he gets a new book. Before he even looks at the book, he counts the pages—625 pages: "I'll never learn all that!" He is defeated before he starts, before he has had a chance to realize that he does not have to learn *all* that. It is not *all* new. He already knows something about it. He has not given himself the chance to learn what he already knows about what he is supposed to know.[3]

Both the teacher and the child can attempt to activate the child's prior knowledge. The reading teacher can do this by trying to relate what the child is going to read to what he or she already knows by asking questions such as these; for example, about a basal reader story taken from the *Little House Series* by Laura Ingalls Wilder:

> Have you read any of the books written by Laura Ingalls Wilder?
> If you have, can you tell us about when they took place? What are some things that you have learned about life at the time that Laura and her family lived?
> What people lived in Laura's family at that time?

The reading teacher also can activate prior knowledge by using television programs, semantic mapping (webbing), a film, filmstrip, a computer simulation, pictures, demonstrations, experiments, and many other devices. These activities should help children to either support or reject the schema which they currently have about the reading selection.

The reading teacher also can pose comprehension questions for the child to read to answer. As much as possible, these should be meaningful, important textually implicit (interpretive) and scriptally implicit (creative) questions which help the child have important purposes for reading the material.

However, after having high-level comprehension questions modeled for them for awhile, children should be encouraged to develop their own questions which they are to read to answer. Student-formulated questions help the child interact with the reading material, improve overall reading comprehension, and make the child more independent as a learner.

Russell G. Stauffer developed the *Directed Reading-Thinking Activity (DRTA)* a number of years ago. Although this technique is not new, it still

---

[3]P. David Pearson and Dale D. Johnson, *Teaching Reading Comprehension.* (New York: Holt, Rinehart and Winston, 1978), p. 192.

remains very valuable primarily because it encourages student involvement and uses prediction strategies. The DRTA normally is most useful in a basal reader achievement group although it also can be used on an individual basis such as an individual reading conference or in the language-experience approach. This technique helps children to learn to predict outcomes, set purposes for reading, and then analyze their reading. To implement it, follow these steps:

1. Have a group of children or an individual child set purposes for reading by reading the title of the selection and then skimming the material.

2. Have the children or child pose questions about the material and form hypotheses to test. The children or child then confirm or reject these hypotheses.

3. The children or child then read the material keeping their purposes and hypotheses in mind.

4. After the material is read, each child then proves his or her prediction to the rest of the group.[4]

Jane L. Davidson studied the DRTA technique a number of years ago and found that teachers who use it asked more interpretive comprehension questions than teachers who did not follow the procedure.[5]

Another strategy for teaching active comprehension directs *the teacher to ask a question to get a question*, not an answer. For example, a first-grade teacher may hold up a picture for the children to look at. Instead of asking questions about the picture such as "Who is on the sled?" or "What is going to happen?" the teacher can say: "Look at the picture. What would you like to know (learn) about the picture?"

Another strategy for attaining the goal of active pupil questioning has been called the *phase-in-phase-out strategy*. In this strategy the teacher phases in the questioning process by taking the first step in modeling questions which are appropriate to the content. The reading teacher then offers additional information about the content to be read or explains additional information about the topic. Some knowledge of the material to be read is necessary in order to generate the appropriate type of questions. Once children have an idea of the kinds of questions which can be asked about different types of content (narrative or expository), they are placed into groups to ask each other questions regarding the material to be read. Final phasing out occurs when the children ask and answer appropriate questions of various types on their own.

---

[4]Russell G. Stauffer, *The Language-Experience Approach to the Teaching of Reading.* (New York: Harper & Row, Publishers, 1980).

[5]"The Quantity, Quality, and Variety of Teachers' Questions and Pupils' Responses During an Open-Communication Structured Group Directed Reading-Thinking Activity and a Closed-Communication Structured Group Directed Reading Activity," unpublished doctoral dissertation, University of Michigan, 1970.

The *ReQuest Procedure* or *reciprocal questioning* is a strategy which has proven very useful in encouraging children to become active questioners at the higher levels of comprehension. The original ReQuest Procedure was developed by Anthony Manzo in 1969, and since then has been used and revised by a number of different reading specialists.[6] Very briefly, here is how this procedure is used:

1. The teacher first tells the children to ask the kind of questions about each sentence in a selection which they think that the teacher might ask.

2. The teacher then answers each question as fairly and fully as possible and tells the children that they subsequently must do the same.

3. Then the teacher and the children both silently read the first sentence.

4. The teacher then closes the book, and a child asks questions about that sentence that the teacher is to answer.

5. Next the child closes the book, and the teacher asks questions about the material. The teacher must provide an excellent model for the child's questions. The questions should be mainly of the higher type such as textually implicit (interpretive and critical) and scriptally implicit (creative) questions.

6. After a number of additional sentences, the procedure can be varied to use an entire paragraph instead of individual sentences. Questioning should continue until the child can answer the question: "What do you think will happen next in this selection?"

The ReQuest Procedure also can be called *reciprocal questioning* and is especially valuable because it demonstrates to a child how to formulate and answer high-type questions instead of just explicit (literal) questions. This strategy also helps children to monitor or evaluate their own reading comprehension or to use the skill of *metacognition*.

One interesting consideration is the technique of asking the same questions *both before and after reading a selection*. Children often do better at answering test questions after reading if they have been asked the same questions earlier since the pre-reading questions serve as attention-getting devices or clues on what to look for in the reading. Pre-questions can be thought of as aids to processing what is read. Thus pre-questions should help the child to process relevant aspects of the material in useful ways: "How will you use this information in your own project or even in your own life?" Questions that force a child to summarize or review the material are likely to improve his or her comprehension. The use of pre-questions also can be a device to activate the learner's prior knowledge (schema) as was explained earlier.

---

[6]Anthony V. Manzo, "The ReQuest Procedure," *Journal of Reading*, Volume 13 (Nov., 1969), pp. 123–126.

Post-Reading Questions to Evaluate Comprehension Ability

There are a number of effective strategies that can be used after reading both to assess and to teach reading comprehension. Some of these can be used equally well during reading for the same purpose.

One of the oldest techniques for evaluating reading comprehension at the end of a selection is called the *retelling* or *tellback strategy*. It was first used in the 1920s as *the way* of assessing comprehension ability on the first standardized tests of reading. However, it has not been very commonly used for many years because of the difficulty of accurately evaluating children's responses on standardized reading tests. Such tests instead normally used the multiple-choice format to assess comprehension ability. However, recently the retelling strategy has been used quite often mostly as a teaching strategy although it also appears on the silent reading test of the *Durrell Analysis of Reading Difficulty*, an individual diagnostic reading test.

To use this technique, simply have the child read a passage on the instructional or independent reading level and say: "What was this material about?" or "Can you tell me all that you remember about this material?" This simple strategy can enable the reading teacher to assess the child's comprehension of the material fairly effectively in a mainly informal manner. It is an example of what can be called *process comprehension*.

Ronald T. Hyman has suggested that the reading teacher use a number of different techniques to improve his or her questioning skills. Most of these ideas have been found to be extremely helpful by reading teachers whom I have taught. Very briefly, some of these suggestions are as follows:

1. Let all students know that they will be called on.
2. In addition to letting all students know that they will be called on, ask students not simply to call out the answers, but rather to make sure that a specific student is called on to answer each question.
3. Do not call on volunteers more than *10* to *15 percent* of the time. If the reading teacher calls only on the volunteering students, he or she does not get a true picture of the number of students who do not know the answers to various questions which are posed.
4. Call on volunteers mainly for those types of questions which ask the student to give his or her own opinion.
5. Be sure that the questions are *passage dependent*; that is, that the child cannot answer the question unless the material has been read. Questions which are not passage dependent can mainly be answered from the child's prior knowledge.
6. The teacher should try to use concise questions. For example, the question "Why was Ronald W. Reagan elected President in 1984?" may not be too meaningful. A more valuable question according to Hyman would be

"What do you believe were some of the most important reasons that people voted for Ronald W. Reagan in 1984?"

7. The reading teacher must give children sufficient time to answer a question. Some research studies have found that teachers give children less than *five seconds* in which to answer a question. The teacher should allow the child from five to ten seconds in which to respond to a question. This gives him or her *thinking time*. However, I believe that this is not commonly done partially because teachers do not wish to embarrass a child who may not know the answer and partially because many other children in the reading group or class are often waving their hands and want to blurt out the answer. Although it is often difficult to do, it still is exceedingly important for reading teachers to give children time to gather and organize their thoughts before attempting to answer a question.

8. All children should be urged to answer at least some of the questions rather than letting them say: "I don't know." Otherwise some children will persist in simply saying "I don't know" in answer to most questions.[7]

An obvious but often overlooked way of improving a child's comprehension after he or she has read a selection is called *text lookbacks*. Obviously, a child should look back in the text for an answer when he or she is uncertain about it. However, students who do not comprehend well are not as skilled in text lookbacks to answer questions as are students who are most effective comprehenders.

A strategy has been developed by Garner and others to improve middle-grade students' use of text lookbacks. The reading teacher uses or prepares short, 200-word passages which are printed on two pages. *Two text-based questions* (the answers are found in the material) and *one reader-based question* (the answers are found in the children's prior knowledge) are written on the third page.

Very briefly, the steps of this procedure are as follows:

What—Children are told that they will be learning to look back in the text to help them answer questions.

Why—Children are told that this is important because looking back can help them find the answers to questions. As elementary as this may sound, a number of children do not use text lookbacks when they would benefit from doing so.

How—The teacher models the text lookback strategy by looking back to the first or second page of the prepared passage to answer the two text-based questions. The teacher then explains that it will not help to look back for the reader-based question.

---

[7]Ronald T. Hyman, "Questioning for Improved Reading," *Educational Leadership*, 39 (Jan., 1982), pp. 307–309. Reprinted with permission of the Association for Supervision and Curriculum Development and Ronald T. Hyman. Copyright © 1982 by the Association for Supervision and Curriculum Development. All rights reserved.

When—Children are told to use this strategy whenever they cannot answer questions about what they have read.

To practice this important strategy, the teacher and children first use several of the short, three-page passage and question sets. Then they use the procedure with questions written for a two- or three-page segment in either their basal reader or content textbook. For independent practice, children first work with several more three-page passage and questions sets and then work with questions written for two- or three-page segments in one of their textbooks. The children can keep a progress chart indicating how many questions they answered correctly and how many times they used the lookback strategy to help them answer questions.[8]

An Example of a Text Lookback Strategy Activity Sheet

The following page presents an example of a text lookback strategy activity sheet at the fifth-grade level. Due to space limitations, it has been printed all on one page. You may duplicate it and use it in its present form if you wish, but more importantly, it should serve as a model for you of this type of activity sheet.

---

[8]Ruth Garner, Victoria C. Hare, Patricia Alexander, Jacqueline Haynes, and Peter Winograd, "Inducing Use of a Text Lookback Strategy Among Unsuccessful Readers," *American Educational Research Journal*, 21 (Winter, 1984), pp. 789–798. Copyright 1984 by the American Educational Research Association. Adapted by permission of the publisher.

TEXT LOOKBACK STRATEGY ACTIVITY SHEET
(Approximately fifth-grade reading level)

Name _____ Grade _____ Teacher _____

Read the two short passages silently. Then look back at the passages to find the answers to the *text-based questions* and answer them. Write an answer to the *reader-based question* based on your own experience.

Page 1   Lewis and Clark made a major journey of discovery for the United States, and their exploration of the Louisiana Territory began in 1804 near St. Louis. On their expedition Lewis and Clark surveyed the land to find the best route to the Pacific Ocean. They made careful records of what they learned about Indian customs and language and about plant and animal life.

The expedition was divided into two groups with Lewis and three men traveling overland to buy horses from the Indians. Clark and the main party were bringing the expedition's equipment by canoe.

Page 2   On the overland trip Lewis and his three companions met an Indian tribe and smoked a peace pipe. After the chief learned that they had eaten no food that day, he gave the men cakes made of dry berries. Later this same chief gave Lewis boiled antelope meat and some roasted fresh salmon.

Later Lewis and his party reached the fork of the two rivers where they were to meet Captain Clark and his party. The next day an Indian scout told Lewis that he had sighted white men in canoes on the river. The canoes came into camp, and the two parties came together, to the relief of both Lewis and Clark. The expedition reached the mouth of the Columbia River several months later.

Page 3   *Text-Based Question:* What were Lewis and Clark trying to locate?

_____

Text-Based Question: Where did Lewis and Clark finally meet again?

_____

Reader-Based Question: Why do you think that the expedition was divided into two parts?

_____

Several Final Considerations and Strategies for Using Questioning to Improve Comprehension Ability

There are several other strategies the reading teacher may wish to consider while using questioning of various types to improve comprehension ability.

For example, T. E. Raphael has developed an interesting instructional program to improve children's ability to answer implicit (interpretive) comprehension questions. Children are taught to identify how they decide on an answer to a question which may be explicit or literal (the question and answer may come from one sentence), implicit or interpretive or critical, and scriptally implicit or creative. Raphael has found that *instruction and reinforcement in identifying question-answer relationships are very effective in terms of improving disabled readers' question-answering ability.*

Very briefly, here is how this strategy works:

How—The instruction begins with the reading teacher's explaining the three different types of *QARs*. It is important to remember that both the question and the answer must be considered in order to arrive at the appropriate label. Here is an example of the QARs:

Explicit QAR—Where did Jerry go?
         to the circus

Implicit QAR—Why was Jerry happy?
         He saw a clown.

Scriptally Implicit QAR—How did Jerry's father know that he was probably happy?
         He probably laughed
         when he saw the clown
         and the dog.

As explained earlier in this section, Explicit QARs are labeled *Right There*, Textually Implicit QARs are labeled *Think and Search*, and Scriptally Implicit QARs are labeled *On My Own*. The reading teacher then presents several short passages and one question from each of the QAR categories for each passage and tells why the QAR label for each question is appropriate. Next children are asked to explain QAR labels for questions and answers related to particular passages. After this, children are given questions and answers related to particular passages. Later children are given reading material, questions, and answers and asked to answer the question and provide QAR labels.

What, Why, and When—In addition to these steps, it is important that the reading teacher explains to children that they will be learning how to figure out where answers to questions come from, and that this is important because answers may come from different places. This understanding should improve their ability to answer questions after reading. The reading teacher also can explain to children that they should use this skill they are reading and studying on their own if they have a hard time answering comprehension questions.

Children then can think about the type of questions that they are answering and label them as either *Right There, Think and Search,* or *On My Own* questions.[9]

A *game was developed* by Raphael and Wonnacott which *encourages discussion of the concepts underlying question-answer relationships.* This game involves having some children pretend to be lawyers. The lawyers must state the type of QAR represented by a question and defend their reasoning by explaining the source of the most appropriate response. The rest of the children may raise objections and present a defense if an alternative QAR is determined. The activity involves children in verbalizing their thinking process and provides an opportunity for clarification of the process and any misunderstanding which may occur.[10]

A SELF-MONITORING CHECKLIST

Carr, Dewitz, and Patberg found that teaching sixth-grade children to ask themselves questions about their answers to implicit (interpretive) questions improved their interpretive comprehension ability. Questions which children asked themselves *focused on forward and backward clues* which could be used to answer implicit (interpretive) questions. *This instruction was found to be very beneficial for disabled readers.* The following are the steps in this strategy:

- HOW—Instruction in the use of this strategy starts with the completion of cloze passages. The teacher first presents several single sentences with one cloze blank per sentence to demonstrate the cloze procedure; for example: "Most of the houses in Jenny's neighborhood in Wisconsin are painted _____." Children then are to suggest a number of possible answers such as *red, brown, blue,* or *black,* and these answers are written on the chalkboard. The teacher and children discuss why some answers may be more appropriate than others. The teacher then tells children that they have to rely mainly on prior knowledge to complete the blank in this type of sentence.

- Next the teacher presents several short passages on which the children use a *forward context clue*; that is, the children must read *past the cloze blank* to fill it in with an acceptable answer. For example: "Most of the houses in Jenny's neighborhood in Wisconsin are painted _____. When it snows there in January there is almost no color at all in her neighborhood." The teacher and children then discuss

---

[9]T. E. Raphael and P. David Pearson, "Increasing Students' Awareness of Sources of Information for Answering Questions," *American Educational Research Journal*, 22, pp. 217–236. Copyright 1985 by the American Educational Research Association. Adapted by permission of the publisher.

[10]R. E. Raphael and C. A. Wonnacott, "The Effect of Metacognitive Training on Question-Answering Behavior: Implementation in a Fourth Grade Developmental Reading Program." Paper presented at the National Reading Conference, Dallas, Texas, 1981.

how *snow is a forward clue* that helps the children come up with the answer *white* for that cloze blank.

- Then the teacher presents several short passages in which children must use a *backward clue*; that is, they must consider the information *before the cloze blank* in the passage to complete the blank with an acceptable answer. For a passage such as the following: "After a sleet storm, Mark took his dog outside and slipped and fell on the _____," the teacher and children discuss how *sleet, storm, outside,* and *slipped* are clues to the word *ice*.

- Next the children are given a three- to five-page passage from a content textbook in which cloze blanks have been inserted. After completing the cloze procedure, the teacher and children discuss acceptable answers and whether *forward or backward clues* were useful in arriving at these answers.

- Next the children are asked implicit (interpretive) comprehension questions about the completed passage. The questions are similar to the cloze exercise in that they require children to use forward and backward clues to find one-word answers. The teacher and children discuss acceptable answers as well as the forward and backward clues which helped them arrive at the answers. Then the children are shown how to use a *self-monitoring checklist* to help themselves fill in cloze blanks and answer implicit questions.

- WHAT, WHY, AND WHEN—The lessons in this strategy should be carried out for about 15 days over a six- to eight-week period. It also is important that the teacher explains to the children that they are learning how to ask themselves questions about their answers to questions on content textbook material and how to use forward and backward clues to help them answer the content textbook questions. Children can learn that using forward and backward clues and the *self-monitoring checklist* can help them in answering implicit (interpretive) comprehension questions much more effectively on their own in content area reading. They should be told to use the self-monitoring checklist whenever they are asked to answer questions about content textbook material.[11]

An Example of a Self-Monitoring Checklist

This section concludes with an example of a self-monitoring checklist at the middle-school reading level. You may duplicate it and use it in its present form if it seems applicable for your students. It also should serve as a model of this type of checklist for you in constructing your own example of this type of device.

---

[11]Eileen M. Carr, Peter Dewitz, and Judythe P. Patberg, "The Effect of Inference Training on Children's Comprehension of Expository Text," *Journal of Reading Behavior*, 15 (October, 1983), pp. 1–18. Used with permission of the authors.

SELF-MONITORING CHECKLIST
(Middle-school level)

Name _____ **Grade** _____ **Teacher** _____

Read each question silently and put a checkmark in the proper blank after it.

		Yes	*No*
1.	Does the answer I gave make sense to me?	_____	_____
2.	Does the answer I gave make sense in the sentence?	_____	_____
3.	Did you use your own prior knowledge about the material to help you find the answer?	_____	_____
4.	Is your answer based on your own prior knowledge of the material and the clues which were found in the passage?	_____	_____
5.	Was there a *forward* context clue in the sentence?	_____	_____
6.	Was there a *forward* context clue in the paragraph?	_____	_____
7.	Was there a *forward* context clue in the passage?	_____	_____
8.	Was there a *backward* context clue in the sentence?	_____	_____
9.	Was there a *backward* context clue in the paragraph?	_____	_____
10.	Was there a *backward* context clue in the passage?	_____	_____
11.	Did the context clues help you change your answers or are the answers the same?	_____	_____
12.	Do you usually use *forward* and *backward* context clues while reading content material?	_____	_____

5

Improving
Comprehension Ability
at the Emergent
Literacy Level

Should the emergent literacy level mainly stress the word identification skills, leaving the teaching of comprehension until the intermediate grades and beyond? Although comprehension always has been taught to some extent even from the beginning stages of reading instruction, contemporary research and teaching emphasize strongly the improvement of all elements of reading comprehension from the earliest stages of reading instruction. Most aspects of comprehension can be stressed in some rudimentary form at all levels.

Section 5 of the *Kit* is devoted to helping the reading teacher learn how to most effectively emphasize the various elements and aspects of reading comprehension at the emergent literacy level. This is extremely important since it is crucial that the child make an excellent start in learning comprehension at the beginning stages of reading if he or she is to be able to master it in the later elementary school and secondary school. The section opens by briefly describing the relation of listening comprehension and reading comprehension and providing several suggestions for improving ability in listening comprehension at the pre-reading and beginning reading levels. Next it discusses how effective picture interpretation can be used as a means of developing readiness for subsequent reading comprehension and briefly describes the *whole language approach* emphasizing the use of predictable books, the patterned language approach, and the use of the shared book experience.

The main part of Section 5 presents a variety of classroom-tested strategies and suggestions for improving comprehension ability at both the pre-literacy and initial literacy levels, including some strategies that can also be used effectively with older students. This part of the section begins by discussing why wide reading is so important in improving comprehension ability. Next it briefly explains the variations of the language-experience approach which currently are used to teach both reading and writing skills. The section then discusses questioning strategies and prediction strategies and provides an activity sheet at the third-grade reading level on the use of prediction.

Next the section describes the directed reading activity, the guided reading procedure, and the directed reading-thinking activity and provides explanations of and activity sheets for the anticipation guide and explicit teaching of reading comprehension. It then discusses and illustrates variations of the cloze procedure, sentence comprehension, and reading to follow directions. The section next discusses visual imagery and provides an activity sheet at the third-grade level. It also discusses retelling, text lookbacks, rereading, metacognition, punctuation, semantic maps, anaphoric relationships, and provides activity sheets in several of these comprehension skills.

The section closes by describing some primary-grade creative activities for improving reading comprehension, how to relate reading and writing, and story frames.

THE RELATION OF LISTENING COMPREHENSION TO SUBSEQUENT READING COMPREHENSION

It has been known for many years that the language arts of *listening* and *reading* are related to some extent. They are both called *receptive language arts*, while *speaking* and *writing* are called *expressive language arts*. It is true that all four of the language arts are interrelated and that improvement in any one of them *may* result in some improvement in the others.

If children at the pre-reading and beginning reading levels are asked different types of comprehension questions (both explicit and implicit) about material which they have heard told or read to them and are thus often motivated to respond at the higher levels of thought, they *may* become more adept at responding to different types of comprehension questions as they are able to read for themselves. It certainly is important for family members in the home and teachers in nursery schools, day care centers, and kindergartens to pose different types of comprehension questions about tradebooks, stories, and other material which the child has heard. As explained in the two following books, listening comprehension also can be used as a measure of a child's *potential or capacity level*, a determiner of whether he or she can make reading improvement in both the primary grades and at the middle-upper level.

Wilma H. Miller, *Reading Diagnosis Kit*. West Nyack, New York: The Center for Applied Research in Education, Inc., 1986, pp. 171–182.

Wilma H. Miller, *Reading Teacher's Complete Diagnosis & Correction Manual*. West Nyack, New York: The Center for Applied Research in Education, Inc., 1988, pp. 43-44.

To improve a young child's listening comprehension ability, many different types of reading material can be used such as old-fashioned nursery rhymes, books with predictable language patterns (see later in this section), many different types of tradebooks, simple articles from children's magazines and newspapers, or stories of various kinds which are read to the child. For optimum improvement of listening comprehension, however, it is important to often ask the child questions that require implicit (interpretive) or higher-order responses. The use of prediction during reading to the child also can be very important in improving comprehension ability. Simply ask the child: What do you think is going to happen next in this story? What would you like to have happen next in this story? How do you think this story might end? What would be a good ending for this story? All of these activities can provide excellent readiness for comprehension when the child is able to read for himself or herself.

PICTURE INTERPRETATION AS A MEANS OF DEVELOPING READINESS FOR READING COMPREHENSION

Most reading specialists believe that pictures and other visual material can activate a child's prior knowledge. At both the beginning reading level and even at the middle school level pictures can help the child to recall his or her schema (prior knowledge) about the topic which is going to be read. For example, pictures relating to a space shuttle may help a child retrieve appropriate prior knowledge about the topic from his/her long-term memory. To use pictures in this manner, many teachers assemble a picture file over a period of years. When a particular story or unit is to be studied, the teacher then posts the pictures or passes them around for the children to look at. As the pictures are shown, the reading teacher should use them to activate the child's prior knowledge by asking questions about them which can help the child remember what he or she already knows about the subject of the pictures. Obviously, much of the discussion should involve the use of higher-order comprehension questions such as implicit or interpretive questions.

It is also important to help children respond at lower and higher levels to pictures which are found in the basal readers and tradebooks at both the pre-reading and beginning reading levels. Parents also should ask their child questions about pictures which appear in the tradebooks that they read to them. As much as possible, these questions also should stimulate interpretive or higher-level thinking. Picture interpretation then as a readiness for subsequent reading comprehension can begin as early as the age of about two for those children who are ready for it. Picture interpretation should continue in the kindergarten as children hear tradebooks of various types read aloud to them. It also should continue in the early primary grades as children begin reading their own simple tradebooks and basal reader stories. As much as possible at these levels also the questions posed abut the pictures should be of the higher type.

Here is a sample tradebook at the reading readiness level and several simple picture interpretation questions which were constructed from it. This should illustrate that it is possible to construct implicit (interpretive) or higher-order comprehension questions even from pictures at the beginning reading levels.

Who Took the Farmer's Hat? by Joan L. Nodset
Pictures copyrighted by Fritz Siebel, 1963.
Harper & Row, Publishers, Inc.
10 East 53rd Street
New York, New York 10022

The farmer had a hat, an old brown hat.
Oh, how he liked that old brown hat.

Why do you think that the farmer needed to wear the brown hat that's shown in this picture?

What are the baby pigs in the picture doing?

What might the farmer use the tractor in the picture for?

What does the bird do that is standing on the pig?

But the wind took it, and away it went.

What is the farmer in the picture doing?

What do you think happened to the trough that the pigs were eating out of?

The farmer ran fast, but the wind went faster.

What is the dog in the picture trying to do?

"Like it?" said Bird.
"I like it," said the farmer.
"Oh yes, I like that nice round brown nest.
It looks a little like my old brown hat.
But I see it is a nice round brown nest."

Why do you think that a brown hat would make a good nest for a bird?

What did the bird put in the hat to make it into a nest?

Why was the hat in the limb of a tree?

THE WHOLE LANGUAGE APPROACH USING PREDICTABLE BOOKS, THE SHARED BOOK EXPERIENCE, AND THE PATTERNED LANGUAGE APPROACH

Predictable books are an excellent way to encourage picture interpretation, language competency, and beginning reading skills. These are books that are written with a repeated pattern. They often sound rhythmic to the child. The text of these books often matches the illustrations closely. One of the more popular predictable books is *Brown Bear, Brown Bear* by Bill Martin, Jr. Predictable books often can help the teacher of beginning reading introduce effective reading and writing skills as well as stress picture interpretation. For example, here is a part of this interesting predictable book:

Brown Bear, Brown Bear
What do you see?
I see a red bird looking at me.

Red Bird, Red Bird
What do you see?
I see a _____ looking at me.[1]
(Children can supply their own variation to create their own story.)

I have seen this activity done in a kindergarten class taught by Mrs. Linda Ball at Metcalf Elementary School in Normal, Illinois. The children each completed and illustrated their own variation of the story, and all of the stories were then bound into a class language-experience booklet.

Dr. Emily Long, a first-grade teacher at this same elementary school and an adjunct professor of education at Illinois State University, also makes extensive use of big books with predictable language patterns both to encourage picture interpretation and to motivate the children's writing of their own materials. *Big books* are large-sized picture books with predictable language patterns that were first used extensively for these purposes in New Zealand. They are said by Dr. Long to be especially useful for these several purposes. One source from which she said they can be obtained is the following:

Reading in Junior Classes
Ready to Read Program
Department of Education
Wellington, New Zealand
Copyright date 1985

Two other excellent sources are the following:

Rigby
P.O. Box 797
Crystal Lake, Illinois 60014

DLM Teaching Resources
One DLM Park
Allen, Texas 75002

Apparently a variation of the approach explained to me by Dr. Long in the literature can be called the *Shared Book Experience*. This approach originated in New Zealand in an attempt to combine the language learning experiences of children by shifting to the center of early reading activities "The enjoyment of a rich, open literature of favorite stories, poems, and songs."[2] It may also be called *whole-language learning*. Donald Holdaway, one of the major advocates of the whole-language approach, has stated that the model underlying the Shared Book Experience has its roots in the same developmental concepts of learning spoken language and acquiring other learning. The oversized (big) books which are used

---

[1] Bill Martin, Jr., *Brown Bear, Brown Bear, What Do You See?* New York: Holt, Rinehart and Winston. Excerpt from *Brown Bear, Brown Bear, What Do You See?* Copyright © 1970 by Holt, Rinehart and Winston, Inc. Reprinted by permission of the publisher.

[2] Barbara Park, "The Big Book Trend—A Discussion with Don Holdaway," *Language Arts*, 59 (May 1982), pg. 815.

in the Shared Book Experience capitalize on good literature and also upon the social dynamics of the classroom stressing cooperative teaching. Shared Books can be used simultaneously with a language-experience approach and followed up by the use of individualized reading.

The *Shared Book Experience* focuses around the use of a large book or overheads of good quality which are predictable stories that can be presented to a class or a group of children. These enlarged materials should be very interesting and contain predictable enough language to motivate children at the emergent literacy level to anticipate what will happen in the story and to participate whenever chosen words or phrases are repeated, as is done quite often with predictable books. As the teacher reads the story, she may use a pointer to be sure that the children follow along. After a big book is used, the children might dictate, write, and publish their own follow-up to the story or dramatize it in a creative manner.

A typical Shared Book Experience involves the following activities:

1. *Tuning-In*—The enjoyment of poetry and song. In this instance the children are given opportunities to participate in and enjoy singing or reading along with other children.

2. *Rereading of a Favorite Story*—Children may be able to make predictions and read along with the story even at the beginning reading level.

3. *Learning About Print and About Language*—This part entails what can be called functional skills—teaching and innovation. Functional skills include such reading skills as comprehension, while innovative skills include the creation of a new statement based upon a familiar theme or pattern such as is illustrated in the footnoted book.[3] Big books as part of the Shared Book Experience always should be used along with other methods of teaching beginning reading skills. If the reading teacher wants more information on this aspect of the concept, he or she can write:

   Shared Book Experience Procedures
   Unit 6 Early Reading Inservice Course
   New Zealand Department of Education
   E. C. Keating, Government Printer
   Wellington, New Zealand, 1978

   This provides an overview of the approach, including suggestions for activities, materials, and slides demonstrating the approach.

Another variation of the Shared Book Experience which can be used to improve comprehension at the beginning reading level is sometimes called the *patterned language approach*. This strategy combines a structured language-experience approach with patterned or predictable stories. This is said to enable beginning readers who cannot read to practice reading since predictable books

---

[3]Robert J. Tierney, John E. Readence, and Ernest K. Dishner, *Reading Strategies and Practices* (Boston: Allyn and Bacon, Inc., 1985), pp. 240–247.

contain repetitive structures that enable readers to predict the next word or line or episode. After hearing such material read aloud, children can join in and "read along" even though at that point they are probably not able to recognize the individual words. However, repeated opportunities to recognize high-frequency words in dependable context helps them develop a sight vocabulary that can soon be recognized in other contexts. This approach can be used in combination with a structured variation of the language-experience approach.

Very briefly, here is how the *patterned language approach* can be implemented at the beginning stages of reading in kindergarten or first grade. Notice that comprehension is stressed in this approach along with graphophonic (phonic analysis) features.

1. The teacher reads the book to the group and then reads it again asking the children to join in when they can predict what is coming.
2. The teacher and children read the story from the book together. Then the story is read from a chart without a picture.
3. The teacher and children read the story from the chart. The children must match sentence strips containing lines of the story by placing the correct strip under each line.
4. The children as a group read the story from the chart. They then must match word cards with words on the chart.
5. The children as a group read the story from the chart. In random order, the teacher places word cards from the story at the bottom on the chart. The children locate each of these words on the story and place them in the order in which they were found in the story. The procedure can be repeated for each section or part of the story.[4]

Here is a fairly comprehensive list of predictable books which can be used by the reading teacher to encourage picture interpretation, beginning reading skills, and beginning writing activities.

Books with Predictable Language Patterns

Aliki, *Go Tell Aunt Rhody*. New York: Macmillan, 1974.

Aliki, *Hush Little Baby*. Englewood Cliffs, New Jersey: Prentice-Hall, 1968.

Asch, Frank, *Monkey Face*. New York: *Parents' Magazine* Press, 1977.

Balian, Lorna, *Where in the World Is Henry?* Scarsdale, New York: Bradbury Press, 1972.

Barohas, Sarah E., *I Was Walking Down the Road*. New York: Scholastic Press, 1975.

Barrett, Judi, *Animals Should Definitely Not Wear Clothes*. New York: Atheneum Press, 1970.

---

[4]*Ibid.*, pp. 247–248.

Barton, Byron, *Buzz, Buzz, Buzz*. New York: Scholastic Press, 1973.

Basking, Leonard, *Hosie's Alphabet*. New York: The Viking Press, 1972.

Becker, John, *Seven Little Rabbits*. New York: Scholastic Press, 1973.

Berenstain, Stanley, and Janice Berenstain, *The B Book*. New York: Random House, 1971.

Brooke, Leslie, *Johnny Crow's Garden*. New York: Frederick Warne, 1968.

Brown, Margaret Wise, *The Friendly Book*. Racine, Wisconsin: Golden Press, 1954.

Brown, Margaret Wise, *Goodnight Moon*. New York: Harper & Row, 1947.

Brown, Margaret Wise, *Where Have You Been?* New York: Scholastic Press, 1952.

Carle, Eric, *Do You Want to Be My Friend?* New York: Thomas Y. Crowell, 1971.

Cook, Bernadine, *The Little Fish That Got Away*. Reading, Massachusetts: Addison-Wesley, 1976.

de Regniers, Beatrice Schenk, *The Day Everybody Cried*. New York: The Viking Press, 1967.

de Regniers, Beatrice Schenk, *How Joe the Bear and Sam the Mouse Got Together*. New York: *Parent's Magazine* Press, 1965.

Duff, Maggie, *Johnny and His Drum*. New York: Henry Z. Walck, 1972.

Emberly, Barbara, *Drummer Hoff*. Englewood Cliffs, New Jersey: Prentice-Hall, 1967.

Ets, Marie Hall, *Elephant in a Well*. New York: Viking Press, 1972.

Ets, Marie Hall, *Play with Me*. New York: Viking Press, 1955.

Galdone, Paul, *Henny Penny,* New York: Scholastic Press, 1968.

Galdone, Paul, *The Three Billy Goats Gruff*. New York: Seabury Press, 1973.

Hutchins, Pat, *Good-Night Own*. New York: Macmillan 1972.

Kalan, Robert, *Rain*. New York: Greenwillow, 1978.

Kent, Jack, *The Fat Cat*. New York: Scholastic Press, 1971.

Kraus, Robert, *Whose Mouse Are You?* New York: Collier Books, 1970.

Langstaff, John, *Oh, A-Hunting We Will Go*. New York: Atheneum Press, 1974.

Langstaff, John, *Over in the Meadow*. New York: Harcourt Brace Jovanovich, 1957.

Mack, Stan, *10 Bears in My Bed*. New York: Pantheon, 1974.

Martin, Bill, *A Ghost Story*. New York: Holt, Rinehart and Winston, 1970.

Martin, Bill, *Little Owl Series*. New York: Holt, Rinehart and Winston, 1965.

Martin, Bill, *Spoiled Tomatoes*. Los Angeles: Bowmar, 1967.

Memling, Carl, *Ten Little Animals*. Racine, Wisconsin: Golden Press, 1975.

Moffett, Martha, *A Flower Pot Is Not a Hat*. New York: E. P. Dutton, 1972.

Peppe, Rodney, *The House That Jack Built*. New York: Delacorte Press, 1970.

Petersham, Maud and Miska Petersham, *The Rooster Crows: A Book of American Rhymes and Jingles*. New York: Scholastic Press, 1971.

Quackenbush, Robert, *She'll Be Coming' Round the Mountain*. Philadelphia: Lippincott, 1975.

Rossetti, Christina, *What Is Pink?* New York: Holt, Rinhart and Winston, 1965.

Skaar, Grade, *What Do the Animals Say?* New York: Scholastic Press, 1972.

Spier, Peter, *The Fox Went Out on a Chilly Night*. Garden City: Doubleday, 1961.

Stover, JoAnn,. *If Everybody Did*. New York: David McKay, 1960.

Wahl, Jan, *Drakestail*. New York: Greenwillow, 1978.

Westcott, Nadine Bernard, *I Know an Old Lady Who Swallowed a Fly*. Boston: Little, Brown, 1980.

Wildsmith, Brian, *Brian Wildsmith's ABC*. New York: Franklin Watts, 1962.

Withers, Carl, *A Rocket in My Pocket*. New York: Scholastic Press, 1967.

Zemach, Margot, *Hush, Little Baby*. New York: E. P. Dutton, 1976.

Zemach, Charlotte, *Do You Know What I'll Do?* New York: Harper & Row, 1958.

STRATEGIES FOR IMPROVING COMPREHENSION ABILITY AT THE EMERGENT LITERACY LEVEL

Much of the remainder of this section describes practical, classroom-tested strategies that can be used successfully by the teacher of reading to improve comprehension ability at the emergent literacy level. As explained in detail in Section 1, today comprehension is thought of as a global process which cannot easily be divided into separate segments as traditionally done in the past. Research has discovered that reading comprehension can be divided into only two major facets: vocabulary knowledge (word meaning) and understanding of the reading material. The strategies in the *Kit* are thus *not* categorized in terms of improving ability in literal (explicit), interpretive and critical (implicit), and creative (scriptally or schema implicit) as was done in my books in the past.

NOTE: However, I sometimes indicate what type of comprehension ability a specific strategy may best improve. This is done to aid you, the reading teacher.

Wide Reading of Relevant Material

Without a doubt the single best way to improve reading comprehension is to encourage the child to *read widely* from interesting, motivating, relevant materials with the major purpose being understanding what is read. Understanding of what is being read makes the most improvement if the child has a purpose for the reading. Such reading can take place in good literature (tradebooks), children's magazines and newspapers, basal reader stories, supplementary reading materials, simple content textbooks, high-interest/low-vocabulary books, relevant computer software, and other types of materials. The child always should have purposes for the reading, should monitor his or her comprehension as the reading is being done, and be prepared in some way to show that he or she has understood the material.

The Language-Experience Approach

The *language-experience approach* is one of the most useful means for developing comprehension skills at the emergent literacy level. Since students have dictated or written the experience stories themselves, comprehension of what is read is obviously not a problem for them. Since they also have experienced what they have dictated or written, they are therefore easily able to understand it. This approach works equally well for older disabled readers and adult non-readers since the reading material is based upon their own experiences and reflects their own language patterns. We have used the language-experience approach to improve sight word recognition, basic phonic analysis skills, and comprehension skills with many disabled readers in various types of tutoring situations other the years.

This approach is mainly based upon the philosophy of Roach Van Allen, professor emeritus of the University of Arizona, under whom I studied in the 1960s. At that time, his conceptualization of the approach was the following:

What I can think about, I can talk about.

What I can say, I can write (or someone else can write it for me).

What I can write, I can read.

I can read what others write for me to read.[5]

In the recent past the conceptualization has taken some variation of this form:

I can think about what I have experienced and imagined.

I can talk about what I think about.

What I can talk about I can express in some other form.

Anything I can record I can tell through speaking or reading.

---

[5]Roach Van Allen and Gladys C. Halvorsen, "The Language Experience Approach to Reading Instruction," Ginn and Company contributions to *Reading*, No. 27 (Lexington, Mass.: Ginn and Company, 1961).

I can read what I can write by myself and what other people write for me to read.

As I talk and write, I use some words over and over and some not so often.

As I talk and write, I use some words and clusters of words to express my meanings.

As I write to represent the sounds I make through speech, I use the same symbols over and over.

Each letter of the alphabet stands for one or more sounds that I make when I talk.

As I read, I must add to what an author has written if I am to get full meaning and inherent pleasure from print.[6]

Here is a brief description of how the language-experience approach can be implemented with one child or with several children who are reading on about the same level:

1. The child must be motivated for the dictating and as soon as possible the self-writing of the story using invented spelling. We have found some type of hands-on activity to be the most effective form of motivation that can be used. My students have used activities such as the following for this purpose: baking cookies or a gingerbread man, making a turkey out of an Oreo® cookie and candy, making butter, carving a pumpkin, making a small black spider out of plaster of Paris with pipe cleaners for legs, sailing a wooden sailboat in a blue lake in a turkey roasting pan, making bubbles, constructing various things, and all kinds of art activities. We also have used field trips of many types to motivate the language-experience story. My students have taken their tutees to safety town, the zoo, the pet shop, the university circus, the university farm, a pig farm, a toy store in the local shopping mall, the top of Watterson Towers (the tallest dorm in the state of Illinois), the university greenhouse, the Nestlé-Beich candy factory, the fire station, and the police station, among many other interesting places.

2. The reading teacher and child can have a meaningful preliminary discussion in which the language-experience story is structured in a very loose manner.

3. The child then can dictate the experience story. At the very beginning stages in the use of this approach, the reading teacher may need to ask a few leading questions to get the child started, but he or she should take care not to structure the story too much. The language-experience story can be transcribed on a piece of chart paper, a sheet of ordinary paper which is lined larger than normal, or on an index card. The child should see his or her language being turned into print as it is dictated. Normally

---

[6]Roach Van Allen, *Language Experiences in Communication* (Boston: Houghton Mifflin Company, 1976), pp. 51–55. Used with permission of the author.

the story is transcribed exactly as the child dictated it although it can be altered slightly if this is done very carefully and tactfully, and if the teacher has excellent rapport with the child.

4. If it is desired, the reading teacher later can type the language-experience story with a primary typewriter, copy it over on a large sheet of chart paper, or put it on a ditto master so that it can be duplicated and used for several purposes.

NOTE: Since it takes a good amount of time to transcribe the individual experience stories, some reading teachers use a parent volunteer to type some or all of the individual experience stories.

NOTE: Steps 3 and 4 can be done effectively on a *word processor* if one is available to the reading teacher. The word processor has been used by reading teachers both to record children's dictated experience stories and to enable them to compose their own stories fairly effectively. Some contemporary research in the area of reading and writing maintains that beginning readers should compose their own experience stories from the initial stages using *invented spelling in the stories*. At this stage a letter could represent an entire word in the story written by the child. A number of researchers believe that this gives children a better introduction to reading and writing than does the more traditional *dictated experience stories*. For example, here is a sample story using *invented spelling* done by a beginning reader:

> i hv a dg.
> H nm s sm
> i l hm vy mc.
> I have a dog.
> His name is Sam.
> I love him very much.

Emily Long, a former graduate student of mine and now a first-grade teacher at Metcalf Elementary School in Normal, Illinois, has used this variation of the language-experience approach for several years and has stated that it results in excellent reading and writing achievement for her children. I prefer to use the more traditional dictated experience stories at the outset until the child has a very rudimentary command of written language although I believe that *invented spelling* is fine when the child has reached that point.

5. After the child has dictated the language-experience story, the reading teacher can read it aloud for the disabled reader. Later, the teacher and child can read it together, and the child should be encouraged to read it alone as soon as possible.

6. The child can circle or underline all of the words which are recognized.

7. A word bank can be made from the child's dictated stories. Each important word is written on a card of some type. All of the cards are then

placed in a container of some type such as a large brown envelope, a file box, or a shoe box. The words can later be used as flashcards for sight word recognition, alphabetizing in rough order, placing into categories, or use in reading games.

8. I normally have my students encourage the child to illustrate each experience story on a separate sheet of paper. My students have had their tutees use marking pens, crayons, watercolors, fingerpaints, and tempera paints for the illustrations. If a booklet is not made, the illustrations can be attached to the story in some way.

9. If the teacher so desires, the children's language-experience stories over a period of time can be bound into a booklet which can be taken home and read to their parents. There are several ways that the covers of the booklets can be obtained. The reading teacher can make his or her own covers which the child can decorate. The reading teacher also can buy pre-bound blank experience books from the local book store or order pre-bound experience booklets with blank pages on which the child can dictate or self-write stories from the following address:

Treetop Publishing
220 Virginia Street
Racine, WI 53405

Here are several language-experiences stories which have been dictated by kindergarten children to some of my undergraduate students in reading:

Going to the Zoo

by Quiana Maple

I like to go to the zoo.
I like to look at the deer.
The lions roar real loud.
I like to see the snakes move.
They stick out their tongues.
I petted the baby crocodile.
I saw the monkeys behind the glass.
I had fun at the zoo.

A Bike Ride

by Sarah Porter

We went past Split Rock. We saw turtles, I ran over a snake and screamed. We stopped and collected sandrocks, one tool that the Indians used, and skull and snail shells.

My Mom found a flower and planted it in her garden and watered it.

We went to Towpath this morning. We went bike riding. Thea, Colin, Dad, Mom, and I went.

I went to Kentucky Fried Chicken. I didn't think I would have fun, but I did.

Today is Bubble Day

by Ashley Zamarron and Bradley Nagle

Once upon a time there were lots and lots of bubbles.

Ashley had yellow bubbles and Bradley had orange bubbles.

Ashley made a big bubble with a tiny mouse inside.

Bradley made a big dinosaur bubble.

Ashley and Bradley popped all the bubbles in the air.

When all the bubbles popped, they went to heaven.

If you desire additional information about the use of the language-experience approach to reading comprehension at the emergent literacy level, you can consult any of the following sources:

Allen, Roach Van, *Language Experiences in Communication*. Boston: Houghton Mifflin Company, 1976.

Allen, Roach Van, and Claryce Allen, *Language Experience Activities*. Boston: Houghton Mifflin Company, 1982.

Hall, Mary Anne, *Teaching Reading as a Language Experience*. Columbus, Ohio: Charles E. Merrill Publishing Company, 1981.

Miller, Wilma H., *Teaching Elementary Reading Today*. New York: Holt, Rinehart and Winston, Inc., 1984, Chapter 4.

Stauffer, Russell, *The Language-Experience Approach to the Teaching of Reading*. New York: Harper & Row, 1980. (This source is very useful if you wish to use the language-experience approach with slow-learning children, hearing-impaired children, visually impaired children, or minority group children of any kind.)

Individualized Reading

Individualized reading is ideally suited to improving comprehension in both the primary and intermediate grades. It can be used along with a basal reader approach, a phonic approach, or an eclectic approach to stress the importance of comprehension. Very briefly, individualized reading is based on the premise that children desire to read, can select their own reading materials, and can pace their own reading.

Individualized reading involves recordkeeping of the reading materials on the part of both teacher and child, and recordkeeping of reading skill needs and interests on the part of the teacher. It also involves meeting periodically with the teacher in *individual reading conferences* during which the child responds to several comprehension questions at various levels about the material, retells the story, gives his or her reaction to the material, and may read aloud a short portion of it to the teacher (often a favorite portion). If you want to learn exactly how this approach can be incorporated into your primary-grade reading program to improve children's comprehension, you can consult the following sources:

Barbe, Walter B., and Jerry L. Abbott, *Personalized Reading Instruction.* West Nyack, New York: Parker Publishing Company, 1975.

Burns, Paul C., Betty D. Roe, and Elinor P. Ross, *Teaching Reading in Today's Elementary Schools.* Boston: Houghton Mifflin Company, 1988, Chapter 6, pages 318–324.

LaPray, Margaret, *Teaching Children to Become Independent Readers.* New York: The Center for Applied Research in Education, Inc., 1982.

Miller, Wilma H., *Teaching Elementary Reading Today.* New York: Holt, Rinehart and Winston, Inc., 1984, Chapter 6, pages 111–137.

Questioning

All types of *questioning strategies* can be used in the primary grades to improve reading comprehension, as explained in detail in Section 4 of this handbook. As stated, it is exceedingly important for the reading teacher to ask many interpretive and critical (textually implicit) comprehension questions both during and after a reading selection, although, especially in the primary grades, it is acceptable to include some literal (explicit) questions also. It is also very important to ask important, relevant questions and to avoid asking too many questions.

As stated in Section 4, many of the basal reader manuals contain more questions for a short selection at the beginning stages of reading instruction than they warrant. Sometimes there are several suggested questions to be asked for only *one* page of reading. A single page does not always warrant the asking of even only one question. I think that this also points out the need for the child in the primary grades to *read much good literature in the form of interesting tradebooks* and respond to a few important comprehension questions about that reading material instead of reading only basal reader stories that often have a limited storyline.

Prediction Strategies

As also mentioned in Section 4, it is very helpful to children's reading comprehension to stress all types of prediction strategies both before and during the reading of a selection. Before reading the teacher can motivate prediction by asking:

What is the title (name) of the story?

What do you think this story might be about?

Look at this picture. What do you think the story might be about?

During the reading of a story, prediction strategies can greatly enhance a child's comprehension and also can enable him or her to be a more active comprehender. Here are several questions that my tutors have used with their children to enhance active comprehension. They often are best used with a story which has clearly delineated story divisions:

What do you think will happen next in this story?

What do you think that _____ (story character) should (will) do now?

What would you like _____ (story character) to do next in the story?

Robert M. Wilson and Linda B. Gambrell have proposed a very interesting *prediction strategy* which will be briefly reviewed here. It involves the cyclical steps of *activation, prediction, reading,* and *verifying.* Here is a brief description of these steps:

1. *Activation*—The reader must be exposed to a basic piece of information that is relevant to the passage in order to activate the prediction process. The teacher has to make a decision on what part of the text passage might be the most appropriate for generating good predictions. It could be the title of the selection, a picture or another graphic presentation, or possibly a paragraph from the text.

2. *Prediction*—The reader then makes predictions about what will happen based upon the text information and the reader's prior knowledge about the content. The children should understand that there are no incorrect predictions. To make a good prediction a child should use prior knowledge in combination with the passage information. The teacher can model such prediction questions as the following:

    What do I think this passage may be about?

    What could I learn from reading this passage?

    What do I think may happen next in this passage?

    The teacher must stress that the child should compare the text information with prior knowledge in order to generate valid, text-relevant predictions.

3. *Reading*—The children read the passage to determine how accurate their predictions were.

4. *Verifying*—The children are to compare the predictions made with what information was gained from the reading. Children should give evidence that the predictions were either:

    1. *True*—If there is support in the material for the prediction
    2. *False*—If there is support in the material that indicates that the prediction was not true

3. *Questionable*—If there is not information to support either the accuracy or inaccuracy of the prediction

Sometimes the children must do additional reading to determine if a judgment was relevant or not. The teacher can code each prediction on the chalkboard as the children discuss their findings. Predictions that are verified as accurate can be starred, while those that are inaccurate or unimportant can simply be crossed out. The predictions that were found to be questionable can have a question mark placed next to them.

Then new predictions about the remaining text material can be generated and the entire process continues. The teacher may say something similar to this to help the children generate more accurate predictions:

Now that you have learned _____, can you make some good predictions about what will happen next?[7]

Sample Activity Sheet Based on This Prediction Strategy

The following pages present a sample worksheet activity on about the third-grade reading level that was loosely based on the prediction strategy of Wilson and Gambrell. You may duplicate and use this activity in its present form if it seems relevant for your children. More importantly, you may use it as a model for your own activity sheets on how to use this strategy with your children in class discussions.

---

[7]Robert M. Wilson and Linda B. Gambrell, *Reading Comprehension in the Elementary School* (Boston: Allyn and Bacon, Inc., 1988), pp. 32–36.

SAMPLE ACTIVITY SHEET USING THE PREDICTION STRATEGY
(Approximately third-grade reading level)

Name _____ Grade _____ Teacher _____

BUBBA, THE TRICKY CROW*

Teacher:

> *Let me show you how the prediction strategy* can help you read with much more understanding. Here is a story that I have read. The name of the story is *Bubba, the Tricky Crow.* I want to read this story and try to understand what it is about. One thing that I can do to help me better understand what I read is to make some predictions about what I think might happen in this story. Making predictions will help me know what to look for as I read the story. I have read the title of the story and know that it is about a tricky crow. I should now think about what I already know about *crows.* I already know that a crow is a big, black bird. Now I should make some predictions based on the title of the story and what I already know about crows.

I.   Now write down as many predictions as you can just based on the title of the story.

_____

_____

_____

_____

_____

Bubba, the Tricky Crow

Bubba is a very smart, big, black crow who lives in the small town of Benson. Although some of the people in this town like Bubba very much, other people are angry at the tricks that Bubba has played on them. These tricks show how really clever a crow can be.

Teacher:

> Now that I have read the first paragraph of this story, I know that my prediction about Bubba being a smart crow who can do tricks is correct. I also now know that some people in this town don't like the crow's tricks, while some people think that they are funny. Now I'm going to predict what some of these tricks might be and why they make some people angry. I'm also going to predict why some of these tricks make other people happy. I can also predict what may happen to Bubba if his tricks make too many people mad.

II. Write down as many predictions as you can about the rest of the story. Then read the rest of the story to see if your predictions are right.

_____

_____

*This is a true story.

©1990 by The Center for Applied Research in Education

_____

_____

_____

_____

_____

Bubba fell out of a nest one spring and was rescued by a woman in the town of Benson. This woman raised Bubba on her back porch until she was old enough to live outdoors. Now that she is grown up, Bubba flies around town looking for trouble.

Sometimes Bubba grabs hold of a small dog's leash up by the neck and walks around the block with him. At other times she flies right up to a person and pecks at their clothes. This really scares some people.

Once Bubba found some keys on the ground and was seen flying away with them in her beak. She has even taken a cigarette out of a man's pocket and flown away with it. Bubba once tried to steal a yellow ball from a little boy playing outside.

One of Bubba's most annoying tricks is to pull clothes off a clothesline letting all of the clean clothes fall to the ground. Often Bubba scares people by flying right toward their heads when they are outside. Once she scared a woman to death who was walking in the cemetery by flying right at her head.

Bubba usually hides all of the things that she takes. Once she stuffed some raw hamburger behind a truck fender. She has hidden a $20 bill and also an expensive piece of cloth that a man was polishing his car with.

Crows can live to be 20 years old. Crows sometimes may fly south for the winter, and some of the people in Benson hope that Bubba will do just that. They are tired of some of her tricks even though they admit that "she is one tricky crow."

III. Now write down all of your predictions that you think were right.

_____

_____

_____

_____

_____

IV. Now write down all of your predictions that you think were wrong.

_____

_____

_____

_____

_____

Answer Key

(Only some possible logical answers can be provided for this activity sheet. Any logical answer should be considered correct in each case.)

I. It's about a crow who can do tricks.
It's about a smart crow.

II.

Tricks That Make People Angry

Bubba could fly right by a person's head.
Bubba might try to pick small fruit off trees.
Bubba might try to steal some of a dog's food.

Tricks That Make People Happy

Bubba might fly in the air crowing loudly.
Bubba might take a piece of food from a person's hand.
Bubba might be a nice pet for a person.

What May Happen to Bubba

Someone might try to shoot her.
Someone might try to trap her and let her loose in the woods.

III. No answer key can be provided for this section as it was impossible to determine what all of the children's predictions could be.

IV. No answer key can be provided for this section as it was impossible to determine what all of the children's predictions could be.

Directed Reading Activity

The *directed reading activity* is undoubtedly the most common way of improving comprehension ability at the primary-grade reading level in contemporary elementary schools. It can be used both with narrative and expository materials. It is best illustrated in basal reader teacher's manuals when directions are provided to the teacher on how to conduct the lesson. Very briefly, here are the steps which comprise the directed reading activity:

Developing prior knowledge for reading the story—In this step the teacher helps the children to relate the story to their own prior knowledge, thus enhancing their comprehension while reading. The children are encouraged to express their own purposes for reading the story with the help of the teacher if necessary.

Presentation of new vocabulary terms—The teacher may choose to present several of the most important new vocabulary terms found in the material. This vocabulary presentation always must be in context and should encourage children to apply their own word attack skills.

Guided silent reading—The children then read a significant portion of the material or the entire material in the light of the purposes and predictions that they formed before doing the silent reading. They also should be encouraged to formulate predictions during the reading and to verify or reject their predictions.

Purposeful oral reading—The children read aloud to answer a specific question or to satisfy a particular purpose.

Extending skill development—During this aspect of the lesson, the teacher presents the word identification or comprehension skills from the basal reader manual relating to that particular basal reader story. These skills later can be reinforced independently with workbook pages, other commercial materials, teacher-made materials, or computer software.

Enrichment activities—The last step of the lesson provides appropriate follow-up activities which add to each child's understanding of the concepts and ideas presented in the story. Some suggested activities may be relevant independent reading, creative writing, art activities, construction activities, dramatic play, or cooking and baking activities.

The Guided Reading Procedure

The *guided reading procedure* was developed by Anthony Manzo in 1975 and is designed to help students recall specifically what they read, improve their ability to generate their own implicit or higher-order questions, develop their understanding of the importance of self-correction while reading, and improve their ability to organize information. Although this procedure is the most appropriate for use with expository material at the intermediate-grade reading level, it can be begun in a rudimentary form in the primary grades.[8]

This procedure is described in detail in Section 6, of the *Reading Comprehen-*

---

[8]Anthony V. Manzo, "Guided Reading Procedure," *Journal of Reading*, Vol. 18 (Jan., 1975), pp. 287–291.

sion Activities Kit since it is most appropriate at the middle-school level. However, here are the steps included in the procedure.

1. Prepare the child for the reading assignment.
2. Children read and recall the information.
3. The children return to the material for additional facts and corrections.
4. The children organize the remembered information.
5. The children must be provided with thought-provoking information.
6. The children must be tested on their knowledge of the information.

Directed Reading-Thinking Activity

The *directed reading-thinking activity (DRTA)* was developed a number of years ago by Russell G. Stauffer, professor emeritus of the University of Delaware. However, it still remains as an excellent, contemporary way in which to improve comprehension ability with all types of readers since it involves prediction and reading material for formulated purposes. This technique is normally most useful in a basal reader achievement group, but it also can be useful when individualized reading is employed. Briefly, the DRTA encourages *active involvement* with the reading material by having children generate hypotheses about the material and then checking the accuracy of their predictions. This is why it can improve reading comprehension so effectively. Very briefly, here are the basic steps of the DRTA:

1. Tell the children the title of the story, have them read it for themselves, or show them an illustration. On the basis of this information, have them formulate predictions about the story. If an informational book is being used, an alternative idea is to have the children tell what is already known about the topic (help them to activate their prior knowledge).
2. Tell the children that they should read to see if the material verifies the predictions that were made. Then have them silently read a portion of the material or the entire selection.
3. Have the children then discuss each of their predictions, indicating which ones were verified and which ones were not. Help the children to determine what criteria should be used in determining whether or not the predictions were verified.
4. If the material was not read at one time, alternate periods of silent reading and discussion until the entire material has been read. In each case, emphasize the validity of the reasoning which the children are using rather than the correctness of the original hypotheses.[9]

In summary, it can be seen that the directed reading-thinking activity helps

---

[9]Russell G. Stauffer, *Directing Reading Maturity as a Cognitive Process* (New York: Harper & Row, 1969), pp. 35–86.

children to learn to predict outcomes, set purposes for reading, and analyze their reading in a meaningful manner.

The Anticipation Guide

The *anticipation guide*, which was developed by Readence, Bean, and Baldwin in 1981, can increase the comprehension of children in both the primary grades and the middle-school level by doing the following:

> activating children's prior knowledge before reading and providing purposes for reading by serving as a guide for subsequent reading

The *anticipation guide* helps children to activate their prior knowledge before reading and also utilizes statements instead of questions before reading as an initial way to get children more involved in their learning. For example statements require children only to recognize and respond, while questions require children to produce a response. The end result of this process should be production of their own questions and statements. Although a start may be made toward this end result in the primary grades, it can be better refined at the middle-school level.

Here is a very brief description of how the anticipation guide can be used:

1. *Identify Major Concepts*—The teacher must first identify the major concepts in the reading selection by careful reading of the material and the teacher's manual if one is available.

2. *Determine Children's Knowledge of These Concepts*—The teacher should attempt to ascertain how the main concepts in the material support or refute what the children already know about the material.

3. *Create Statements*—The teacher should create about three to five statements about the material. These statements are those in which the children have enough knowledge to understand what the statements say, but not enough to make any of them totally known.

4. *Decide Statement Order and Presentation Style*—The order of the statements ordinarily should follow the order of the statements presented in the material. The guide can be presented on a ditto sheet, the chalkboard, or an overhead transparency. The set of directions and blanks for children's responses should be included.

5. *Present Guide*—When giving the guide to children, the reading teacher usually should read the directions and statements orally. Children should be told that they will share their thoughts and opinions about each statement by defending their agreement or disagreement with the statements. Children can work individually or in a small group while making the response.

6. *Discuss Each Statement Briefly*—The teacher should first ask for a show of hands from children to indicate their agreement or disagreement with

each statement. The teacher then tallies the various responses. Children should be encouraged to judge their own view in terms of the views of other children.

7. *Have Children Read the Material*—The children then are told to read the material with the purpose of deciding what the author may say about each statement. As they read, children should keep two things in mind: their own thoughts and beliefs as well as those provided by other children and how what they are reading is related to what was earlier discussed.

8. *Conduct Follow-Up Discussions*—After reading the material, the children can respond again to the statements. Then the anticipation guide serves as the basis for a post-reading discussion in which children can share the new information gained from the reading and how their previous thoughts may have been modified by what they believe that the reading said. They should understand that they do not have to agree with the author depending on what type of material is read.[10]

Sample Anticipation Guide

The following page presents a sample anticipation guide at about the third-grade reading level which the reading teacher can duplicate and use in its present form if it seems relevant. It also can serve as a model for the reading teacher while he or she constructs this type of guide for use with his or her own children from the appropriate narrative or expository (content) reading material.

---

[10]Adapted from J. E. Readence, T. W. Bean, and R. S. Baldwin, *Content Area Reading: An Integrated Approach* (Dubuque, Iowa: Kendall/Hunt Publishing Company, 1981). Used by permission of Kendall/Hunt Publishing Company.

SAMPLE ANTICIPATION GUIDE
(Approximately third-grade reading level)

Name _____   Grade _____   Teacher _____

CAN BEARS TAKE A NAP IN A WALNUT TREE?*

Directions: Here are some statements about bears sleeping in a walnut tree. Read each statement to yourself and put an *X* next to each statement that you agree with. Be sure to be able to defend your ideas when we talk about the statements later.

_____ 1. A 300-pound black bear is able to sleep in a tree.

_____ 2. Five bears were found sleeping in a tree very near a house.

_____ 3. People were able to walk right up to the bears and encourage them to get in a truck.

_____ 4. The captured bears were caught and then released deep in the woods.

Now read the story to yourself. Remember what you should look for as you read the story so we can discusss later what you learned from reading the story.

Can Bears Take a Nap in a Walnut Tree?

A man and his wife in central Wisconsin were very shocked one autumn morning when they heard their dog barking outside their house. They looked out the window and saw five bears sleeping in a large walnut tree only 15 feet from the house.

A 300-pound mother black bear and her four cubs were dozing in this tree, which was so near to their house that the couple could almost touch them from the window.

Conservation wardens spent the whole morning trying to get the bears out of the tree. They finally used tranquilizer darts and a long pole to capture the mother bear and three of her cubs. The other cub got away but was later caught in a nearby cornfield.

Highway 10 was blocked to traffic for several hours as the bears were being captured.

The captured bears then were taken to the Wisconsin City of Green Bay to be weighed. Later they were taken in a truck to an isolated area in northeastern Wisconsin where they were released in the deep woods where they would be safer.

_____

*This is a true story.

Explicit Teaching of Reading Comprehension

The *explicit teaching of reading comprehension* is a framework for developing reading comprehension skills and strategies which the child can apply to various reading situations without teacher direction. It is based on the concept that reading comprehension and other problem-solving abilities can be changed with appropriate intervention. It was discovered by a number of research studies that children can be taught reading comprehension skills that will transfer to other reading situations. Explicit teaching of reading comprehension is a generic plan for presenting and reinforcing many reading comprehension strategies, and it seems to be adaptable for use in both the upper primary grades and in the middle school. It is briefly described both in this section and in Section 6, and an activity sheet at the appropriate reading level is provided in both sections.

Very briefly here are the steps in the explicit teaching lesson:

Step One—Introduction to the skill or strategy through examples and review. Discuss how, when, where, and why the strategy or skills are used. If the skill has been used previously by the children, review what they already know about that skill.

Step Two (Optional)—Have the children volunteer additional examples and discuss them.

Step Three—Label, define, model, and explain the skill or strategy. The skill or strategy should be given a specific label and its application demonstrated with teacher modeling.

Step Four—Guided practice. In this step, examples are done together in order to prepare the children for independent practice and to determine who is incurring difficulty with the skill or strategy.

Step Five—Independent practice. The children work through the sample type of exercise, but do so independently.

Step Six—Application. Children are given a variety of situations in which they are encouraged to apply the skill and discuss its application. This may involve applying the skill or strategy to other reading materials or situations outside of school.[11]

Sample Lesson and Activity Sheet on Explicit Teaching Applied to the Implicit (Interpretive) Comprehension Skill of Discriminating Between Fact and Opinion

The following briefly illustrates how to apply explicit teaching of the implicit (interpretive) reading comprehension skill of discriminating between fact and opinion. The procedure is very briefly illustrated, and a sample activity sheet is

[11]Robert J. Tierney, John E. Readence, and Ernest K. Dishner, *Reading Strategies and Practices: A Compendium* (Boston: Allyn and Bacon, Inc., 1985), pp. 84–94.

included at about the third-grade reading level which the reading teacher can duplicate and use if it is appropriate. It can also serve as a model for the reading teacher to use in constructing his or her own explicit teaching lesson on any aspect of reading comprehension which is emphasized at the primary-grade reading level. Some examples are locating the directly stated main idea, locating significant details, reading and carrying out directions, placing a number of items in correct sequence, and using visual imagery.

I. *Introduction to Skill or Strategy*
The teacher can discuss with the children television advertising and newspaper advertisements which may contain biased statements. The teacher should ask the children how such statements can be evaluated or judged. The teacher can say the following to activate the children's prior knowledge: *Tell me what you know about statements of fact and about statements of opinion. How are they alike and how are they different?*
Possible Answers:
A fact is always true.
You can show that a fact is true.
An opinion can be true, but it isn't always.
Some people have opinions that are wrong.
A fact is better than an opinion.
All of these answers can be written by the teacher on the chalkboard or on an overhead transparency.

II. *Labeling, Defining, Modeling, and Explaining the Skill or Strategy*
The teacher can say something like this:
Can any of you give us a statement of fact?
The teacher can write examples such as these on the chalkboard or on the overhead transparency. The teacher can provide some of his or her own examples if necessary.
It is warmer in Florida than in Alaska.
Hollywood is in the state of California.
Christmas always comes on the 25th of December.
My dog is black, brown, and white.
Every elephant has a trunk.
The teacher then can say something like this to the children: *How can you tell whether all of the statements that you made are statements of fact or not?*
The following possible answers can then be written on the chalkboard or on a transparency:
You can read about it in a book.
You can ask someone who knows all about it.
You can look it up yourself.
You can count.
It is important that the children understand that some proof is required for the statement to be evaluated as true.

The teacher then can have the children provide some examples of statements of opinion such as the following, which are written on the chalkboard or on a transparency:

My mother is the best cook in the whole world.

I am the prettiest girl in my class.

A brick house is better than a stone house.

A farm is a better place to live than the city.

My school is the best one in Peoria.

Then the teacher can attempt to help the children arrive at the generalization that statements of opinion normally cannot be proven to be true. At this point the children probably can be given some key words for both statements of facts and statements of opinions. *Here are some key words for statements of fact: age, location, dates, temperature, and actual physical characteristics such as eyes, nose, and mouth. Here are some key words for statements of opinion: niceness, beauty, meanness, goodness, happiness, sadness, and "bestness."*

III. *Guided Practice of the Skill or Strategy*

Next the teacher can say the following: *If I read that Chicago is farther north than Miami, you can ask yourself if that is a statement of fact. It is a statement of fact or not?*

Possible Answer:

It's not a statement of fact because it's not true.

The teacher can say: *How do you know that it's not a statement of fact?*

Possible Answer:

Chicago is farther north.

The teacher can say: *How can you know that?*

Possible Answer:

I looked on the map, atlas, or globe of the United States.

Next the teacher might say: *You can prove that the statement is wrong. Since we decided that statements of fact contain things that can be proven, even if it is proven to be wrong, it is still a statement of fact. For example, the following statements of fact are still false:*

Valentine's Day always is in July.

New York is the capital of the state of Illinois.

The President of the United States lives in Mexico.

The teacher can then provide some type of review such as the following: *Statements of fact can be proven. They can be proven either true or false. However, statements of opinion are very hard or impossible to prove.*

ACTIVITY SHEET FOR THE EXPLICIT TEACHING OF READING COMPREHENSION SKILLS OF DETERMINING FACT AND OPINION
(Approximately third-grade reading level)

Name _____ Grade _____ Teacher _____

Read each of these sentences. Some sentences are *statements of true facts,* some sentences are *statements of false facts,* and some sentences are *statements of opinion.* In the blank before each sentence: write the letters *TF* if it is a statement of a *true fact,* write the letter *FF* if the sentence is a statement of a *false fact,* and then write the letter *O* if the sentence is a *statement of opinion.* Then try to write a place or person that you could use to check your answer such as a science textbook, a library book, the encyclopedia, a person, the zoo, or your teacher.

ANIMAL FACTS—ANIMAL MYTHS

_____ 1. A turtle can walk right out of his shell.

_____

_____

_____ 2. A cat is the nicest pet that a child can have.

_____

_____

_____ 3. A porcupine can use its quills to protect itself.

_____

_____

_____ 4. A bat uses its ears as well as its eyes to find its way in the dark.

_____

_____

_____ 5. A person should be afraid to touch a snake since snakes feel strange.

_____

_____

_____ 6. A snake bites with its forked tongue.

_____

_____

_____ 7. A raccoon sometimes dips its food into water before eating it.

_____

_____

_____ 8. An ostrich often buries its head in the sand.

_____

_____

_____ 9. A large dog is a better pet for a child than a little dog is.

_____

_____

_____ 10. Many bees are able to sting only once.

_____

_____

_____ 11. An owl has a small brain for a bird of its size.

_____

_____

_____ 12. Wolves usually live in packs or groups.

_____

_____

_____ 13. Crickets usually chirp faster on a hot day than they do on a cold day.

_____

_____

_____ 14. The most interesting animals in the circus are the elephants.

_____

_____

_____ 15. Cats can jump and move around very easily.

_____

_____

```
┌─────────────────────────────┐
│      Answer Key             │
│                             │
│   1. FF       9. O          │
│   2. O       10. TF         │
│   3. TF      11. TF         │
│   4. TF      12. TF         │
│   5. O       13. TF         │
│   6. FF      14. O          │
│   7. TF      15. TF         │
│   8. FF                     │
└─────────────────────────────┘
```

Sources for the Information

Any appropriate source that can be drawn from logical analysis. However, an especially good source is the following tradebook which has both fascinating information and *very charming* illustrations:

Seymour Simon, *Animal Fact/Animal Fable* (New York: Crown Publishers, Inc., 1979).

Simple Variations of the Cloze Procedure

Introduction to the *cloze procedure and various readiness activities* for this technique can be used effectively in the primary grades as one important means of improving both comprehension ability and ability in contextual analysis. The cloze procedure was developed in 1953 by Wilson L. Taylor and is based upon the psychological theory of *closure,* which indicates that a person normally wants to complete any pattern which is incomplete. The cloze procedure emphasizes the *prediction element of reading* which is obviously very important to effective reading comprehension, as stressed many times previously in this resource. Prediction is used in the cloze procedure since a child wishes to predict the unknown words encountered while reading. The cloze procedure makes use of both *semantic (word meaning)* and *syntactic (word order) clues* to help a person deduce the unknown words that are met while reading.

The *traditional cloze procedure* is more appropriate for use in improving comprehension at the middle-upper level and is therefore described in detail in Section 6. This section emphasizes those variations of cloze which are the most suitable for use in the primary grades and provides a ready-to-use example of one of these variations.

It is extremely important that any variation of the cloze procedure be preceded by many relevant cloze readiness activities. For example, when the cloze procedure is used in kindergarten or first grade, the reading teacher can read several sentences orally or record them on cassette tape, omitting one word in each sentence which then can be completed with one or several pictures cut from magazines. The children can choose the correct picture to complete each of these sentences.

At the emergent literacy level, the reader can omit words from dictated language-experience stories which the child can supply with words that make sense in sentence context. Also at this level, the reading teacher can say a sentence aloud omitting a word which the child is supposed to provide. Any word which makes sense in sentence context is considered to be acceptable. The reading teacher can print a short passage on the appropriate reading level on a transparency and place masking tape over the word or words which are to be omitted. Then an individual child or a small group of children can try to guess each omitted word. I have had a number of tutors use this masking tape technique with books which have fairly large print. After each guess, the teacher or one of the children can remove the masking tape and the children can compare the actual deleted word with their guess to see how appropriate each guess or prediction was. This technique normally is called *zipper cloze*.

For another cloze readiness activity which a number of my tutors have used successfully, print sentences on strips of poster board or tagboard, deleting one word in each case and placing slits before and after it. Then print each deleted word on a word card. Have the child place the correct word card in each sentence strip.

Most written cloze procedures are constructed from basal reader stories, supplementary reading materials, tradebooks, or content textbooks at either the instructional or the independent reading level depending upon the difficulty of the procedure. To construct most cloze procedures, select a passage of approximately *250* words and type the first and last sentences of the passage with no deletions on a ditto master, stencil, or word processor. Every *nth* word is then omitted throughout the remainder of the passage unless that word is a proper noun. Each deletion should be replaced by a typewritten space 15 spaces long. I recommend that every *tenth word* be omitted at least through the second-grade reading level, and every tenth or eighth word be omitted at about the third-grade reading level. When variations of the cloze procedure are used to improve comprehension ability at the primary-grade reading level, I believe that synonyms for each omitted word should be counted as correct.

Here is a brief description of some of the variations of the cloze procedure that I believe are useful in the primary grades:

1. Write all of the omitted words in columns in random order at the bottom of the sheet containing the passage. Have the child select and write in the correct word in each of the blanks.

2. Write two or three options for each of the omitted words below the blank and have the child select the correct one for use in sentence context. Here is a sample sentence from such a cloze exercise:

   My older brother wants to get a new
   _____ for Christmas.
   bicycle
   broken
   breeze

3. Construct a cloze procedure which has random deletions with the deleted word being fairly easy to deduce in most cases.

4. Construct a variation of the cloze procedure which combines practice in phonic analysis and contextual analysis. In this version the initial letter or the first two letters of each deleted word are placed at the beginning of each blank space. The reading teacher should be careful not to divide a consonant blend or consonant digraph from the remainder of the word in this variation. We have used this version very effectively many times in both the second-grade and the third-grade reading levels. The children that we have used it with liked it very much and found it very interesting to complete. Here is an example of one sentence from this variation of the cloze procedure:

   Joey hopes that his m _____ will buy him a skateboard for his birthday.
                      mother

5. One variation that I recommend for use at about the third-grade reading level combines *word length clues* and *meaning clues*. Each deleted word is replaced by a typewritten space as long as the omitted word. For example, this is how the word *raccoon* would appear if it were deleted from this type of cloze procedure.

   _ _ _ _ _ _ _

   We have used this variation of cloze successfully many times with children at the upper primary reading level.

6. A newer version of cloze may also be helpful in improving comprehension ability. In this procedure more than one word at a time is deleted. This variation probably would be the most effective with children at about the third-grade reading level and above. Material can be written by omitting in every other sentence the main verb phrase and all of the information following that verb. For example, a portion of such a passage may be as follows:

   A new family with three children moved in next door to us yesterday. They had _____.
   This family seemed very nice and friendly when we met them yesterday.

I hope _____. Both the father and mother in our new neighbor family teach in a high school.

Robert J. Tierney and others have presented a sequence in which cloze exercises can be presented that may be useful in the primary grades. Very briefly, here is that sequence:

1. Sentences in which the teacher omits one word and there is a multiple choice format with the choices. The two choices first include the correct item and an incorrect item which is different graphically and is a different part of speech.

1. clown

Elsie saw a   at the circus.

2. make

2. The same format as above but with the incorrect choice somewhat graphically similar to the correct item and a different part of speech.

1. clap

Ellie saw a   at the circus.

2. clown

3. Two choices both of which are the same part of speech.

1. clown

Ellie saw a   at the circus.

2. cloud

4. Three choices which include the correct answer, a word of the same part of speech, and a word which is a different part of speech.

1. clown

Ellie saw a   2. cloud   at the circus.[12]

3. clapped

The Maze Technique

The reading teacher may notice that this variation of the cloze procedure is quite similar to the *maze technique* which also can effectively be used to improve comprehension ability in the primary grades. I have had countless tutors use the maze technique effectively with children at this level over the years, and the children have enjoyed completing it. Very briefly, here is how a maze technique is constructed:

Select a page of about *120-150 words* from a basal reader, content textbook, supplementary reading materials, or a tradebook and separate it into sentences. Then three alternatives are placed in place of every *fifth word* in the passage. One alternative is the correct word; another alternative is the same part of speech but incorrect; while the third

---

[12]*Ibid.*, pp. 166–167.

alternative is both incorrect and another part of speech. If you wish to see a ready-to-use maze technique, you can consult either of the two following sources:

Wilma H. Miller, *Reading Diagnosis Kit*. West Nyack, New York: The Center for Applied Research in Education, Inc., 1986, pp. 327–329.

Wilma H. Miller, *Reading Teacher's Complete Diagnosis & Correction Manual*. New York: The Center for Applied Research in Education, Inc., 1988, pp. 121–122.

Sample Cloze Procedure with Deleted Words Placed at the Bottom in Random Order

The following page contains a sample cloze procedure with the deleted words placed at the bottom of the page in random order. It is appropriate for use at about the second-grade reading level. You may duplicate and use it if it seems appropriate for your students. More importantly, it can serve as a model for you as you construct your own cloze procedure of this type.

SAMPLE CLOZE PROCEDURE WITH DELETED WORDS
AT BOTTOM OF PAGE
(Approximately second-grade reading level)

Name _____ **Grade** _____ **Teacher** _____

Read this story about *sea horses* to yourself. Then find *one word* at the bottom of the page which makes sense in each blank and write it in. When you are done, read the story again to be sure that it all makes sense.

SEA HORSES

The sea horse is an interesting creature with the tail of a monkey, the pouch of a kangaroo, and the head and neck of a horse.

The sea horse is a fish that swims while _____ is standing up. Its two eyes can look up _____ down at the same time. One eye can be _____ for food, while the other eye watches for an _____. The sea horse even can play hide and seek _____ changing colors or pretending to be a piece of _____.

Sea horses are very unusual because the father sea _____ has the baby sea horse instead of the mother. _____ father sea horse has from ten to more than _____ babies at one time. The babies go to the _____ of the water for the first several hours of _____ life. These young babies tumble about playfully grabbing the _____ of their brothers and sisters.

The baby sea horses _____ very rapidly, eating tiny shrimp and sea weeds. Many _____ horses are about 6 to 8 inches long when _____ are grown. It takes about a year for a _____ horse to grow up.

There are many different kinds _____ sea horses. Sea horses are found in the seas _____ oceans all over the world except in those that _____ very cold water. They certainly are one of the most interesting creatures that a child can ever see.

by	sea	A
it	and	their
seventy	of	weed
surface	have	horse
tails	looking	grow
sea	and	
they	enemy	

```
┌─────────────────────────────────────┐
│              Answer Key              │
│                                      │
│   it          surface      have      │
│   and         their                  │
│   looking     tails                  │
│   enemy       grow                    │
│   by          sea                     │
│   weed        they                    │
│   horse       sea                     │
│   A           of                      │
│   seventy     and                     │
│                                      │
└─────────────────────────────────────┘
```

Every-Pupil Response Techniques

There are several *every-pupil response techniques* that can be used at the primary-grade reading level to improve ability in lower-level comprehension (explicit or literal) comprehension. In such a strategy, each child has multiple chances to respond in a basal-reader achievement group setting instead of only one or several chances.

One variation is to have the child make two small cards of posterboard or tagboard and then print the word *yes* on one card and the word *no* on the other card. Ask lower-level comprehension questions about a story which the children in a basal reader achievement group have read and have the children answer each question by holding up the *yes or no card*.

Other variations of every-pupil response techniques may consist of cards with faces, stick figures, letters, sight words, homonyms, or numbers printed on them. After the teacher asks a question, each child must select the most appropriate answer and hold up the correct response card for the teacher to see. By looking at all of the raised cards, the teacher can easily ascertain which children have mastered that skill and which have not. Such a technique enables all children to participate actively in the lesson and helps the more reluctant children to respond also.

Sentence Comprehension

Recently we have tutored several children in the upper intermediate grades who could pronounce words very effectively on grade level but had no understanding of what they were reading. The same can be true with *primary-grade children*. This is a much more difficult problem to remediate than is the child who miscalls up to half the words in oral reading but can comprehend the material very well. The latter problem fortunately is both much more common and much easier to correct.

If a child, therefore, has great difficulty with reading comprehension even when he or she can pronounce the words well, it usually is best to first emphasize *sentence comprehension* before proceeding to the comprehension of paragraphs and longer passages. One of the most effective first steps in sentence comprehension is to place directions such as the following on sentence strips which the child is to read and then carry out:

Go to the window and open it.

After this very rudimentary aspect of sentence comprehension is mastered, the reading teacher can next focus on comprehension of less concrete sentences such as this:

Jason bought a loaf of bread and a gallon of milk at the grocery store.

Subsequently, it should be possible to emphasize paragraph comprehension and passage comprehension at the appropriate reading level, often at the independent reading level. However, it is important to keep the activities concrete and mainly at the explicit level for as long as necessary to insure effective comprehension.

Sample Activity Sheet for Sentence Comprehension

The following page presents a sample activity sheet which contains a number of concrete directions that the child can read and carry out. Although the child can simply be asked to read and follow these directions directly from this activity sheet, it probably will be most effective for the reading teacher to print each one of them on a separate sentence strip for the child. They are designed to be used with a child who has great difficulty with comprehension but is an excellent word-caller. I used such sentence strips effectively myself with a 13-year-old junior high school student who could pronounce words effectively on the eighth-grade level but had absolutely no comprehension of what she read when I was a doctoral student. They worked very well in beginning her program of comprehension improvement.

SAMPLE DIRECTIONS FOR IMPROVING READING COMPREHENSION
(Primary-grade comprehension ability)

Name _____ **Grade** _____ **Teacher** _____

Go to the door and open it.

Walk to the bathroom and back.

Look inside of your desk. You may keep what you find inside of it.

Stand up and jump up and down three times.

Walk to the window in this room.

Print your name on the chalkboard.

Touch your toes five times.

Clap your hands four times.

Show me a green crayon and a red crayon.

Draw a flower on a sheet of paper.

Look inside of your desk for your reading book.

Run to the door and back here.

Get a drink of water.

Draw a picture of a man on the chalkboard.

Touch your nose, eyes, and mouth.

Go to your favorite part of the classroom.

Walk to the principal's office and back.

Draw a picture of a tree on a piece of paper.

Look inside my desk for a very big surprise.

Skip around the room one time.

Following and Carrying Out Directions

Learning to *read and follow directions* is a very important aspect of explicit (literal or lower-level) comprehension in which even many adults have not attained a high degree of competency. A beginning can be made in this very important reading skill in the primary grades. It should be presented and reinforced in many relevant situations at the early stages of reading if it is to be mastered by the middle-upper and adult levels.

At the beginning stages of reading instruction, the teacher can present oral directions of one step and then later of several steps. Subsequently, written directions can be presented containing one step at first and later several steps. These written directions can be made relevant by trying to relate them to some type of actual classroom situation.

If children can make an excellent beginning in learning how to read and follow directions in the primary grades, they will be well on the way to mastering one of the most relevant of the reading skills. Then further progress can be made in this important skill in the intermediate grades as is explained in detail in Section 6.

Sample Activity Sheet in Reading and Following Directions

The following pages present two sample activity sheets for reading and following directions which are appropriate for use at about the second-grade reading level. You may duplicate and use them in their present form if you wish or use them as a model for this kind of activity sheet of your own.

ACTIVITY SHEET FOR READING AND FOLLOWING DIRECTIONS
(Approximately second-grade reading level)

Name _____   Grade _____   Teacher _____

Read each set of directions carefully. Then follow the directions in the space below them. Be sure to read each set of directions before following them.

1. Draw a picture of a tree.

2. Draw a picture of yourself standing beside the tree.

3. Draw a picture of your pet or the pet that you would like to have standing beside you.

4. Put a sun in your picture.

5. Draw three flowers in your picture.

ACTIVITY SHEET FOR READING AND
FOLLOWING DIRECTIONS (*cont.*)

Name _____ **Grade** _____ **Teacher** _____

1. Print your favorite day of the week.

2. Print your own first name.

3. Write the numbers from 1 to 10.

4. Print your favorite color.

5. What color are your eyes?

6. Print the name of your school.

7. Print your favorite season of the year.

8. Write the name of the grade you are in at school.

9. Write the name of your best friend.

10. Write the name of your favorite food.

11. Write what kind of pet you have or that you would like to have.

12. Print the name of your teacher.

13. Write the name of the town that you live in.

14. Write the name of your favorite person.

15. Don't follow any of these directions.

Visual Imagery

Visual imagery, sometimes called *mental imagery,* often has been taught in schools as a way of appreciating literature but rarely has been taught as a strategy for the improvement of comprehension. However, it can be very effective for this latter purpose if the child is reading material that lends itself to making mental images of what is read. Many children do not use this technique unless they have specific instructions and practice in how to do so.

Although the use of visual imagery can be extended and refined at the middle-upper level, it certainly can be begun at the primary-grade reading level. For example, G. M. Pressley taught eight-year old children to construct mental pictures for the sentences and paragraphs which they read. When he compared these children with a control group whose members merely read the story, the imagery group remembered more of the story's events.[13]

John D. McNeil described one set of procedures for helping children to find out what is important in reading material and to change this material into mental images. This procedure is called *Mind's Eye* and very briefly consists of the following elements:

1. *Key Words*—Children should be taught to recognize important words in sentences and passages. Children first underline key words, then form mental images only from these key words. Later children pick out key words on their own and immediately create mental images for them.

2. *Discussion of Images*—After silent reading of key words, children are asked questions that help them formulate clear mental pictures, such as: Tell me about the picture that you see. What kinds of pictures do you see? This discussion may also focus on prediction: What do you think might happen next?

3. *Oral Reading*—After discussing their mental images, children read orally to verify that their images reflect the material.[14]

If you want to assess the value of mental imagery to your students, you should first discuss its usefulness and model for your children how it can be helpful to them. You might want to use an adaptation of the following strategy which is loosely based on one described by John D. McNeil in his useful book *Reading Comprehension: New Directions for Classroom Practice:*

1. Choose reading material that is unfamiliar to the children and is excellent for stimulating visual or mental imagery.

2. Divide the group into two random groups.

3. Read the entire passage to both groups. Ask the members of one group to

---

[13]G. M. Pressley, "Mental Imagery Helps Eight-Year Olds Remember What They Read," *Journal of Educational Psychology* 68 (January, 1976), pp. 355–359.

[14]From *Reading Comprehension: New Directions for Classroom Practice* by John D. McNeil, Copyright © 1984 by Scott, Foresman and Company. Reprinted by permission.

draw several pictures that depict what is described in the passage. Ask the members of the other group to draw several pictures of anything that interests them.

4. A few days later ask the children in both groups to write a short summary of what was found in the passage.

5. Evaluate the summaries in terms of main ideas and significant details.

6. Determine whether or not the group which formulated mental images seemed to remember more of the passage than the group which did not.

According to McNeil, this strategy probably can be begun at about the third-grade reading level and may be effective from that point on.[15]

Sample Activity on Using Visual Imagery as an Aid to Reading Comprehension

The following pages present a sample activity on using mental or visual imagery as an aid to comprehension at about the third-grade reading level. It probably should be used only after the child has had some instruction and modeling in the use of this strategy. If you wish, you can duplicate and use this activity in its present form. However, it also can be used as a model of this type of activity sheet.

---

[15]*Ibid.*

ACTIVITY SHEET ON USING VISUAL IMAGERY AS AN AID
TO READING COMPREHENSION
(Approximately third-grade reading level)

Name —————————————— Grade ———— Teacher ——————————

Read this short passage about Grand Canyon National Park to yourself. Then follow the directions to complete the rest of the activity sheet.

THE GRAND CANYON NATIONAL PARK

Sarah, Jerry, and their parents decided to visit Grand Canyon National Park in Arizona one July.

When they arrived at the park, the two children rushed to get out of the car. They saw the great gorge of the Grand Canyon National Park far below them. Also far below were the mountains and valleys, pink and brown, red and yellow, and black and white. Way at the bottom of the gorge Sarah and Jerry saw the Colorado River winding along like a gray-colored snake. Their parents told them that the river was a mile below them at the bottom of the majestic gorge.

The family pitched their tent at a campground in the Grand Canyon National Park. The camp ranger told Sarah and Jerry that many deer, squirrels, and lizards live in the park. He also told them that many, many years ago there was a large sea here, and weather and time cut out the huge gorge that now is the Grand Canyon.

The whole family went for a hike along a trail that next morning, and Sarah and Jerry saw several deer and squirrels, and they even saw a lizard crawl under a rock. The children also saw some people riding mules down the narrow trail toward the bottom of the gorge. Sarah and Jerry wished so very much that they could ride mules too, but they knew that they were too young. They both decided that they would come back some day and ride a mule down to the bottom of the canyon to see the river.

That evening the whole family sat around a campfire and saw some Indians dance a feather dance. They also saw pictures of some of the animals that live in the park.

The next morning the family drove out of the park. Sarah and Jerry knew that they would come back again some day and then ride mules down to the bottom of the beautiful gorge.

Now think about the story that you just read. Make several pictures in your mind about the story, and then draw *two* of these pictures here.

(Continued on following page)

Now write a one- or two-sentence summary of the story on these lines.

_____

_____

_____

_____

Retelling Techniques

The *retelling strategy* may be very helpful in improving comprehension ability. This strategy may also be called *tell-back technique* and is certainly not new. Indeed it first was used around 1920 as the major way of assessing comprehension ability on the first standardized reading tests. It was discontinued after a time due to the difficulty in accurately assessing the child's response. Such tests then used multiple-choice items to assess comprehension ability because of the ease of evaluating such items. However, in the recent past the retelling technique has been used again fairly commonly, mainly as a teaching strategy. As discussed earlier, it is still used in the *Durrell Analysis of Reading Difficulty* as an assessment device of reading comprehension.

To use this valuable technique, simply have the children read a passage on their instructional or independent reading levels and ask:

What was this passage about?
Can you tell me all that you remember about this passage?
What do you remember about the passage that you just read?

This simple strategy will enable you to assess the child's comprehension of what was read and thus serve also as a teaching strategy in an informal way. It is an example of what now is called *process comprehension*. It can be used at the primary-grade reading level quite effectively and extended in use at the middle-upper grade reading level.

Text Lookbacks

Text lookbacks are another obvious but still useful strategy for improving reading comprehension which can be begun at the primary-grade reading level and refined and extended at the middle-upper reading level. Children with comprehension difficulties often are simply unaware of the value of using look-backs to improve their reading comprehension.

To use this technique, the child simply is encouraged to look back in the reading material and reread that part of it in which the answer to the question being posed is located. A number of poor comprehenders are simply unaware that this is an acceptable and valuable process. This strategy first should be explained to children and then modeled for them. Finally children should be able to apply it whenever they cannot answer questions about what they read. This strategy was explained in detail and illustrated in Section 4.

Rereading

Another very basic strategy for improving reading comprehension which can first be presented at the primary-grade reading level is *rereading*. Good readers frequently state that if they do not understand what they are reading, they go back and reread the material. Poor comprehenders apparently are much less likely to do this unless they are specifically helped to do so.

This very basic comprehension strategy should first be presented to primary-grade children using the *think-aloud procedure*. The teacher should select a difficult reading passage. While reading the passage, the teacher should model comprehension difficulty by stating something like: "I don't understand this material very well. The thing that I can do when I don't understand is to go back and read the passage again. This time I should reread only this paragraph to see if I can understand it." To show children the usefulness of the rereading strategy, children can share situations where they had difficulty with the material during the first reading but could understand it much better after reading it again. Having children describe what caused their comprehension difficulty and suggesting reasons why the rereading helped them to understand it illustrates the importance of recognizing comprehension difficulty when it happens and being able to use a certain strategy to correct the difficulty. This also is an example of *metacognition*, which was described earlier in the *Kit* and will be mentioned very briefly again here.

Metacognition for Monitoring Reading Comprehension

As explained in detail in Section 2, *metacognitive strategies* have been emphasized a great deal by recent researchers in cognition and reading as one of the more important ways of improving comprehension ability. *Metacognition* simply means teaching children to think about or monitor their own comprehension. Often children with reading difficulties are unable to monitor their own comprehension as well as the typical good or average reader. Steven D. Rinehart and Jennifer M. Platt state that disabled readers may have difficulty with comprehension because they have deficits in metacognition. They state that disabled readers often have difficulty in areas such as these:

1. Understanding the purpose of reading
2. Modifying reading strategies for different purposes
3. Considering how new information relates to what is already known
4. Evaluating the reading material for clarity, completeness, and consistency
5. Dealing with failure to understand
6. Identifying the important information in a passage
7. Deciding how well the material has been understood[16]

Children in the primary grades can make a beginning in *metacognition* which can be refined at the middle and upper reading levels. They should learn to recognize what parts of reading may cause them comprehension difficulties and

---

[16]Steven D. Rinehart and Jennifer M. Platt, "Forum for Reading," Volume 15 (Spring/Summer 1984), pp. 54–62.

what to do when this happens. They also should understand the great importance of always reading for meaning.

Example of a Simple Metacognitive Checklist

The following page presents a very simple metacognitive checklist for reading comprehension that should be appropriate for use in about the second and third grades. You may duplicate and use it in its present form or modify it in any way you like.

SAMPLE CHECKLIST FOR METACOGNITION
OF READING COMPREHENSION
(Upper primary-grade reading level)

Name _____ Grade _____ Teacher _____

After you have read a story in your basal reader, put an *X* on the line under the words *Yes or No*.

		Yes	*No*
1.	I knew what I wanted to learn from reading this story before I read it.	____	____
2.	I knew what to do when I saw a word in the story that I didn't know.	____	____
3.	I knew what to do when I saw the periods, commas, or question marks in the story.	____	____
4.	I knew how carefully to read the story.	____	____
5.	I knew quite a bit about the material that the story had in it.	____	____
6.	I understand what the story was about.	____	____
7.	I could answer the questions about the story that my teacher asked.	____	____
8.	I know what the most important idea in this story is.	____	____
9.	I can retell the story if I want to.	____	____
10.	I can summarize this story if I want to.	____	____

Marks of Punctuation

Children at the upper second-grade and third-grade reading levels can learn to be aware of the different marks of punctuation. Some children are word-by-word readers who do not pause at periods, questions marks, or commas. This lack of awareness of punctuation often contributes greatly to the child's difficulty in comprehension. My students have emphasized the purpose of punctuation marks with their tutees in a number of different ways which have been successful in helping them to improve their comprehension. This has proven most effective at the upper primary-grade reading level.

One tutor made each important punctuation mark (period, comma, question mark, and exclamation point) into a "person" and placed it on a card. The tutor and child first discussed each punctuation mark, and then the tutor held up the appropriate card as the child read orally. Other tutors have colored the punctuation marks in a printed passage in different colors such as red and yellow. Still others have used the taped oral reading of the children to help them notice their lack of attention to punctuation marks as they followed along in a copy of the printed material. Others have provided simple sentences in which the child must place the correct punctuation marks. Awareness of punctuation usually greatly improves comprehension ability, and this awareness can be begun at the primary level and continued into the middle-upper level.

Semantic Maps

Semantic maps can be used in both the primary and intermediate grades as a motivator for writing as well as an aid to reading comprehension. *Semantic maps* are also called *semantic webs, story maps, story webs, advance organizers,* and *think-links* by various reading specialists and researchers. In any case, they are graphic configurations of representations which illustrate the relationships among an event's components and the important ideas and details from a topic which may have been read. They illustrate the concept that ideas are tied together in reading and thus the use of the term "web."

I have seen Dr. Emily Long, the first-grade teacher at Metcalf Elementary School mentioned earlier in this section, use semantic maps prior to children's writing to help them become aware of the relationships between the terms that will be used in the writing and to understand how the various elements being discussed are related. I was especially impressed when the teacher made a semantic map about dinosaurs on her chalkboard with the help of the children. This first-grade class had studied dinosaurs for several weeks, and the semantic map was used as a summary of the unit about them as well as a help with some of the items that each child could use in his or her writing of a short expository story about dinosaurs. Every child in this heterogeneous first-grade class attempted the story with further teacher help, and most of them did very well because of the help provided by the semantic map which remained on the chalkboard while the stories were being written.

As a follow-up to reading, a semantic map can help children become involved in the reconstruction of the author's passage and thus their comprehension of the material can be greatly improved. Semantic maps can organize a story in several ways. For example, an *inductive web* organizes the information by generalizations or conclusions about the characters and their interactions with other characters. An *episodal web* organizes the story information according to its actions and events. An *emotional web* organizes the story information by the attitudes, feelings, or impressions of the characters for each other.

In formulating a semantic map or web, I think it is useful to put a completed one first on a transparency or the chalkboard and tell the children how it can help them improve their comprehension of what they read. At the primary-grade reading level, the map obviously has to be a simple one. Tell the children how this representation illustrates the relationships between the main ideas and important details. Then place a partially completed semantic web on the transparency or chalkboard after the children have read a basal reader story or a simple content selection.

Only after they have had considerable experience with this technique should they be required to construct one independently. At first a partially completed semantic map can be placed on a ditto master for them to complete. Later, several children at this level may want to work together to construct the map. It may be too difficult for any children but good readers to construct their own map at the primary-grade reading level. If this technique is not presented carefully with much preparation, a child can experience much frustration with the strategy and it becomes a hindrance rather than a help to comprehension.

Sample Semantic Map

The following pages present a partially completed semantic map about gorillas at about the third-grade reading level. It may be helpful for several children to work together at completing it if you wish. You may duplicate this map and use it in its present form, but it also may serve as a model for you of one form of semantic map. There are many other forms that this technique can take in addition to the one illustrated.

SAMPLE STORY MAP
(Approximately third-grade reading level)

Name _____   Grade _____   Teacher _____

Read this story about *gorillas* to yourself. Then finish the story map that is found after the story. You can look back at the story if you want.

Gorillas—Are They Really Monsters?

A gorilla may look like a monster to many people. A large male gorilla may stand 5½ feet tall, weigh more than 500 pounds, and may have an arm-spread of 8 feet. Its face has huge jaws, sunken eyes, large nostrils, and gigantic teeth.

Some gorillas may act like they would be ferocious monsters too. They may beat their chests with their fists and let out a mighty roar.

In fact, gorillas were thought of as ferocious monsters for many years. Those who were captured alive often were mistreated and therefore could be quite mean.

Gorillas have been studied by scientists seriously for about 30 years. These scientists usually lived among the gorillas to observe their behavior. Apparently the gorillas accepted the scientists as other "gorillas" like them.

All of these scientists have discovered that gorillas are really peace-loving animals. For example, male gorillas beat their chests with their fists to help the members of the gorilla troop find each other. Gorillas live in groups containing females and young gorillas along with males who wander in and out. Every group of gorillas has a leader who is called a big silverback because he has silver-gray hairs on his back.

Gorillas of different groups usually avoid fighting with each other. In fact, several gorillas who have lived in captivity apparently loved their masters very much. One young gorilla named Toto, for example, lived with a woman happily for many years until its death.

Even though a gorilla looks like a perfect monster, it usually really is a fairly gentle giant.

©1990 by The Center for Applied Research in Education

(Continued on following page)

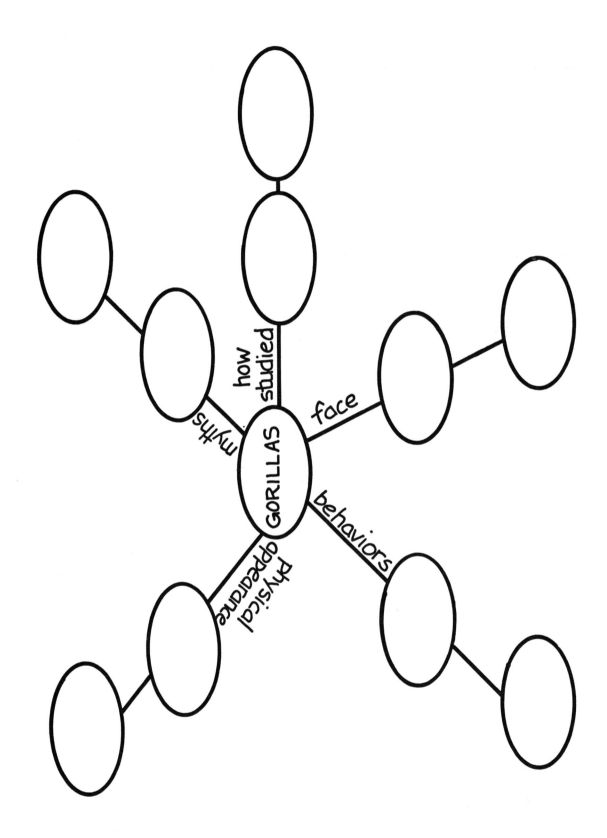

GORILLAS

how studied

myths

face

behaviors

physical appearance

Anaphoric Relationships

Rudimentary anaphoric relationships can be presented in the primary grades, with most emphasis being placed on it at about the third-grade reading level. *Anaphora* is the ability to recognize and identify pronoun antecedents. This is an element of inferencing or implicit (interpretive) comprehension. For example, take these sentences: "The Finnish people sometimes are good ski-jumpers. *They* often can learn this skill as young children." The child must be able to infer *they* the pronoun stands for *Finnish people*. Anaphoric relationships often are determined both by prior knowledge as well as by linguistic conventions in dictating antecedents.

According to John D. McNeil, children often are only about *60 to 80 per cent* accurate in recognizing pronoun antecedents. Although this skill certainly must be refined at the middle-upper level, it can be begun in the primary grades. McNeil has defined the following ways of teaching and/or reinforcing anaphoric relationships:

Metacognitive Awareness—The children must be conscious of pronoun antecedents and their ability to interpret them correctly.

Question Probing—The children can be asked to respond to probes such as the following about antecedents: Bob said, "I'm going to the zoo." "Me, too," said Joy. "We will both go to the zoo."
Name the person or persons who are going to the zoo. (Bob and Joy).

Antecedent Matching—Put numbers over linked terms found in an appropriate passage. Children must write the same number over the words which are linked in an anaphoric relationship. An example of this type of activity sheet follows.

Rule Generation—Have children formulate rules or strategies to interpret the anaphoric relationships which they know. They can use any appropriate statement of the rule which makes sense to them.[17]

Sample Activity Sheet on Anaphoric Relationships

The following page presents a sample activity sheet at about the second-grade reading level on the use of anaphoric relationships. You may duplicate and use it in its present form or modify it in any way. It also may serve as a model for you in developing your own variation of this type of activity sheet.

---

[17]From *Reading Comprehension: New Directions for Classroom Practice* by John D. McNeil, Copyright © 1984 by Scott, Foresman, and Company. Reprinted by permission.

ACTIVITY SHEET FOR USE OF ANTECEDCENT MATCHING
(Approximately second-grade reading level)

Name _____   Grade _____   Teacher _____

Write the same number over the words which are linked in an *anaphoric relationship*. The first number is included for you in each sentence.

1. The school *bus*[1] picked up *Jenny*[2] every morning at *her* aunt's house, and every afternoon *it* dropped *her* there again.

2. As the *woman*[1] put the kettle on the fire, *Donald*[2] looked at *her* again. *She* certainly was a funny little lady. *She* was no bigger than *he*.

3. Many Eskimo *dogs*[1] are tan or gray, but *Nanook*[2] is white. *His* heavy bushy *coat*[3] is so thick that *he* can sleep in the snow when the temperature is 60 or 70 degrees below zero.

4. My *father*[1] climbed out over the door, opened the gate, climbed back into *his Ford*[2], drove *it* through, climbed back into *it*, and *he* drove on to the next gate.

5. *Mr. Paulos*[1] went to town and then *he* came back carrying the softest, purringest *cat*[2] that you ever saw. *She* had fur the color of twilight.

6. The *mouse*[1] just got fatter and fatter. Every few days *he* would turn up and make the *cat*[2] chase *him* all over without letting *her* get anywhere near enough to catch *him*.

7. *Evelyn and Jamie*[1] received a *computer game*[2] for Christmas. *They* had a good time playing with *it* even though *they* thought that *it* was hard to learn how to play it.

8. My *sister*[1] wants a *puppy*[2] more than anything else, but *she* can't get *it* since our family lives in an apartment.

9. *Deer*[1] are beautiful, interesting animals. *They* should be afraid of the *hunters*[2] who may try to shoot *them* during the hunting season when *they* are in the woods.

Answer Key

1. her[2]
   it[1]
   her[2]

2. her[1]
   She[1]
   She[1]
   he[2]

3. His[2]
   he[2]

4. his[1]
   it[2]
   it[2]
   he[1]

5. he[1]
   She[2]

6. he[1]
   him[1]
   her[2]
   him[1]

7. They[1]
   it[2]
   they[1]
   it[2]

8. she[1]
   it[2]

9. They[1]
   them[1]
   they[2]

Creative Activities to Improve Comprehension Ability

Many *creative activities* can also be used to improve elements of comprehension. These are mainly activities that follow-up or relate to reading in some way. We have used many of these types of activities at the primary-grade reading level and have found them to be very successful.

All types of *construction and art activities* can be used to follow-up reading. The basal reader teacher's manual contains many examples of such activities in the enrichment part of the basal reader lesson. The language-experience approach is excellent for this purpose also, as has been explained earlier. Since there undoubtedly are as many creative activities in the art and construction realm as there are creative teachers, it would be impossible to list them all here. However, here are just a few of these kind of activities that we have used successfully in various tutoring situations in the primary years over the years: making a turkey out of an Oreo ™ cookie, candy corn, and toothpicks; making a shell picture; sailing a toy sailboat in a turkey roasting pan filled with blue water; decorating a pumpkin to be a Jack-o-lantern; stuffing a Santa Claus for Christmas; making a Me-Doll; decorating a picture with fall leaves; and making snowflakes.

Cooking and baking activities also can be used as a follow-up to reading in the primary grades. Often my students have constructed a recipe with *rebuses* (pictures) in place of some of the ingredients. The tutor and child have then followed the recipe to make the item. Here are some of the items which have been made by primary-grade children with the help of their tutor: butter, baked bread, frosted cupcakes, cookies of various kinds, deviled eggs, peanut butter on crackers, pretzels, gingerbread men, a macaroni-and-meatball dinner, and candy.

As mentioned earlier, one of the most important and valuable emphases in the late 1980s and probably the early 1990s is the attempt to *relate the instruction of reading and writing*. For far too long, reading and writing have been taught in most elementary schools as separate entities with the greatest emphasis being placed on reading instruction. As noted earlier, *the whole-language approach* (which uses big books, books with predictable language patterns, the patterned language approach, and the language-experience approach with dictated and child-written stories) now is emphasizing the relationship between reading and writing.

However, it still is important to note that "for every $3,000 spent on children's ability to receive information, $1 was spent on their power to send it in writing," and "for every two hours spent on teaching reading, only five minutes are spent on teaching writing."[18] If the reading teacher combines this with the research of Linda Gambrell who discovered that children actually spend very little time reading during the teacher-directed reading lesson in a typical classroom day, the teacher of reading can understand how very little emphasis

---

[18]Donald H. Graves, "A New Look at Writing Research," *Language Arts 57* (November/December, 1980), p. 914.

writing instruction has received in the past. Gambrell, for example, found that children in the first to the third grades spend only two to five minutes during the teacher-directed part of the reading lesson engaging in silent reading.[19] Dishaw discovered that children in the primary grades engage in silent reading only seven or eight minutes per day.[20]

Both creative writing of prose and poetry as well as simple expository writing can be begun effectively in the primary grades. District #150 in Peoria, Illinois, for example, requires all children in the elementary school to write each school day, and a number of their products are scored in a *holistic manner* by teachers trained in this type of scoring. *Invented spelling* is used in this process although children are taught correct mechanics also at the appropriate times in both the primary and intermediate grades. Topics are assigned or they can be child-generated. I have seen the products of this concerted emphasis on writing, and they are quite remarkable. I have also seen the writing of children who used the IBM Computer Program *Writing to Read,* and even children in first grade wrote superb stories both on the word processor and with pencil and paper. As stated earlier, the word processor can be an extremely effective tool in motivating children to write both creative and expository stories.

Summarization is also an excellent tool to relate the teaching of reading and writing. Summaries can first take an oral form in the primary grades. Later in the second and third grades, children can be encouraged to do written summaries, progressing from one-sentence summaries to summaries of several sentences or perhaps a short paragraph.

Gerald L. Fowler recently authored an article in which he illustrated how "story frames" can help children to improve comprehension ability by encouraging them to monitor their comprehension. Fowler illustrated several different types of short frames which are shown on the following page. The story frame can be displayed on the overhead projector following the reading of a story. The children then are asked to complete the blanks in the story frame. Usually there is no exact response for a blank in a story frame.

After the children have had some experience with this technique, the story frame can be constructed prior to the reading of the story. Not all story frames are equally appropriate for all stories. Of the five different types of story frames suggested by Fowler, I believe that the first three are the most appropriate for use at the upper primary-grade reading level. These are as follows: story summary with one character included, the important idea or plot, and the setting. The other two story frames are illustrated in Section 6 since they probably are most appropriate for use in the intermediate grades.

---

[19]Linda B. Gambrell, "Reading in the Primary Grades: How Often, How Long?" In M. R. Sampson (Ed.) *The Pursuit of Literacy* (Dubuque, Iowa: Kendall/Hunt, 1986).

[20]Mark Dishaw, "Descriptions of Allocated Time to Content Areas for the A-B Period" (Beginning Teacher Evaluation Study Technical Note IV—11a). San Francisco: Far West Regional Laboratory for Educational Research and Development, 1977.

STORY SUMMARY WITH ONE CHARACTER INCLUDED*

Name _____ Grade _____ Teacher _____

Our story is about _____

_____. _____

is an important character in our story. _____

tried to _____.

The story ends when _____

_____.

Important Idea or Plot

In this story, the problem starts when _____

_____. After that,

_____.

Next, _____

_____. Then, _____

_____. The problem is

finally solved when _____

_____. The story ends _____

_____.

Setting

This Story takes place _____

_____. I know this because

the author uses the words "_____

_____." Other clues

that show when the story takes place are _____

_____.

*Gerald L. Fowler, "Developing Comprehension Skills in Primary Students Through the Use of Story Frames," *The Reading Teacher* 36 (Nov., 1982), pp. 176–179. Reproduced by permission of Gerald L. Fowler and the International Reading Association.

6

Improving
Comprehension Ability
at the Middle-Upper
Reading Levels

What do you think is the single most common reading problem evidenced by the hundreds of students we have tutored at the middle and upper grade levels over the years? Without a doubt, such students have demonstrated by far the most difficulty with interpretive (implicit or higher-type) comprehension. I believe this results from the fact that higher-level comprehension skills pose great difficulty for some students and that this level of comprehension has not been taught as effectively as it could have been in both the primary and intermediate grades. Most disabled readers at the middle-upper levels also experience the greatest degree of difficulty with interpretive comprehension in reading the various content materials.

As stated earlier, today's reading researchers are giving most attention to the various elements of comprehension. Fortunately, they also are trying to translate this research into practical classroom strategies and materials which reading teachers can use to improve the comprehension skills of all the students with whom they are working. This section of the kit focuses on improving comprehension at the middle and upper reading levels.

The section begins with a brief discussion of the extreme importance of placing great emphasis on improving comprehension skills at the middle-upper reading levels. Also mentioned are some of the special reading skills that are exemplified by the various content areas of literature, social studies, science, and mathematics. The bulk of the section presents many classroom-tested strategies and activity sheets that can be used to improve specific components of comprehension at the middle-upper reading levels. Most of these strategies and materials attempt to improve ability in various elements of implicit (interpretive) comprehension. They mainly reflect the contemporary understandings of reading comprehension explained and illustrated in Section 1 of this resource. The section contains numerous ready-to-duplicate activity sheets of various types which the reading teacher can use to improve ability in different elements of reading comprehension. These activity sheets should save the teacher much valuable time and effort. The teacher will notice that some of the strategies described in Section 5 are briefly mentioned again as they can be used at both the primary and middle-upper school levels.

Very briefly, here are some of the strategies and activity sheets described and illustrated in this section: wide reading of relevant materials, using prior knowledge to improve comprehension (the Anticipation Guide, the Pre-Reading Plan [PReP], and a Questionnaire-Inventory to Assess Prior Knowledge), student-generated predictions prior and during reading, questioning strategies of various types, self-questioning about the main idea, metacognitive strategies for monitoring reading comprehension, story grammars, semantic mapping, and advance organizers, the Directed Reading-Thinking Activity (DRTA), the Guided Reading Procedure, sentence combining, and various study techniques such as Survey Q3R, the REAP Technique, Guide-O-Rama, and the Herringbone Technique.

The Section also provides many ways of stressing the relationship between reading and writing skills, thus hopefully improving ability in both of them simultaneously. Some of these means for stressing reading and writing together are as follows: summarization skills, the GIST Procedure, the Guided Writing Procedure, Authors Chair/Peer Conferencing, Dialogue Journals, and ECOLA. The Section closes by briefly describing how knowledge of the various patterns of paragraph organization can improve comprehension, and providing an activity sheet which illustrates that concept.

It is hoped that the teacher of reading will find this section extremely useful in improving the teaching of reading comprehension skills at the middle-upper reading levels—an absolutely essential task.

IMPORTANCE OF TEACHING COMPREHENSION SKILLS AT THE MIDDLE-UPPER READING LEVELS

As stated earlier, it is the higher-level comprehension skills that cause students the greatest degree of difficulty in reading at both the middle and upper levels. Most students at both levels with the exception of severely disabled readers have relatively good word identification skills and an adequate sight vocabulary. Many also can respond adequately at the literal (explicit) level of comprehension. However, faced with the challenges of responding at the higher levels, they may experience great difficulty and frustration. Unfortunately for them, most of the comprehension required at the middle-upper levels is of the interpretive (implicit) type at which they are the least competent.

Indeed, often if a student does not master the important elements of interpretive comprehension in the middle grades, he or she does not have the opportunity to do so at either the secondary level or the adult level and may be handicapped in this skill for the rest of his or her life. Thus it is essential that middle-school students gain competency in interpretive comprehension skills as much as possible. It they do not do so, they will have special difficulty in comprehending their content textbooks.

All of the various content areas of literature, social studies, science, and mathematics involve unique reading skills that impact upon a student's comprehension ability in those areas. The teaching of these unique reading-study skills should be correlated with the teaching of interpretive comprehension skills as much as possible. The strategies and activity sheets included here are all based upon content reading materials.

As stated earlier, content materials are composed of *mainly* expository material and not the narrative reading material most commonly found in basal readers. Although the *content area of literature* does contain some narrative material, it also involves certain unique reading-study skills that should be presented to students reading at the middle-school level or higher. Some of these skills are as follows:

- understanding of specialized vocabulary terms
- recognition of figurative language, slang, and word connotations
- knowledge of polysemous words (words with multiple meanings) and word origins
- developing mental (visual) imagery
- evaluating critically what is read
- responding creatively to the author's ideas and concepts
- using the card catalog, reference books, and the *Reader's Guide to Periodical Literature* to research material
- developing reading flexibility

Some of the different *genre in literature* are fairly difficult for students to comprehend, while others usually do not cause them quite as much difficulty. For example, *poetry* is difficult because it contains rich spoken language with imagery and figurative language playing a crucial part. An *essay* focuses on a detailed expansion of one idea or piece of information and requires the student to think logically, to recognize patterns of organization, and to do critical analysis. *Biography*, which is an account of one or more lives written by someone other than the writer, may be best understood by having the child write an autobiography or the biography of a friend. It generally is not an exceedingly difficult genre. The *short story* is a compressed segment of fiction with some kind of plot. It has no length or rigid form. On the other hand, *drama* is a difficult type of literature which demands a great deal from the children who must read it. Children who read drama must be able to visualize the details of the characters, the setting, and the action. It may be of help to have a small group of children read a play together and then perform it for a group of classmates or adults.

The *content area of social studies* also requires a number of unique reading-study skills if children are to attain competency in this area. Effective reading of social studies material is crucial if children are to develop an understanding of how people interact in various cultures, in societies, and in the world. Unfortunately, the content materials in this area are very difficult because they are often written at a higher reading level than many of the children who must read them. This poses an especially difficult problem for disabled readers who are reading significantly below grade level.

Here are some of the most important reading-study skills necessary for effective comprehension in social studies:

- understanding of extremely difficult specialized vocabulary terms, some of which have a unique meaning in this area, such as the word *cabinet*
- knowledge of the meaning of some useful prefixes and suffixes that can aid in recognition of specialized vocabulary
- finding the main ideas and significant details in the reading material
- following a sequence of events, especially in history
- identifying cause-effect relationships
- reading critically to identify propaganda techniques, an especially important reading skill in a democratic society
- distinguishing fact from opinion
- understanding of some of the following patterns of organization that may be found in social studies textbooks: *enumeration, cause-effect*, and *comparison-contrast*
- using graphic aids such as maps, graphs, diagrams, tables, and pictures
- using textbook aids such as the table of contents, chapter introductions, summaries, vocabulary lists, glossaries, and footnotes
- using the card catalog, all types of reference books such as encyclopedias and atlases, and the *Reader's Guide to Periodical Literature*
- understanding of time-and-space relationships
- using a study technique such as Survey Q3R (explained in detail later)

The *content area of science* is extremely difficult even for otherwise able readers. Thus, it is virtually impossible for disabled readers. The science textbooks selected for a grade level are often much above the reading level of many of the students who are to read them. In addition, they are difficult for a number of other reasons, perhaps most importantly, the large number of specialized, polysyllabic terms that they contain.

Here are some of the most significant reading-study skills which make reading *science textbooks* so difficult for most students:

- understanding of extremely difficult (technical) vocabulary
- knowledge of the meaning of prefixes and suffixes that may help the student decode the polysyllabic technical vocabulary

- reading and remembering many important details
- distinguishing fact from opinion
- understanding and effectively carrying out directions
- performing scientific experiments after reading how they should be conducted (creative reading skill)
- recognition of some of the patterns of organization found in science textbooks, such as the *sequential pattern* or the *enumeration pattern*
- organizing ideas from reading and understanding the relationships between the ideas in order to draw acceptable conclusions
- understanding of cue words, such as *few, several, many*, and *some*
- reading to test, prove, or predict outcomes
- interpreting graphic and visual materials correctly
- using a study technique such as Survey Q3R
- using library research to locate and study a topic
- identifying symbols, formulae, and abbreviations
- being a good problem-solver and hypothesis-tester

The reading of *mathematical verbal problems* often poses serious difficulty for otherwise good readers, including this writer. Reading in the content area of mathematics causes extreme difficulty for many students in the middle and upper school levels. In reading in this area, the student must know how to read mathematical materials and must understand the concepts and their applications.

The following are some of the unique reading-study skills that are required for effective comprehension in mathematics:

- understanding of specialized vocabulary terms
- understanding of the meaning of some relevant prefixes and suffixes
- knowledge of mathematical symbols
- understanding that some common terms have entirely different meanings in mathematics, such as the term *square* in *square root*
- reading very carefully for significant details
- determining the relevant and irrelevant data in a verbal problem
- comprehending many different kinds of graphic and tabular materials
- finding and understanding reference materials on topics such as famous mathematicians
- interpreting formulae, equations, principles, and axioms
- understanding visual materials such as diagrams and geometric forms
- reading for main ideas
- pronouncing difficult multisyllabic words
- solving word problems

William P. Dunlap and Martha Brown McKnight have written a useful article on how to help children conceptualize difficult mathematical word problems. They point out that one major problem which affects children's ability to solve mathematical word problems is the three-level translation of the vocabulary included in that problem. Students must be able to translate from the general to the technical to the symbolic vocabularies. The authors explain that the translation process among the vocabularies is essential to the conceptualization of the message included in that word problem, then give some concrete examples of these vocabulary translations.[1]

STRATEGIES AND ACTIVITY SHEETS FOR IMPROVING COMPREHENSION ABILITY AT THE MIDDLE AND UPPER LEVELS

The remainder of this section provides numerous classroom-tested strategies and activity sheets the reading teacher can use to improve the comprehension ability of every student with whom he or she works at the middle or upper levels. Although most of these ideas and materials are designed to improve ability in implicit (higher-order) comprehension and reflect the contemporary research in reading comprehension, a few are more traditional but are included because I believe they remain relevant and meaningful. All of the strategies and activity sheets are written in a manner I hope the reading teacher will find easy to understand although some of them involve fairly difficult concepts. The activities have been used in tutoring situations of various types and found extremely useful in improving the reading comprehension of students at these levels.

Wide Reading of Relevant Materials

Although it may seem simplistic and self-evident, *wide reading of relevant, meaningful narrative and expository (content) material at the appropriate reading level in the middle and upper grades is the single best way to improve reading comprehension.* The more that a student reads with the purpose of understanding what is read, the more effective his or her comprehension skills will become since reading is a skill that *improves best with motivated, meaningful practice.* This is why good readers who enjoy reading usually become better readers who enjoy reading for information and pleasure even more because they understand what they read and find reading to be rewarding, challenging, and self-fulfilling. They read for meaning using context clues effectively, make excellent use of prior knowledge, use appropriate fix-up strategies such as rereading or self-correction when needed, and use prediction strategies and have set purposes for reading.

However, *reluctant or disabled readers* do not find reading rewarding and therefore often avoid doing it if possible. They do not make good use of their prior knowledge, do not set purposes or make predictions prior to reading, do not make

---

[1]William P. Dunlap and Martha Brown McKnight, "Vocabulary Translations for Conceptualizing Math Word Problems," *The Reading Teacher* 32 (Nov., 1979), pp. 183-189.

good use of context clues, and do not self-correct. Therefore, their comprehension skills do not improve to the extent they should. We have found it *extremely difficult* to motivate such children to do wide reading from either narrative or expository materials unless they are provided with unique strategies or materials which will aid them in some way to improve their reading comprehension. That is why I believe this statement made by a colleague of mine is correct but sometimes not practiced with such students: "Children learn to comprehend best by simply reading." Although this is certainly true, we have found that we must provide some intervention if these children are to learn to read effectively and thus improve their comprehension ability. The remainder of this section is designed to help the reading teacher do just that.

Using Prior Knowledge to Improve Comprehension Ability

As mentioned in previous sections of this resource, *the student's prior knowledge (background of experiences) is the single most influential factor on his or her subsequent comprehension of the reading material.* The greater the student's prior knowledge, the less dependent he or she need be on the printed material which he or she must read. It is extremely difficult for a child to comprehend reading material effectively for which he or she has limited prior knowledge. It therefore is very important for the reading teacher to help the student to activate prior knowledge before reading either narrative or expository (content) material.

There are a number of fairly self-evident ways of activating prior knowledge which are useful. Undoubtedly the most common is a *class or small-group discussion* in which the teacher helps the children to activate prior knowledge by relating what is going to be read to what they already know or have read about in the past. In this process it is important to avoid diversionary questions, as explained earlier. Such questions tend to distract children away from the actual topic of the subsequent reading. Many types of vicarious experiences such as the following can be used to activate students' prior knowledge: computer simulations, experiments, demonstrations, films, filmstrips, videotapes, recordings, cassette recordings, pictures, and dioramas.

As explained and illustrated in Section 5 and briefly discussed again later in this section, *semantic webs or maps* also can be very useful in activating the prior knowledge of several or more students. For this purpose, it may be helpful to have a jointly composed semantic map by the teacher and students since the students otherwise may lack enough prior knowledge to formulate a completely useful web or map especially prior to reading expository (content) material.

In a recent article Betty C. Holmes and Nancy L. Roser discuss five ways to assess a reader's prior knowledge. They are as follows:

(1) *free recall*—This strategy requires the least time and effort but may not be very productive in yielding useful information.

(2) *word association*—This strategy yields a little more information and should not take much teacher time to prepare.

(3) *structured questioning*—This strategy requires much preparation, but conversely much information may be acquired by the teacher in how much and what types of prior knowledge the student possesses.

(4) *recognition*—This strategy may take the form of a multiple choice activity and may be useful in locating information and misinformation which the student(s) possess(es).

(5) *unstructured discussion*—Although this strategy can be very motivating for the child, it is generally considered the least helpful in determining the prior knowledge possessed by one or more students.[2]

As explained in Section 5, the *Anticipation Guide* Readence, Bean, and Baldwin developed in 1981 can increase a student's comprehension ability by activating prior knowledge and by providing purposes for reading by serving as a guide for subsequent reading. Since this strategy is detailed in Section 5, only the major points are reviewed here. Very briefly, here are the major steps included in an anticipation guide:

1. Identify the Major Concepts
2. Determine Children's Knowledge of These Concepts
3. Create Statements
4. Decide Statement Order and Presentation Style
5. Present Guide
6. Discuss Each Statement Briefly
7. Have Children Read the Material
8. Conduct Follow-Up Discussions[3]

The following pages present a sample anticipation guide at about the sixth-grade reading level that the reading teacher can duplicate and use in its present form if it seems relevant. More importantly, it also can serve as a model in constructing this type of guide.

---

[2]Adapted from Betty C. Holmes and Nancy L. Roser, "Five Ways to Assess Reader's Prior Knowledge," *The Reading Teacher* 40 (Mar., 1987), pp. 646-648.

[3]J. E. Readence, T. W. Bean, and R. S. Baldwin, *Content Area Reading: An Integrated Approach* (Dubuque, Iowa: Kendall/Hunt Publishing Company, 1981).

SAMPLE ANTICIPATION GUIDE
(Approximately sixth-grade reading level)

Name _____ **Grade** _____ **Teacher** _____

Directions: Here are some statements about the *science of robotics*. Read each statement to yourself and put an *X* next to each statement that you agree with. Be sure to be able to defend your ideas later when we talk about the statements.

_____ 1. Although robots are not really very smart, they can do such things as paint cars, assist in brain surgery, and hear and speak.

_____ 2. Very few American factories have purchased robots to do some of the work because they are so expensivce that they take many years to pay for themselves.

_____ 3. The robots working on factory assembly lines today might well be said to have the intelligence of chimpanzees.

_____ 4. There may well be a robot in the future that can be a household helper who prepares light meals, cleans house, and clears snow.

_____ 5. Robots may be as intelligent as humans in about ten years.

Now read the following story to yourself. Remember what you should look for as you read the story so we can discuss later what you learned from reading this story.

ARE ROBOTS REALLY AS SMART AS HUMANS?

Scientists in the 1950s proclaimed the *robot* to be the wave of the future and said that robots would free housewives of drudgery and fill factories with a tireless steel-collar work force. However, this prediction has not come true in many ways.

Robots are now significantly better than they were 40 years ago, but orders for them peaked in 1984 and have been falling ever since. Today, about 33,000 robots work in the United States, mostly in manufacturing jobs, with automakers using at least *40%* of them.

Although robots still are not really very smart at all, they can:

— see by recognizing forms and shapes, and measure distances through sonar and laser
— hear and speak by recognizing thousands of words
— smell by their sensors detecting smoke and fumes
— move on wheels, hop on one leg, or walk on eight legs like a spider

The industrial robot can weld, paint, assemble, and load but is only about as smart as an insect. The robots working on contemporary assembly lines might be compared to spiders who do their job competently, but it is a narrow job.

Service robots can now help the disabled, work in hazardous environments, or sweep floors. Some doctors in California have performed more than 35 brain operations with the help of a robot which guides surgeons as they drill into human skulls.

In the future a "dream" robot may be developed: a $50,000 household helper that would prepare light meals, clean house, make beds, and clear snow. However, it may take up to $14,000,000 and several years to develop if that much money can ever be obtained.

The concept of building a mechanical man is fairly old since there were clock-work automatons built by Swiss and French clockmakers in the 17th and 18th centuries. The term *robotics* was coined in 1942 in a science fiction story by Isaac Asimov from the word *robot* which was coined in 1921 by a Czech playwright named Karel Capek. Some scientists believe that technology may well enable robots to have human-like intelligence in about 50 years. Will you really be ready for that?

```
┌─────────────────────────────────┐
│         Answer Key              │
│                                 │
│   X   1                         │
│   X   2.                        │
│   X   4.                        │
│                                 │
└─────────────────────────────────┘
```

Pre-Reading Plan (PReP)

The *Pre-Reading Plan* (PReP) to assess and activate students' prior knowledge for key concepts in a content reading assignment is explained and illustrated in detail in Section 2 and therefore will be mentioned only very briefly here. As you may remember, this procedure can be used with a group of students before they read a content assignment. *PReP* is a quick, practical means for the reading teacher to use in assessing students' level of prior knowledge for a content reading assignment. It also should improve their comprehension of the reading material. To use it, the teacher selects about three major concepts from a 700- to 800-word content textbook passage, and a diagram is made with their responses to the key concepts found in this assignment. An example of this type of diagram about *corn farming* is found in Section 2 and can serve as a model for the reading teacher.

Thomas G. Devine has described some indirect ways to assess students' prior knowledge. Very briefly, here are some of the more useful ways:

1. *Simple questionnaires and inventories*—The teacher may have students complete a short, 20- to 30-item, duplicated activity sheet of questions that contain some true-false items, fill-in-the-blank items, and incomplete sentence items (only the first part of the statement is given).

2. *Open-ended inventories*—The students must write out responses to such questions as: *What do you now know about the koala bear?* or *The koala bear* _____.

3. *Informal content checks*—These pretests help to determine how much students know about an area before they must study it.

4. *Informal concept tests*—The students list words on the chalkboard that label the concept or the sentences containing the concepts. This technique

helps the teacher locate students who have inaccurate schemata in that subject.

5. *Synonym and definition tests*—In these tests the teacher lists words and concepts on the board or an activity sheet with a parallel list of synonyms placed in incorrect order. The student must draw a line from each word to the correct synonym.[4]

A Sample Questionnaire-Inventory to Assess Prior Knowledge

The following page presents a model questionnaire-inventory for assessing prior knowledge on the topic of the Australian koala bear. It is on approximately the fifth-grade reading level. The questionnaire-inventory is followed by a brief passage about the koala bear which students can read after completing the questionnaire inventory. This prereading device incorporates both structured and open-ended forms. Although the reading teacher can duplicate and use it in its present form if it seems applicable, it is mainly designed to serve as a model for this type of device which reading can construct.

---

[4]Thomas G. Devine, *Teaching Reading Comprehension: From Theory to Practice* (Boston: Allyn and Bacon, Inc., 1986), pp. 79-81.

QUESTIONNAIRE-INVENTORY FOR ASSESSING PRIOR KNOWLEDGE
(Approximately fifth-grade reading level)

Name _____ Grade _____ Teacher _____

In a few minutes you are going to read a story about the *koala bear*. The following part of this activity is trying to find out just how much you know about the koala bear before you read the story about it. Complete all of the items the best that you can and then read the story to yourself. Then see how well you did on the items you marked.

1. T F   The koala bear usually is about 4 feet high.

2. T F   The koala bear is able to eat only the leaves of certain eucalyptus (gum) trees.

3. T F   The baby koala bear remains in the mother's pouch for three months.

4. T F   A mother koala bear may sometimes spank her baby.

5. T F   There are now more koala bears than there were 100 years ago.

6. A koala bear has a rounded stump of a _____.

7. Koala bears live almost completely in _____.

8. Koala bears do not drink _____ but get moisture from their food and from dew.

9. Koala bears have _____ toes on each of their front feet.

10. Koala bears have mainly ash-gray _____.

11. The koala bear has cheek pouches _____

_____.

12. The koala bear lives almost completely _____

_____.

13. The mother koala bear carries _____

_____.

14. The koala bear's normal voice _____

_____.

15. The koala bear's fur _____

_____.

Continued on following page

LEARNING ABOUT KOALA BEARS

The koala or native bear is one of the most fascinating and charming animals of Australia. The koala bear is small, being about 2 feet tall, and has a rounded stump of a tail. Its body is covered with dense, thick fur that is mainly ash-gray with tinges of brown, yellowish-white, and white. Its ears are tufted, and it has a prominent beak-like snout. The koala has cheek pouches for storing food temporarily, and the female has a pouch which opens backwards.

Koala bears are no longer as common as they once were because they can only eat the leaves or tender shoots of certain types of eucalyptus (gum) trees. They live almost completely in gum trees but will sometimes come to the ground only to move to another tree to look for food. Koala bears do not drink but get their moisture from their food and the dew found on the leaves.

Koala bears sleep curled up in the forks of trees during the day. They are very agile, lithe, and active and can easily live in the top-swaying branches of the giant eucalyptus trees. They do not fall out of trees unless they are dead or paralyzed because they have such powerful toes. The five toes of their front feet are grouped two and three with a wide gap between to give them a strong grip on the branch. On the back feet, the first toe is large and opposite to the rest, acting like a thumb in grasping. The second and third toes are joined together, and these toes are used for combing the koala bear's fur.

Thirty-five days after the parents have mated, a single cub is born. It is only three-fourths of an inch long and stays in the mother's pouch for three months. It is fully furred at six months, and it rides on its mother's back until it is a year old.

Koala bears have an innocent, babyish expression and are gentle, but unintelligent animals. Their whole face has a human appearance because of its beak-like snout which resembles a human nose. Their normal voice is hoarse and grating, but it can truly cry like a hurt child when it is wounded. Koala bears also are like humans in that they may spank their young as adult parents do. Interestingly, koala bears do not panic when frightened but simply look calmly, demonstrating no fear.

Although most people do not have the opportunity to see live koala bears in person except perhaps in the zoo, these animals still remain fascinating to people because of their unique, interesting appearance and characteristics.

Answer Key

1. F	9. five
2. T	10. fur
3. T	11. for storing food temporarily
4. T	12. in eucalyptus (gum) trees
5. F	13. her baby in a pouch for three months
6. tail	14. is hoarse and grating
7. trees	15. is dense and ash-gray
8. water	

Student-Generated Predictions Before and During Reading

As explained in Sections 4 and 5, *prediction strategies* which are used both before and during reading have proven to be extremely useful in improving comprehension of students at all reading levels. We have found them to be especially useful with the students at the *middle-school level* in tutoring.

Before reading either narrative or expository (content) material, the reading teacher can motivate prediction by asking:

What is the title of this story or article?

What do you think this story or article might be about?

What type of material would a story on this topic probably contain?

During the reading of narrative and expository material, we have found that prediction strategies can greatly improve the child's implicit (interpretive) comprehension and also can enable him or her to be a *more active comprehender*. Here are several questions that my tutors have used with intermediate-grade children to improve their comprehension of the material. They may be best used with a story that has clearly delineated story divisions:

What do you believe will happen next in this story (article)?

What would you like to have happen next in this story (article)?

What do you think that _____ (story character) will (should) do now?

As explained in detail in Section 5, Robert M. Wilson and Linda B. Gambrell have described a prediction strategy that includes the cyclical steps of *activation, prediction, reading,* and *verifying.* Consult this section about how to best use the strategy. It can be very easily adapted for use at the middle-school level.

Questioning Strategies of Various Types Emphasizing Textually and Scriptally Implicit (Higher-Level) Responses

As explained in Sections 2 and 4 of this resource, *questioning* is undoubtedly one of the most significant means of improving comprehension ability at the middle-upper reading levels, especially if mainly textually and scriptally (higher-order) questions are used. A number of the contemporary tests of reading comprehension such as the *Illinois Goal Assessment Program (IGAP)* use comprehension questions to which several different responses are considered acceptable, as illustrated in Section 2. It is imperative that students at the middle-upper reading levels respond to questions at the higher levels if they are to become competent in this most important aspect of comprehension.

It also is crucial that students learn to ask themselves implicit (interpretive) questions prior to reading in order to formulate their purposes for reading. Section 4 also explains QARs, and the importance of teaching students to recognize the various kinds of questions such as: *Right There, Think and Search,* and *On My Own.* When students are made aware of the *Think and Search* and *On My Own questions,* they are much more likely to formulate these types of questions for themselves.

As also explained earlier, *reciprocal questioning* undoubtedly is one of the most useful questioning strategies that can be used with students at the middle-upper reading levels. We have used *reciprocal questioning* extensively as a teaching strategy with middle-school students who showed considerable difficulty with comprehension. Reciprocal questioning was especially successful with Matt, a fourth-grade student whom we tutored for two consecutive semesters. During the fall of 1988, the tutor used activity sheets and game-like activities in an attempt to improve Matt's ability in implicit (interpretive) comprehension. Although he had good explicit (literal) comprehension ability, Matt gave illogical responses to interpretive questions of any type. He also, had a very difficult time remaining on task.

Therefore, when we tutored Matt a second time during the spring of 1989, we directed a new tutor to use *reciprocal questioning* with him as one major strategy to improve his implicit (interpretive) comprehension ability. The tutor mainly used his own social studies and science textbooks for practice in reciprocal questioning. Matt did remarkably well in interpretive comprehension using this strategy and also stayed on task very well. He especially enjoyed asking his tutor questions about the material which she could not answer! Reciprocal questioning improved Matt's interpretive (implicit) comprehension ability very much, and he also found it highly motivating. Several other fourth-grade students we tutored also used this strategy with some improvement, though not as much as Matt's.

This indicates why such a strategy normally should not be used as the *only means* of improving comprehension ability, but merely as one of many strategies and materials used for this purpose.

J. P. Helfeldt and Rosary Lalik found that *reciprocal teacher-student questioning* had positive effects on fifth-grade students' comprehension. Very briefly, here are the main steps used in this variation of the strategy:

What—Students are told that they will be learning how to formulate their own questions which ask readers to interpret materials or draw conclusions and generalizations. Often these are high-level questions that are *how* and *why questions* instead of *what, when,* or *where questions.*

Why—Students are told that if they ask interpretive (implicit) questions about material that they have read, their comprehension of the material usually improves.

How—The teacher first tells the students to ask the kinds of questions about each sentence in a selection which they think that the teacher might ask. The teacher then answers each question as fully and fairly as possible and tells the students that they later must do the same. Then the teacher and student both silently read the first sentence. The teacher closes the book, and the student asks questions about the sentence which the teacher is to answer. Next the student closes the book, and the teacher asks questions about the material. As stated earlier, the teacher should provide an excellent model for the student's questions, and the questions should mainly be of the interpretive (implicit) type. After a number of additional sentences, the procedure can be varied to use an entire paragraph instead of individual sentences.

NOTE: If the reading teacher wishes, reciprocal questioning can be used with a small group of students in the following manner. The teacher introduces new vocabulary and asks several questions to set the purposes for reading. Then the students read the material and answer the initial questions in a small-group discussion. Next the teacher asks several implicit (interpretive) comprehension questions about the material. Every time a student answers a question correctly, the student asks the teacher a question. The student question then is followed by another teacher question.

When—Students are told that after reading an assignment, they can work in groups to ask each other implicit (interpretive) questions about the material which has been read.[5]

Some reading specialists believe that some of the questions in instructional materials such as basal readers do not help students organize and integrate the material. They state that teachers should ask questions based on the logical

---

[5]Adapted from J. P. Helfeldt and Rosary Lalik, "Reciprocal Student-Teacher Questioning," *The Reading Teacher* 30 (December, 1976), pp. 283-287.

organization of events and ideas and their interrelationships—an example of the *story grammar* which will be explained shortly in this section.

Harry Singer and Dan Donlan have developed *schema general questions* that attempt to help students organize and integrate the story which they just have read. Here are the questions designed to help students synthesize the story information:

1. *The Leading Character*
    Who is the leading character?
    What action does the character initiate?
    What did you learn about the character from this action?

2. *The Goal*
    For what does the leading character appear to be striving?
    What did you learn about the character from the nature of the goal?
    What courses of action does the character take to reach the goal?
    What did you learn about the character from the courses of action taken?

3. *The Obstacle*
    What is the first (last) obstacle that the character encounters?
    How does the character deal with it?
    How does the character alter the goal because of this obstacle?
    What does this tell you about the character?

4. *The Outcome*
    Does the character reach the original goal or a revised goal?
    If successful, what helped most?
    _____ Forces within the character's control
    _____ Forces outside the character's control
    If unsuccessful, what hindered the character most?
    _____ Forces within the character's control
    _____ Forces outside the character's control
    Name them

5. *The Theme*
    What does the story basically show? A struggle with self, nature, or other people?[6]

Self-Questioning About the Main Idea

M. E. D. A. Andre and T. H. Anderson have created a *self-questioning study technique* that may improve comprehension ability among middle-upper level students who have difficulty in this area. In this technique students are taught to identify the main idea of each paragraph as they are reading and then are shown

[6]Adapted from Harry Singer and Dan Donlan, "Active Comprehension: Problem-Solving Schema with Question Generation for Comprehension of Complex Short Stories," *Reading Research Quarterly* 17 (1982), pp. 166-187.

how to formulate and answer a question about the main idea. They repeat this procedure then with the next paragraph.

Very briefly, here are the basic steps to follow in this *self-questioning study procedure*:

What—Students are told that they will be learning how to ask and answer questions about the main ideas of the paragraphs as they read narrative text.

Why—Students are told that this is crucial because they will have a better comprehension of the material they are studying.

How—The teacher first models how to identify main ideas in a paragraph. The reading teacher then decides on one or two words which state the topic of the paragraph. Next a main idea sentence about the topic is formulated. The teacher can provide several examples of possible main idea sentences for a particular paragraph as well as several unacceptable main idea sentences. Then the students should be shown how to generate and answer a question about the main idea and are provided with several examples of a possible question that could have been formulated for a particular paragraph. Several unacceptable questions also are discussed.

When—Students can be told to employ the *self-questioning technique* whenever they are reading content (expository) material that seems very difficult to understand. They should then begin again identifying main ideas for the paragraphs and formulating and answering questions about these main ideas.[7]

Sample Activity Sheet for Self-Questioning About the Main Ideas

The following pages present a sample activity for self-questioning about the main ideas on about the sixth-grade reading level. The reading teacher may duplicate and use this activity in its present form if it seems applicable. More importantly, it can serve as a model.

---

[7]Adapted from M. E. D. A. Andre and T. H. Anderson, "The Development and Evaluation of a Self-Questioning Study Technique," *Reading Research Quarterly* (14), pp. 605-623.

ACTIVITY SHEET FOR SELF-QUESTIONING ON MAIN IDEAS
(Approximately sixth-grade reading level)

Name ——————————————— Grade ——— Teacher ——————————

Read the following passage about using bears and their hibernation habits in medical research to yourself. Then *make a statement of the topic of each paragraph on the line below it. On the next line, write the main idea of the paragraph.* Lastly, *make up a possible question for that paragraph.* You may work with one or several partners in completing this activity. The first paragraph has been done for you as an example.

USING BEARS IN MEDICAL RESEARCH

An elderly cattle farmer in central Illinois is caring for several unlikely animals—three large black male bears. The bears live in a 20-foot by 40-foot building and cage complex in culvert-pipe hiberation dens. These three black bears will contribute to the medical research that is aimed at improving the treatment of kidney disease, burns, trauma, anorexia nervosa, and bone weakening.

Topic of paragraph 1: bears and medical research ————————————————

Main idea of paragraph 1: Bear's hiberation habits are now being studied

in medical research. ————————————————————————————

Possible question for paragraph 1: Why is bear's hibernation being studied

for medical research? ———————————————————————————

The bears are being studied because of what their bodies can do during hibernation—a period of time about five months long when they don't eat or drink, but stay in a den and lose about 100 pounds. During that time, bears do not eliminate body waste or lose body strength. Mother bears even carry out pregnancies, give birth, and nurse cubs while they are hibernating. The hibernation of the bears is called a "metabolic marvel" by medical researchers.

Topic of paragraph 2: ———————————————————————————

Main idea of paragraph 2: ——————————————————————————

——

Possible question for paragraph 2: ——————————————————————

——

The three black bears are named Amonzo, Caruso, and U.P. after the Upper Peninsula of Michigan. They were "nuisance" bears in northern Wisconsin and the Upper Peninsula, wreaking havoc in garbage dumps and farm fields. If they had not been captured and sent to the research center, they would have been shot. They are about 5 feet tall and their post-hibernation weights range from 250 to 280 pounds. They are young, ranging in age from three to seven years, with a possible life span of up to 30 years in captivity.

Topic of paragraph 3: _____

Main idea of paragraph 3: _____

_____

Possible question for paragraph 3: _____

_____

The medical researchers use a hypodermic needle on the end of a pole to tranquilize the bears when they are to be studied. Even when black bears are hibernating, they can be fully alert and dangerous within seconds. The researchers take blood and urine samples and weigh the bears periodically. The researchers are very interested in the fact that although bears do not urinate or defecate during hibernation, toxic wastes do not accumulate in their bodies. If a diet can be designed for humans that will minimize the waste products in the blood, the number of dialysis sessions needed by human patients without functioning kidneys may be able to be reduced.

Topic of paragraph 4: _____

Main idea of paragraph 4: _____

_____

Possible question for paragraph 4: _____

_____

The biggest step forward may be when scientists discover what they believe is a substance in bears' blood that "triggers" hibernation. There apparently is a substance in the bears' winter blood that is not found in the bears' summer blood. This difference may be the key to some exciting medical breakthrough for humans.

Topic of paragraph 5: _____

Main idea of paragraph 5: _____

_____

Possible question for paragraph 5: _____

_____

Answer Key

Topic of paragraph 2: bears and hibernation characteristics

Main idea of paragraph 2: Bears are being studied because of the unique characteristics of their bodies during hibernation.

Possible question for paragraph 2: What do bears' bodies do during their period of hibernation?

Topic of paragraph 3: characteristics of the three bears

Main idea of paragraph 3: The three black bears that are being used in medical research would have been destroyed otherwise.

Possible question for paragraph 3: What are the three bears like that are being used in the medical research?

Topic of paragraph 4: how medical researchers are studying the bears

Main idea of paragraph 4: The medical researchers are trying to determine why body wastes do not accumulate in bears during hibernation.

Possible question for paragraph 4: Why are researchers trying to determine that toxic wastes do not accumulate in bears' blood during hibernation?

Topic of paragraph 5: discovering a substance that triggers hibernation

Main idea of paragraph 5: Scientists are trying to discover a substance in bears' blood that triggers hibernation.

Possible question for paragraph 5: Why are scientists trying to discover a substance in bears' blood which triggers hibernation?

(The answers are given only for illustrative purposes. Students' answers may vary considerably from the ones given.)

USING METACOGNITIVE STRATEGIES FOR MONITORING READING COMPREHENSION

As explained in detail in Sections 2 and 5 of this resource, *metacognitive strategies* have been stressed a great deal by contemporary reading and cognitive researchers as one of the most important ways of improving reading comprehension. As you remember, *metacognition* simply means teaching children to think about or monitor their own reading comprehension. Often children with reading difficulties cannot monitor or evaluate their own comprehension as well as the typical good or average reader.

A number of techniques can be used to help students at the middle and upper reading levels learn to monitor their reading comprehension. Some variation of a *checklist* such as the ones included in Sections 2 and 5 may be of help.

> NOTE: However, as one of my graduate students who also is a sixth-grade teacher told me recently: "Students at this level may respond to this kind of checklist in the way they think you want them to." I agree with her statements, and that is why the answers to such a checklist must be evaluated with caution.

Some other strategies such as *underlining, annotating, mapping, prediction,* and *writing* can be used as means for monitoring comprehension. As one excellent example, Beth Davey and Sarah M. Porter have developed a four-step instructional procedure that was found to be especially effective in improving low-achieving readers' comprehension monitoring ability. The procedure was designed to help students do the following: understand the purpose of print, focus their attention on meaning while reading, evaluate their comprehension while reading, and develop fix-up strategies to improve their comprehension.

Very briefly, here are the main steps of this procedure:

How—The first step involves teacher demonstration and modeling. Through the use of the cloze procedure the reading teacher can show students that they can understand what they read even if they do not read every word in that passage. *Fix-up strategies* such as rereading, the use of context, or the use of the dictionary also can be introduced. The reading teacher also should model comprehension monitoring while reading aloud to the students.

The second step involves focusing attention during reading on comprehension and consists of a comprehension-rating task. The students are given simple sentences to read and rate for comprehension. Some should make sense, while others should not because of incorrect words or faulty logic. Two examples are the following: *My father's car was made* and *I ate breakfast after I went to bed last evening.* Working first in small groups and later independently, students rate their comprehension of each *sentence* using a + for sentences which they understand and a − or 0 for sentences which they do not understand.

Later students are given *paragraphs* to read and rate for comprehension. Some paragraphs should make sense, while some should not due to sentences that are out of sequence, concepts that do not make sense, or faulty logic. Children in groups and then independently, rate paragraphs as being sensible by the use of a + or not making sense by the use of a − or 0.

The third step is to help the students establish their criteria for understanding, which involves a three-point rating task. Again first working in groups and then working individually, students rate sentences, paragraphs, and longer text in the following way. *I understand this very well; I kind of understand it; or I don't understand this at all.* The teacher and student then share their ratings for various sentences, paragraphs, and longer passages and discuss their reasons for the ratings. Students then are shown how to locate sources of comprehension difficulty in text. An example of an activity sheet based on this precept is included later in this section.

The fourth step is devoted to developing fix-up strategies and is implemented when students have developed a competence with the first three steps. The children should be shown and have practice with both *word fix-up and concept fix-up strategies. Some of the word-level fix-up strategies may be as follows:*

- *Skip the word* if you think that it will not interfere with comprehension very much.
- *Use your context clues* to predict or decode the word. Often *approximate* meaning and pronunciation is sufficient.
- *Use structural analysis clues* such as prefixes, suffixes, and syllables or meaning units within the word to determine the meaning.
- *Use phonic analysis* to sound out the word.
- *Use a dictionary* to locate the meaning and pronunciation of the word.
- *Ask your teacher (parent)* or a classmate for help.

Some concept-level fix-up strategies are as follows:

— Read on in the passage.
— Reread just the part that you did not understand.
— Ask yourself questions about the material as you read.
— Examine the titles, headings, pictures, and graphic aids again.
— Visualize the ideas in your mind as you read.
— Relate the ideas to your prior knowledge.
— Ask someone to help you understand the passage.
— Change your rate of reading by slowing down for difficult places and speeding up if the material is easy.
— Hypothesize by saying to yourself: I think that the author is trying to say this _____?
— Suspend judgment in the hope that the author will add more information later.[8]

What, Why, and When—To ensure that middle-upper level students will actually use this model of monitoring their own comprehension and employ

---

[8]Thomas G. Devine, *Teaching Reading Comprehension: From Theory to Practice* (Boston: Allyn and Bacon, 1986), p. 170.

appropriate fix-up strategies, it is important for the reading teacher to do the following:

What—Tell the students that they will be learning how to monitor or evaluate their own reading comprehension.

Why—Tell them that this is important because the *only purpose of reading is comprehension of what is read.*

When—Tell students that they should monitor their own comprehension every time that they read. They should pause at various intervals and ask themselves if they are understanding what they are reading. If not, they should use the appropriate fix-up strategy (ies).[9]

Example of a Passage to Use with One Variation of the Comprehension-Rating Model

The following pages present an activity based upon the previously described model of comprehension monitoring and rating. It is on approximately the fifth-grade reading level. The reading teacher may duplicate and use this activity sheet in its present form if it is applicable or use it as a model.

---

[9]Adapted from Beth Davey and Sarah M. Porter, "Comprehension-Rating: A Procedure to Assist Poor Comprehenders," *Journal of Reading* Volume 26, (December, 1982) pp, 197-202.

EXAMPLE OF A PASSAGE TO USE WITH A COMPREHENSION RATING MODEL
(Approximately fifth-grade reading level)

Name ——————————— Grade —— Teacher ——————

Read the following passage about the *Virgin Islands* to yourself. There are some *nonsensical words and ideas* in this passage. Rate each paragraph *by placing a + on the line beside it if it makes sense and a − on the line beside it if it does not make sense to you.*

THE VIRGIN ISLANDS

The Virgin Islands are a series of 80 islands which lie about 1,000 miles from Florida. More than half of the islands belong to the United States. The three main American islands are Saint Thomas, Saint Croix (Croy), and Saint John. Most of the people who now live in the American Virgin Islands came from other parts of the Caribbean. Born Virgin Islanders make up only one-quarter of the population. The great-great grandparents of born islanders were Africans who more than 125 years ago were slaves to the Danes.

———

When the Danish obtained the islands, they discovered that Mediterranean sugar cane planted in the soil there grew very well. The Danes then became impoverished and built themselves handsome homes overlooking terraced hillsides. Although these sugar plantations could be prosperous, there were many dangers to plantation life, such as drought, fire that could turn sugar cane fields to ashes, and hurricanes that could flood out the crops.

———

Slaves did all of the hard work on the plantation. They began working at dawn when the slave driver blew into a conch shell to wake them up. Four hours later they had a breakfast of salt meat and cornbread. Work in the windmills crushing juice from the sugar cane was the most feared by the slaves because the sugar cane stalks sometimes could be tossed out with enough force to kill a man. Any slave who tried to run away could be given a special present such as money.

———

Later due to the terrible conditions that they worked under, the slaves rebelled and demanded freedom which they received. The end of slavery also saw the end of the sugar cane plantations. The freed slaves fished, and grew pumpkins, eggplant, and okra. They also picked the wild fruits of the jungle. Many of the old-time foods are popular in the Virgin Islands today. Island children are particularly fond of the jungle fruits.

———

The United States bought the Virgin Islands from Denmark in 1917, and mainland Americans began to come there about 40 years later. Many visitors moved to the Islands because of their wonderful climate, beautiful sand beaches, and lovely scenery. Some of the visitors learned the native dancing, which is done to string bands. It is a very difficult style of dancing to learn. The string band uses instruments made of oil drums sawed off at the bottom and hammered at the top until different sections reproduce the notes of the scale.

———

©1990 by The Center for Applied Research in Education

The children of the Virgin Islands are almost universally friendly. However, the schools still often need to be improved. There are not enough textbooks for all of the children, and there also are not enough teachers either. Some of the school buildings were put up so quickly that parts of them collapsed. Some of the buildings have so many windows that the children cannot get enough fresh air and perspire a great deal. It is interesting to learn that many of the children of the Virgin Islands go down to the beaches to clean up the litter left by careless adults.

———

Perhaps you will have the opportunity to visit the fascinating Virgin Islands some day. I am sure that you would have a lot of fun there.

———

Answer Key

+ The paragraph is totally correct.
− The following sentence is incorrect: The Danes then became impoverished and built themselves handsome homes overlooking terraced hillsides.
− The following sentence is incorrect: Any slave who tried to run away could be given a special present such as money.
+ The paragraph is totally correct.
+ The paragraph is totally correct.
− The following sentence is incorrect: Some of the schools contain so many windows that the children cannot get enough fresh air and perspire a great deal.
+ The paragraph is totally correct.

STORY GRAMMARS, SEMANTIC MAPS, AND GRAPHIC ORGANIZERS

Although *semantic maps or webs* were mentioned and illustrated briefly in Section 5, they are discussed in more detail here with stress on their applicability to the middle and upper reading levels. As explained briefly in Section 5, the concept of attempting to visually diagram the material prior or subsequent to reading in the attempt to improve comprehension and writing ability can variously be called *story maps, semantic maps, semantic webs, story grammars, idea mapping, graphic organizers, think-links,* and *advance organizers* among other terms. In any case, they are all an effort to motivate learning and organize schema (prior knowledge) and specialized vocabulary. I believe that they are very useful in both the narrative and content areas at the middle-upper reading levels. There probably are as many variations of the basic technique as there are reading researchers in the area, and the reading teacher is encouraged to experiment and formulate the variation which best meets his or her own students' unique needs.

The importance of a *student's recognition of the sense of a story* to its comprehension has been recognized in reading instruction for at least 40 years. *A story grammar* is mainly a way of enhancing a student's awareness of the structure of stories. A story grammar or story structure can be as simple as *helping students to recognize the setting, the plot, and resolution of a story.*

On the other hand, a *story map* may be used to generate questions for the guided reading of any narrative material. To construct a story map, the teacher lists the major events and ideas which make up the story. This framework serves as the basis for formulating questions for the story. It helps to promote questions that match the progression of ideas and events in the story. It may take approximately the following form:

STORY MAP

THE SETTING
    Character(s):
    Place
THE PROBLEM
THE GOAL
    EVENT 1
    EVENT 2
    EVENT 3
    EVENT 4
    EVENT 5
THE RESOLUTION
A SERIES OF QUESTIONS WHICH ARE RELATED TO THE STORY.[10]

The more traditional *semantic map* is a way of eliciting from students their prior knowledge about a content topic. Brainstorming about the topic prior to reading is done by the students but is normally directed by the teacher, who acts as the secretary. Rather than writing randomly all of the concepts and vocabulary terms which the students contribute, the teacher attempts to organize them under headings as the discussion moves along. Semantic maps also can serve as assessment devices and as *guides during reading* as students add to their own personal maps in their notebooks while they silently read a selection. In addition, they can be used as *post-reading tools* when students use them for review and as the basis of post-reading discussion. In content area subjects, an exercise in semantic mapping becomes a lesson in both the content area and the ways in which people think about the content.

Sample Partially Completed Semantic Map

The following page presents a partially completed semantic map about the Native Americans of the Southeast at approximately the sixth-grade reading level. It may be helpful for several students to work together to complete it if you wish. However, it also may serve as a model for you of one form of semantic map.

---

[10]Robert J. Tierney, John E. Readence, and Ernest K. Dishner, *Reading Strategies and Practices: A Compendium* (Boston: Allyn and Bacon, 1985), pp. 155-156.

SAMPLE SEMANTIC MAP
(Approximately sixth-grade reading level)

Name _____   Grade _____   Teacher _____

Read the following story about the *Native Americans of the Southeast* to yourself. Then complete the semantic map which is found after the story. You can work with a partner if you want. You also can look back at the story if you need to do so.

MOUND-BUILDERS OF THE SOUTHEAST

One of the most interesting groups of Native Americans inhabited the southeastern part of this country many hundreds of years ago. They had countless unique characteristics which have been studied by scientists of various kinds in the past 100 to 200 years.

These Native Americans were called the *mound-builders of the southeast* for very obvious reasons. There are mounds of various kinds in a region which stretches from Pennsylvania to Missouri, and as far north as Wisconsin to as far south as Florida. The first Indian people to build mounds lived in the Ohio River Valley, and one site in Kentucky is tentatively dated back to 700 B.C. and is called the Adena Mounds. Some of these early mounds were as high as 70 feet and had bodies buried inside of them along with stone pipes and copper, shell, and mica ornaments.

The Hopewall Mounds in Ross County, Ohio, are very large and elaborate and surrounded by miles of earthen walls. The objects found in these mounds along with the buried bodies included objects of superb beauty and workmanship such as pearl necklaces, birds and fish made of beaten copper, and blades made of glass called obsidian. The obsidian came from what is now known as Yellowstone National Park, indicating that the Indians of that time must have been inveterate traders.

One of the greatest mound sites of the time is the Cahokia Mounds near East St. Louis, Illinois. Unbelievably, one of the mounds there, Monks Mound, measures approximately 100 feet high, 1,000 feet long, and 700 feet wide. Since it covers 16 acres, it is thought to be the largest man-made earthen structure in the entire world.

Some Native Americans of the southeast also constructed another kind of mound—the effigy mound which was in the shape of some living creature. Effigy mounds are found mainly in southern Wisconsin and nearby areas of Illinois and Iowa. All types of animals are represented by these effigy mounds, such as bears, deer, wolves, panthers, turtles, and various kinds of birds. Although the mounds are low, they are very large. One mound in the shape of a bird is 6 feet high with a wingspread of 624 feet. The Great Serpent Mound in Ohio is only 2 feet high but spreads its coils over an area of 1,000 feet. Occasionally, bodies were buried in the effigy mounds, usually at the location of the brain or heart.

One can deduce several things about the mound-building Indians. They certainly had advanced cultures as evidenced by the artifacts found in the mounds. They were farmers instead of nomadic hunters as were many of the early Native Americans. They undoubtedly lived and worked together in organized communities since it took cooperation to construct the earthen mounds even without the help of wheelbarrows. Eventually for some unknown reason the Indians of the southeast stopped making mounds.

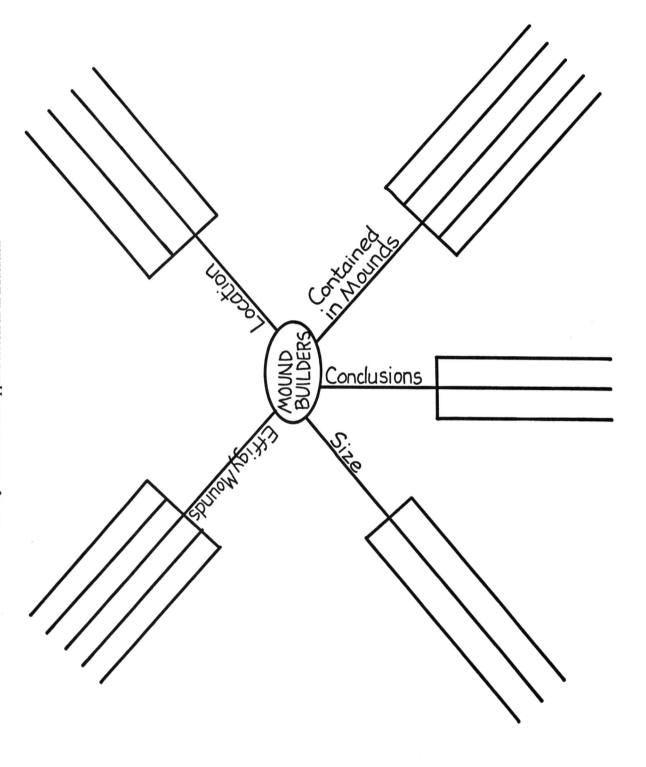

MOUND BUILDERS

Location

Contained in Mounds

Conclusions

Size

Effigy Mounds

Sample Answer Key

MOUND BUILDERS

Contained in Mounds
- buried bodies
- stone pipes
- ornaments of copper, shell and mica
- obsidian blades

Locations
- Western Illinois
- Ross County, Ohio
- Kentucky
- Ohio River Valley
- Area around Southern Wisconsin

Conclusions
- Advanced Cultures
- Farmers
- Organized Societies

Size
- Monks Mound - 100' high, 1000' long, and 700' wide
- Bird Mound - 6' high and 624' wide
- Great Serpant Mound - 2' high and 1000' wide

Effigy Mounds
- Turtles
- Bears
- Deer
- Wolves
- Panthers
- Birds

A related visual representation that can be used prior to reading a content assignment is called an *advance organizer*. Advance organizers apparently were first proposed in 1968 "to bridge the gap between what the reader already knows and what the reader needs to know before he/she can meaningfully learn the task at hand."[11] Their function is to provide a *conceptual scaffolding* for the incorporation of the new material which the textbook contains to the prior knowledge provided by the students. Students are thus prepared to gain information from reading which they could not have gained otherwise.

As you can see, a class discussion followed by reading of a semantic map provides two examples of *advance organizers. Each* helps students to determine what is coming and to fit it into a conceptual structure. It should be written at a higher level of generality than the material to be read. Some content teachers especially at the junior or senior high school level find it helpful to give students a brief overview orally or in print of the material which is to be read. Such an organizer can activate prior knowledge and help students relate it to the material which they are going to read. A number of textbook authors now provide advance organizers within the books to help students. If the content textbook possesses such organizers, the reading or content teacher obviously should use them; if not, he or she may wish to write his or her own.

DIRECTED READING-THINKING ACTIVITY (DRTA)

Since the *Directed Reading-Thinking Activity (DRTA)* was explained in detail in Section 5, it is only briefly mentioned here. As you remember, the DRTA is extremely effective in improving reading comprehension since it encourages active involvement with the reading material in the use of prediction strategies. It may be especially helpful in improving comprehension ability in the middle grades.

Very briefly, it consists of the following steps:

1. Have the student(s) make predictions prior to reading the material.
2. Tell the student(s) that he or she should read to see if the material verifies the predictions.
3. Have the student(s) discuss the predictions to determine which ones were verified and which ones were not.

THE GUIDED READING PROCEDURE

The *Guided Reading Procedure*, mentioned very briefly in Section 5, is most appropriate for use in reading content assignments at the middle-upper reading levels and is therefore described in detail and illustrated here. It can improve

---

[11]David P. Ausubel, *Education Psychology: A Cognitive View* (New York: Holt, Rinehart and Winston, 1968), p. 148.

students' ability to formulate their own implicit (interpretive and critical) questions, develop their use of self-correction while reading, and improve their ability to organize information.

Here briefly are the steps of this procedure and how it can be implemented:

1. *Prepare the Students to Read the Assignment*—The teacher should use some type of prereading activity (See Section 5) or the directed reading-thinking activity (DRTA) prior to reading the material. The students must understand why they are to read the material.

2. *Students Read and Remember the Information*—Remembering their purposes for reading, the students should be directed to read the material silently and turn the material face down upon completing the assignment. When most of the students have finished, the teacher asks the students to retell (tell back) what they remember, and writes what is given using abbreviations if possible.

3. *Return to the Material for Additional Factors and Corrections*—When the students cannot remember additional information, they are allowed to look at the article again, and the teacher writes the additional information on the chalkboard.

4. *Organize the Remembered Material*—The students are now to organize the material into a modified outline form. The outline should show the main ideas and supporting details. Questions such as these may be useful: "What happened first in the material?" "What happened next?"

5. *Give Students Thought-Provoking Questions*—The teacher next helps the students see how the new information relates to material that they already have learned (prior knowledge). In a gradual manner the teacher gives the students more independence in seeing how the new material relates to previously learned material such as by saying: "Do you see how this information and what we learned last week are related?"

6. *Test Students on Their Knowledge of the Material*—Since this strategy is very intense and demanding, the teacher should check students' recall of the concepts presented by providing a short quiz to show how much they have learned by using this procedure. Any type of test format could be used for this purpose.[12]

Sample Guided Reading Procedure

The following pages present a sample guided reading procedure at about the sixth-grade reading level. It is designed as a concrete example of how this strategy can be used to improve comprehension. It should also serve as a model for you in using this strategy with your own students in reading content assignments—especially in social studies and science.

---

[12]Adapted from Anthony V. Manzo, "Guided Reading Procedure," *Journal of Reading* 18 (January, 1975), pp. 287-291.

EXAMPLE OF THE GUIDED READING PROCEDURE
(Small-group activity)
(Approximately sixth-grade reading level)

Name _____ Grade _____ Teacher _____

HARRY S TRUMAN

I. *Preparation for the Reading Assignment*

    1. What do you know about Harry S Truman, the thirty-third President of the United States?

    2. What are some of the things that you would like to learn about Harry S Truman?

    3. What do you think are some of the important concepts (ideas) that you might need to learn about Harry S Truman?

    4. What is your major purpose for reading this passage about Harry S Truman?

II. *Silent Reading*
Now think about the questions you posed and your purpose for reading and then read this passage about Harry S Truman to yourself. *When you are finished, turn the material face down on your desk.*

HARRY S TRUMAN

Harry S Truman was born in the sleepy, southwestern Missouri village of Lamar on May 3, 1884. During his early years, Harry's family kept moving from town to town since his father was unsuccessful in some of his ventures. When Harry was six, his father started a livestock trading business in the town of Independence. As soon as he moved to Independence, Harry's mother took him to Sunday School, and he was assigned a seat in back of the most beautiful little girl with the prettiest golden curls that he had ever seen. Although her name was Elizabeth Virginia Wallace, everyone called her Bess, and Harry later said that he loved her from the moment that he saw her for the rest of his life.

Although Harry was a very bright boy, he had great difficulty in learning to read, and therefore his mother would not let him go to school as she did not want him to be embarrassed. Finally, when he was eight, his parents discovered that he could not see well enough to read. As soon as he received a very thick pair of eyeglasses, he went to school and learned to read very well. Indeed he was a voracious, motivated reader the rest of his entire life although he never achieved a college education.

When Harry was ten, he contracted diptheria, a common childhood illness of the time, could not move his legs and had to be wheeled around the house in a baby buggy for six months. Finally, he caught up in school and was in the same class as Bess Wallace. He carried her books home every afternoon, and they studied Latin together along with doing other things such as skating on the pond together. Harry had also learned to play the piano as a young boy and did so very well. When he graduated from high school, Harry greatly desired to go to college but could not go because his father had lost all of his money and Harry had to go to work instead.

During the next few years Harry tried all sorts of jobs such as working in a newspaper office, a bank, and for the railroad. Although he could not afford to go to college, he tried to satisfy his interest in American history by reading about it. In his secret desires, he knew that he wanted to be a United States senator someday although he knew that this would be difficult to do without a college education

When he was 20, Harry and his family moved to his grandmother's farm where Harry put on overalls and became an ordinary farmer for the next 13 years putting his dream of becoming a senator on hold. Harry studied farming from the experts and soon his farm became one of the most productive in the area. On Sundays Harry put on dress clothes and drove his new car to Independence to see Bess whom he still hoped to marry even though she was wealthy and he was not.

At the age of 33, Harry entered the Army as a lieutenant and was put in charge of his own company of soldiers. At the army camp in Oklahoma, he also opened a center where the soldiers could buy supplies, and it proved to be extremely successful. He also was a very competent lieutenant whose rowdy, rough men followed him bravely into the heat of battle. Since Harry was so brave, he proved himself to be a leader of men, a trait which changed his life.

After Harry was discharged from the Army, he finally realized his dream of marrying Bess, the girl he had loved since the age of six. Harry first opened a clothing store in Independence with a friend, but it went bankrupt after a short time. In 1924 Harry and Bess had a baby daughter named Mary Margaret, and Harry became county commissioner at about that time, a position he held for some time during which he proved to be an honest man with a talent for taking care of business.

However, when he was 50 years old, he entered the contest for United States senator, and although Bess did not particuarly want to live in Washington, she could not allow her husband to give up his dream. Miraculously, Harry won the election and went to Washington with a great sense of awe that he had fulfilled his lifelong ambition without the benefit of a college education. Harry characteristically worked extremely hard at being an outstanding senator by studying all of the issues, and he also was highly respected by his colleagues. Since Harry appealed to the common people, he was reelected to a second term in the Senate against overwhelming odds.

During his second term as senator, Harry gained a reputation for saving the taxpayers billions of dollars from military spending. Since he was a popular senator, President Franklin Roosevelt chose Harry to be his Vice-President. Harry became President of the United States only about three months later when Roosevelt suddenly died.

Although he had been a popular senator, Harry was at first not a very popular President, especially when he ordered that atomic bombs be dropped on Japan to end World War II. Harry was re-elected President in 1948 against tremendous odds by traveling across the country on a train in what was called a "whistle-stop campaign." During his Presidency, Harry always did what he thought was right no matter how unpopular that course of action might be.

Harry and Bess returned to Independence, Missouri, in 1952 after his Presidency concluded. Harry at that time always told children to be honest and study history if they wanted to go into politics. Harry S Truman died in 1972 at the age of 88 wanting only to be remembered as the *people's President*.

©1990 by The Center for Applied Research in Education

III. The teacher should now say: *"Now tell me everything that you can remember about the passage about Harry S Truman."*
(The teacher then records this information on the chalkboard.)

IV. The teacher then says: *"Now look at the article again and see what additional information you can learn about Harry S Truman and notice anything on the chalkboard that is not correct."*

V. The teacher now adds the new information to the chalkboard.

VI. *Outline of the Harry S Truman Selection*

Complete this unfinished outline about the passage you just read.

I. Harry's Childhood
    A. The first six years of his life
        1.
        2.
        3.
        4.
        5.
    B. The years in school
        1.
        2.
        3.
        4.
        5.

II. The years before the Army
    A. Doing a variety of jobs
        1.
        2.
        3.
    B. On the family farm

III. In the Army
    A. The supply store (canteen)
        1.
        2.
        3.

    B.   As a leader of men
        1.
        2.
        3.

IV. Early Politics
    A.   As a county commissioner
        1.
        2.
        3.
    B.   As a United States senator
        1.
        2.
        3.
        4.
        5.

V. Vice-President and President
    A.   As the Vice-President
        1.
        2.
        3.
    B.   As the President
        1.
        2.
        3.
        4.
        5.

VI. Retirement
    A.   The end of his life
        1.
        2.
        3.

VII. *Thought-Provoking Questions*

"How does this information compare with what you knew about Harry S Truman before?"

"How does the Presidency of Harry S Truman compare with the Presidency of George Bush?"

"What have you learned from reading this selection that you can apply to your own life?"

"Tell me how this material compares with the material you read about some other Presidents."

True—False

T   F   1. Harry learned to read easily at an early age in school.

T   F   2. Harry proved to be a true leader of men during his Army days.

T   F   3. Harry loved Bess during nearly all of his life from the age of six on.

T   F   4. Harry was considered to be an honest and highly competent senator.

T   F   5. Harry pleased everyone when he was the President of the United States.

Multiple Choice

6. During his early years after high school graduation, Harry worked:
   a. on a farm
   b. in a bank
   c. on the railroad
   d. all of the above

7. In the Army, Harry was
   a. an incompetent soldier
   b. extremely brave
   c. unpopular with his men
   d. dishonest

8. Harry's first political job was
   a. a county commissioner
   b. a senator
   c. a mayor
   d. the vice-president

9. During his second term as senator, Harry earned a reputation for:
   a. being slovenly
   b. being unpopular
   c. being unworthy for the job
   d. saving the taxpayers much money

10. As President Harry always:
    a. did what he thought was right
    b. did the popular thing
    c. was very popular with everyone
    d. was completely predictable

Answer Key

VI. *Outline of the Harry S Truman Selection*
(The answers on the outline included are only for illustrative purposes. A student's answers could vary somewhat from these and be correct.)

   I. Harry's Childhood
      A. The first six years of life
          1. born in Lamar, Missouri, in 1884
          2. kept moving from town to town
          3. father was not successful in business
      B. The years in school
          1. met a pretty girl in Sunday school
          2. had great difficulty in learning to read
          3. needed thick eyeglasses
          4. contracted diptheria at the age of ten
          5. carried Bess Wallace's books home from school

  II. The Years Before the Army
      A. Doing a variety of jobs
          1. in a newspaper office
          2. in a bank
          3. for the railroad
      B. On the family farm
          1. moved to grandmother's farm
          2. was a farmer for 13 years
          3. became an expert farmer

 III. In the Army
      A. The supply store (canteen)
          1. opened a canteen in Oklahoma
          2. it was very successful
          3. the soldiers bought supplies there
      B. As a leader of men
          1. led some rough, rowdy men

          2. was a very brave soldier

          3. was a competent lieutenant

 IV. Early Politics

    A. As a county commissioner

          1. first political job

          2. was highly successful

          3. was an honest man

    B. As a United States senator

          1. became senator at the age of 50

          2. fulfilled his lifelong ambition

          3. he worked extremely hard

          4. he was an outstanding senator

          5. saved the taxpayers much money

  V. Vice-President and President

    A. As the Vice-President

          1. was chosen by Franklin Roosevelt

          2. his term only lasted three months

    B. As the President

          1. became President when Roosevelt died

          2. was not very popular at first

          3. dropped the atomic bomb on Japan

          4. was re-elected in 1948

          5. always did what he believed to be right

 VI. Retirement

    A. The end of his life

          1. returned to Independence in 1952

          2. told children to be honest

          3. died at the age of 88

1. F		6. d
2. T		7. b
3. T		8. a
4. T		9. d
5. F		10. a

SENTENCE COMBINING

Sentence combining is one strategy which stresses the relation between reading and writing and *may possibly* improve reading comprehension. It may do so because it encourages the interrelationships between syntax (word order) and language processing. Sentence combining instruction encourages students to read two or more short sentences and combine them into one sentence. Sentence combining is based on the assumption that sensitizing students to the methods by which ideas are expressed and related in text will develop their ability to compose and comprehend.

Students should be introduced to the concept of sentence combining through examples given by the reading teacher of using sentences which demonstrate the use of a connective or some other method of combining sentences. Students should learn to notice how sentences are combined based upon the meaning they imply and "how they sound" rather than on any set rule. To help students determine the value of a certain combination, they can share their combinations and judge as a group which combinations of the same sentence are the most preferable. Sentence combining can be taught by units dealing with separate and somewhat distinct skills. For example, one unit might deal with the use of a *connective* (and, but, or), while another might deal with oppositives (subordinate clauses).

Sample Activity Sheet on Sentence Combining

The following page presents a sample ready-to-use activity dealing with sentence combining on approximately the fifth-grade reading level. The reading teacher may duplicate and use this activity in its present form if it seems applicable, but more importantly, it can serve as a model.

ACTIVITY SHEET ON SENTENCE COMBINING
(Approximately fifth-grade reading level)

Name _____ Grade _____ Teacher _____

Read each of the following sets of sentences to yourself. Then *combine each set of sentences into one longer, more interesting sentence and write it on the lines below.* The first one is done for you as an example.

JAMES BECKWOURTH, BLACK MOUNTAIN MAN

1. James Beckwourth was the most important black hero of the frontier.
   James Beckwourth was a dramatic black figure of the frontier.
   James Beckwourth who was the most important black hero of the frontier was a dramatic figure.

2. Jim's mother was a slave.
   Jim's father was the son of a wealthy plantation owner.

   _____

   _____

3. Jim learned to be a blacksmith.
   Jim wanted to roam the frontier.

   _____

   _____

4. Jim headed West from St. Louis at the age of 19.
   He took a bowie knife, a gun, and a hatchet with him.

   _____

   _____

5. Out West Jim became a member of the Crow Indian tribe.
   Jim's Indian name was "Morning Star."

   _____

   _____

6. Jim was a fierce fighter.
   General Stephan Kearney asked Jim to help California in its struggle for independence.

   _____

   _____

(Continued on following page)

7. Jim discovered a pass through the Sierra Nevada Mountains in California.
    That pass was an important gateway to California during the Gold Rush days.

    _____

    _____

8. The pass was named after Jim.
    The pass is now known as Beckwourth Pass.

    _____

    _____

9. Jim built a hotel and trading post in Beckwourth Valley.
    Jim was not an innkeeper for very long.

    _____

    _____

10. Jim knew that he did not have much time to live.
    Jim returned to die among the Indian people who loved him and whom he loved.

    _____

    _____

Answer Key

(The following answers are included only for illustrative purposes. There are other possible correct answers.)

2. Jim's mother was a slave, and his father was the son of a wealthy plantation owner.
3. Although Jim learned to be a blacksmith, he wanted to roam the frontier.
4. When Jim headed West from St. Louis at the age of 19, he took a bowie knife, a gun, and a hatchet with him.
5. Out West Jim became a member of the Crow Indian tribe, and his Indian name was "Morning Star."
6. Since Jim was a fierce fighter, General Stephan Kearney asked him to help California in its struggle for independence.
7. Jim discovered a pass through the Sierra Nevada Mountains in California, and that pass was an important gateway to California during the Gold Rush days.
8. The pass which is now known as Beckwourth Pass was named after Jim.
9. Although Jim built a hotel and trading post in Beckwourth Valley, he was not an innkeeper for very long.
10. Since Jim knew that he did not have much time to live, he returned to die among the Indian people who loved him and whom he loved.

SURVEY Q3R

There are several different study strategies that can be presented and used at the middle-upper school levels to aid in the comprehension and retention of the content material which the students must read. If such a study technique is learned at the middle-school level, students normally will apply at least part of it when they are in secondary school and college. The best known of these is *Survey Q3R—Survey, Question, Read, Recite, and Review. Survey Q3R* was developed by Francis P. Robinson during World War II to aid military personnel in the comprehension and retention of the material which they had to read. It is based upon the *information-processing theory of learning*. Each part of Survey Q3R is designed to facilitate the processing of incoming print so that the child can deal with it effectively.

Although Survey Q3R necessarily must vary with the content area in which it is used, it contains the following basic steps:

Survey or Preview—The student surveys the entire textbook chapter to gain an overall impression of its content. In this survey or preview, the student reads the introduction and summary of the chapter and the first sentence in each of the paragraphs. He or she also may examine the pictures, maps, graphs, tables, diagrams, and other aids contained in the chapter.

NOTE: The *survey or preview* is the most useful aspect of Survey Q3R. It always should be used when reading content material even when no other part of this study technique is used. The use of the survey or preview alone will greatly add to the student's comprehension and retention of content material. I have found that many students feel that Survey Q3R is too time-consuming when it is used in its entirety, but they are willing to use the survey part alone. When this is done, *the survey alone can be very useful in improving their comprehension and retention of content material.*

Question—The student poses questions which he or she wants to read to answer in this step of the study strategy. Each subheading can be turned into a question and additional questions can be formulated to read to answer. Thus this step helps a student to set purposes for reading and makes the reading more active and meaningful.

Read—The student reads the entire chapter on a selective basis to attempt to answer the questions that have been posed. In this selective reading, he or she attempts to fill in the gaps in the reading by capitalizing on prior knowledge. This step of the procedure helps a student become an active participant in reading.

Recite—This step applies only to one section of the material at a time. After the student has read a section purposefully, he or she can recite the important information in either an oral or a written form depending on which is more efficient.

Review—This step is taken after the student has read the chapter. He or she attempts to review the important concepts, generalizations, and facts gained from the chapter. He or she often can use the written notes which were made in the fourth step of the chapter.[13]

Some variations of the Survey Q3R can be called the following:

Survey Q4R: Survey, Read, Recite, Record, and Review

PQRST: Preview, Question, Read, State, and Test

The Triple S Technique: Scan, Search, and Summarize

---

[13]Francis P. Robinson, *Effective Study* (New York: Harper & Row, Publishing, 1961).

PQ5R: Preview, Question, Read, Record, Recite, Review, and Reflect

OARWET: Overview, Achieve, Read, Write, Evaluate, and Test

PQ4R: Preview, Question, Read, Reflect, Recite, and Review[14]

The reading teacher should remember that the survey step of any of these study strategies must be used judiciously, if at all, in the content area of *English* if the student is reading to answer his or her predictions since the survey otherwise could destroy the pleasure in reading the material. However, the survey may be usable with a novel, short story, essay, or poetry if the ending does not contain a surprise element. Since few of these literary forms contain subheadings, students usually must formulate their own purposes for reading in the light of prior knowledge. The final steps of Survey Q3R may be valuable in summarizing what was learned from the reading.

Survey Q3R can be used in its original form with most *social studies textbooks*. For example, in a history textbook at the middle-upper level, the student can use the survey, can turn each subheading into a question, can read each section to answer the questions, can review the material in that selection, and can subsequently summarize the entire chapter.

When a student uses Survey Q3R to study a *science textbook*, he or she surveys the entire chapter, turns the subheadings into questions and uses this step to understand the author's pattern of writing, reads to answer the formulated questions and to recall details and processes, tries to recall the main ideas and specific details, and writes a brief outline of what was read.

On the other hand, Survey Q3R must be modified considerably in problem-solving in *mathematics* in the following manner:

Survey—Skim the verbal problem to gain an overall impression of it.

Question—Decide what the question is in the problem, what facts are needed to solve it, and the order of the steps that are needed to solve it.

Read—Read the verbal problem very carefully to understand the question thoroughly and to determine the steps that are needed for the solution.

Recite—Decide what facts the answer depends upon.

Review—Estimate the answer and later check the answer after the problem has been solved.

A METACOGNITIVE STUDY STRATEGY

Marjorie Montague and Michael L. Tanner have written an article about a study strategy for comprehension and retention of content area material. Very briefly, this specific cognitive and metacognitive strategy contains the following steps:

---

[14]Thomas G. Devine, *Teaching Reading Comprehension: From Theory to Practice* (Boston: Allyn and Bacon, 1986), p. 157.

Prereading—This step is to create awareness, activate content knowledge that the learner brings to the situation, set a purpose for reading, analyze the text structure, and develop vocabulary.

During the Actual Reading—The student should take notes, summarize, outline, answer textually explicit and implicit questions, and monitor the reader's success.

Postreading—In this step the student reorganizes, integrates what was read, and reviews the textual material in preparation for a test.[15]

REAP TECHNIQUE

A related study strategy is the *REAP technique*, which is designed to improve students' comprehension skills by helping them to synthesize an author's ideas into their own words and to develop their writing ability as an aid to the recall of the concepts which they gained through the reading. The REAP strategy is based on the idea that a student comprehends most effectively when asked to write the ideas gained from a passage which he or she has read. It is thought to be an alternative to the *Directed Reading Activity* (See Section 5) and the *Guided Reading Procedure* (see the example earlier in this section). The student is to internalize a text-based understanding by the use of this strategy.

The REAP Strategy consists of these four steps:

R—Reading to discover the author's ideas

E—Encoding the author's ideas into one's own language

A—Annotating these ideas in writing for oneself or for sharing with others

P—Pondering the significance of the annotation

The most important aspect of the REAP technique is in helping students to develop the ability to write annotations about what they have read. Therefore, the discussion of the REAP strategy follows these steps:

writing annotations

teaching children to write annotations

thinking about the annotations which were written

When a child writes annotations, he or she must interact with the ideas of the author to synthesize them into his or her own language.

There are several types of annotations which can be understood in detail by checking the footnote:

summary annotations

thesis annotations

---

[15]Adapted from Marjorie Montague and Michael L. Tanner, "Reading Strategy Groups for Content Area Instruction," *Journal of Reading* (May, 1987), pp. 716-723.

question annotations

critical annotations

intention annotations

motivation annotations

The students must be taught how to write annotations by these four steps:

recognizing and defining

discriminating

modeling

practicing

Lastly, the student must think about or ponder the annotations to process them.

The REAP technique is most useful for students in the secondary school in relating reading and writing and for offering students a way to interact with their textbook. Although the annotation may serve as a foundation for critique writing in English classes, the writing of annotations can be a very difficult and time-consuming task for even good and average readers, much less below average readers.[16]

SELECTIVE READING GUIDE-O-RAMA

A very interesting strategy for improving comprehension ability at the middle-upper reading level is called the *Selective Guide-o-Rama* and was developed by Cunningham and Shablak. This technique is designed to help students locate the major ideas and important details within a content textbook chapter and to teach them flexibility in their reading. This strategy assumes that most students are not "experts" in the subject matter which they are reading, and that they cannot validly select the most important information in the textbook. Most students seem to read the material as if everything in that chapter were of equal importance. The content instruction, however, should guide students through a content reading assignment by giving them clues as to which information is important and which material they can read very rapidly.

The *Selective Reading Guide-o-Rama* is designed for students in approximately sixth-grade and above who need additional help in comprehending and studying their content material. Before the instructor formulates this strategy, he or she must decide what students should know and what they should be able to do when they finish the chapter.

The content teacher can follow approximately these six steps in using the technique:

---

[16]Adapted from M. G. Eanet and A. V. Manzo, "REAP—A Strategy for Improving Reading/Writing Study Skills." *Journal of Reading* 19 (May, 1976), pp. 647-652.

(1) The content teacher first must identify the important information in the text chapter that he or she wants the students to understand.

(2) The instructor then goes through the content textbook and selects those portions of the text that provide students with the previously chosen important information. The teacher marks the margin with the letters "M" for *main ideas* and "D" for *important details*.

(3) Then the teacher should imagine that he or she has already completed the introduction to the lesson (such as with the Directed Reading Activity—see Section 5).

(4) The teacher then constructs the guide in a way in which the students will recognize the important information in the content reading assignment.

(5) The teacher should point out unimportant as well as important information to show students that they must be flexible in their reading.

(6) The completed guide should be in logical order and should move the student from the beginning of the chapter through to the end.

NOTE: The *Selective Guide-o-Rama* can be used for several months and then removed gradually. It may work best with those students who need the assistance and who can profit from a very structured approach used to teach these skills. *The instructor also can design a cassette tape version of this technique if the student cannot read a printed copy.* For example, the instructor may tell the student: "Turn the recorder off and read these first two paragraphs on page 24 very carefully. When you have finished, turn the recorder on again and I will discuss the material which you have read."[17]

Sample Guide-o-Rama

The following pages present a sample Guide-o-Rama from the content area of science at about the sixth-grade level. The reading teacher can duplicate and use this activity in its present form if the appropriate content textbook is available. However, more importantly, it should serve as a model for you in constructing your own Guide-o-Rama from your own content textbook at the appropriate reading level.

[17]Adapted from Dick Cunningham and S. L. Shablak, "Selective Reading Guide-o-Rama: The Content Teacher's Best Friend," *Journal of Reading* 18 (February, 1975), pp. 380-382.

SELECTIVE GUIDE-O-RAMA
(Approximately sixth-grade reading level)

Name —————————————— **Grade** ————— **Teacher** ——————————

George G. Mallinson, Jacqueline B. Mallinson, William L. Smallwood, and Catherine Valentino, *Silver Burdett & Ginn Science.* Lexington, Massachusetts: Silver Burdett & Ginn, 1987, Grade 6. Copyright 1987 by Silver, Burdett & Ginn Inc. *Chapter 12, "Forecasting the Weather," pp. 283–305.*

Now that we have briefly already discussed what you now know about forecasting the weather and what you want to learn about this topic in science, read the chapter. It should better help you to understand and remember the important ideas in the chapter if you use this *Guide-o-Rama.*

Page 284—Second paragraph. You should understand and remember the terms *meteorology and meteorologist* from this section.

Page 285—Write down the device mentioned on this page that can show both wind speed and wind direction.

———

Page 286—Look at the picture of the wet-and-dry bulb thermometer on this page. Then read the third paragraph on this page to determine how this device is used to measure relative humidity.

Page 287—This page is important only if you want to make your own wet-and-dry bulb thermometer to measure relative humidity. This, however, would be an interesting scientific experiment if you want to do so.

Page 288—Second paragraph. Remember the term *barometer*. Read to find out what a "falling barometer" and a "rising barometer" mean.

Page 289—Just skim the first paragraph on this page. Read the next two paragraphs fairly rapidly trying to gain an overall impression of the material.

Pages 290–291—Read the material on weather satellites and their role in meteorology very carefully on these two pages. You probably should remember the names of the two weather satellites found near the top of page 291.

———

Page 291—Look at the television picture at the top of the page. Do you remember seeing a similar picture on your own television set?

———

Page 292—Read the second paragraph to determine where the weather changes occur. ————————————————————— This is the border between two air masses that are not alike.

(Continued on following page)

Page 293—Read this entire page to find out how the jet stream can influence weather temperature in a region.

Page 294—The section on *climatologists* can be read fairly rapidly for a general impression.

Page 295—Study the material in the brown box very carefully. Then observe the weather in your region for several months trying to see if it seems accurate.

Pages 296–297—On page 296 remember the terms *isotherm and isobar* which are found in the second and third paragraphs. Study the weather map on page 297 very carefully. What do the blue line and the red line mean?

Pages 298–303—This section on storms can be read fairly rapidly to gain an understanding of what kind of storms exist. You should read the second paragraph on page 298 to find out what two conditions are needed for a thunderstorm to occur. _____
Look at the picture on the bottom of page 299 to determine what causes the lightning in a thunderstorm.
Read pages 300 and 301 to see how a *tornado funnel* appears.
On page 302 read the second paragraph to find out how a *hurricane* and a *tornado* are alike.

_____

Answer Key

Page 285—wind sock
Pages 290–291—TIROS (Television Infra-Red Observation Satellite) and GOES
(Geostationary Operational Environmental Satellite)
Page 292—a front

Pages 298–303—updrafts and much water vapor
the air in the center is low pressure

THE HERRINGBONE TECHNIQUE

One useful study technique which is a structure outlining procedure is called the *Herringbone Technique*. This strategy indicates that the important information can be obtained by asking six basic comprehension questions—*Who? What? When? Where? How?* and *Why?* An outline then is provided to record this information and thus provide the structure for notetaking. The Herringbone Technique is designed for use with students at the fourth-grade through the twelfth-grade reading levels.

As with any content reading assignment, the classroom teacher should first prepare for the instruction by determining what are the most important concepts and vocabulary terms found in that assignment. Students then are prepared for the content reading assignment by using the Directed Reading Activity (see Section 5) or the Directed Reading-Thinking Activity (DRTA) (see earlier in this section).

The *Herringbone Form* can be placed on standard 8½" by 11" paper and duplicated for the students. They are told that they will be looking for the answers to the questions found on the form and will be writing them on the form as they read the content chapter for which they have been prepared. To introduce this strategy, the reading teacher should put the *Herringbone Form* on the chalkboard or on a transparency. As the entire class learns the strategy, the teacher can write the information on the transparency or the chalkboard as the student also writes it on his or her form. After students understand this technique and have been prepared to read a specific chapter in a content textbook, they can begin reading the chapter and recording the responses on their own copy of the *Herringbone Form*. The form attempts to help students locate the answers to these questions:

Who was involved? This answer is the name of one or more persons or groups of persons.

What did this person or group do?

When was it done?

How was it accomplished?

Why did it happen?

The *Herringbone Technique* helps students to discover the important relationships within this information. After the students have completed this technique, a follow-up group discussion often is valuable. Students can be helped to note that the textbook does not always provide all of the information needed to complete this technique or that some of the information which is required on the sheet is not particularly important to the comprehension and retention of the material. If the students think that the missing information is important, they may be encouraged to complete it by using a variety of research sources. If the teacher considers some of the answers provided on the form to be rather superficial, additional questioning may help the students to understand the material more effectively. Interestingly, the *Herringbone Technique* contains the *Main Idea* on the midline. Students are asked to give a statement of the main idea of the chapter. This is an important step in helping them grasp and remember the most important concept in the chapter.[18]

Sample Herringbone Technique

The following pages attempt to illustrate the Herringbone Technique for the reading teacher in a way that is meaningful. First an incomplete form is provided which can be duplicated and given to students. This is followed by a completed Herringbone form which was constructed from a sixth-grade social studies textbook. The latter form should serve as a model of what a completed Herringbone technique can look like. It also can be used in its present form if the content textbook used is appropriate for the reading teacher's needs.

---

[18]Robert J. Tierney, John E. Readence, and Ernest K. Dishner, *Reading Strategies and Practices: A Compendium* (Boston: Allyn and Bacon, 1985), pp. 203-207.

SAMPLE HERRINGBONE TECHNIQUE
(Approximately fourth-to-twelfth-grade reading level)

Name _____ Grade _____ Teacher _____

Complete this sample outline as you read the chapter from your content (social **studies** or science) textbook. Be sure to also write your statement of the *main idea* on the proper line on the outline.

Terms:

SAMPLE COMPLETED HERRINGBONE TECHNIQUE
(Approximately sixth-grade level)

Name _____   Grade _____   Teacher _____

From SCOTT, FORESMAN SOCIAL STUDIES, Grade 6, OUR WORLD: *Yesterday and Today* by Dorothy Drummond and Bruce Kraig. Copyright © 1988 by Scott, Foresman and Company. Reprinted by permission.

Terms:

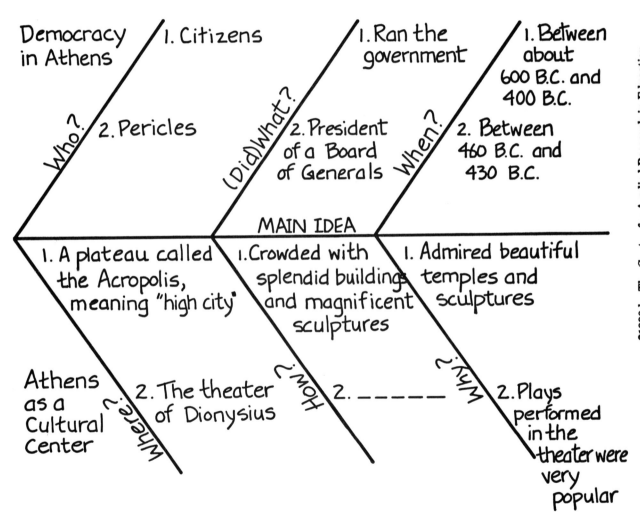

©1990 by The Center for Applied Research in Education

PARAGRAPH PATTERNS OF ORGANIZATION

As explained earlier, expository or content material is normally extremely difficult for most students who are to read it. One strategy that can be used to aid in their comprehension of content textbooks is the *teaching and illustration of different types of paragraph patterns of organization or structure.* There are several different listings of text structures that can be taught to children at the middle and upper levels. One of the more useful ones was developed by Olive Niles some time ago and follows shortly.

Any pattern of organization normally should be presented and then illustrated to the students using sample content material to be meaningful to them. This instruction, modeling, and illustration then can be followed up by practice in the patterns of organization using the students' own textbooks or activity sheets such as the one that is provided shortly.

Here is one useful listing of *paragraph patterns of organization:*

Simple Listing—In this type of text structure, the exact order in which information is presented is not very important. Descriptions or definitions of objects, events, or concepts are often given.

Ordered Listing—The listing in textbooks with this structure follows a time sequence, operating procedures, spatial dimensions, or some other type of order.

Problem and Solution—In this type of text structure, the problem is stated and the solution is then described.

Cause and Effect—One or more antecedents are described that then lead to a result.

Comparison and Contrast—This text structure is based on a description of similarities or differences between statements or the pros and cons of two or more objects, approaches, or concepts.[19]

Another type of pattern of organization was proposed by Thomas G. Devine. According to Devine, teachers need to show students how these work and how to use them as they read. Here are the patterns of organization as proposed by Devine:

Generalization—In using this pattern the writer makes a broad statement (a generalization, an inference, or an expression of opinion), and then supports it with evidence, examples, explanations, or reasons. This pattern is more commonly used in expository prose. Students are taught it when they are taught to find main idea sentences and supporting details.

Enumeration—This pattern is the easiest for students to recognize and use themselves since the author simply lists related items. Students may be

---

[19]Olive Niles, "Organization Perceived," in Harold L. Herber (editor), *Perspectives in Reading: Developing Study Skills in Secondary Schools* (Newark, Delaware: International Reading Association, 1965).

introduced to this pattern through scrambled lists such as school-day activities.

Comparison and Contrast—In this pattern of organization one item may be better understood if it is compared or contrasted with another.

Sequence —Sequence is like enumeration in that items are presented to the reader within the paragraph. However, in the enumeration pattern the order of items presented is not a primary concern, whereas it is of the utmost importance in the sequence pattern. In the sequence pattern the writer is guided by some predetermined sequence or order.

Cause and Effect—In this pattern items are given as causes or effects of other items. One item is subordinated to another in the relationship, implying that it is dependent on the other item in some way.

Question and Answer—In this pattern the writer asks a question and then answers it himself or herself. Both the question and the answer are needed by the reader since one of them can never be enough by itself.[20]

Sample Activity Sheet on Cause-Effect Relationships

The following page presents a sample activity sheet using cause-effect relationships. It was constructed from the content area of social studies at about the fifth-grade reading level. The reading teacher may duplicate it and use it in its present form if it seems applicable, or it may be used as a model of this type of activity sheet.

---

[20]Devine, op. cit., pp. 201-205.

ACTIVITY SHEET ON CAUSE-EFFECT RELATIONSHIPS
(Approximately fifth-grade reading level)

Name _____ Grade _____ Teacher _____

Match the number from each *cause listed on the left* of this activity sheet *to its effect listed on the right* of the activity sheet. All of the items are related to the *country of Australia.*

AUSTRALIA

Cause

1. Since Australia is in the Southern Hemisphere, the seasons are the reverse of those in the United States.

2. There are no permanently snow-capped mountains in Australia.

3. Eucalyptus trees are a variety of evergreen trees.

4. Marsupials have no placenta or membrane through which the young draws sustenance before it is born.

5. The koala bear can eat only certain kinds of eucalyptus leaves

6. The echidna or spiny anteater has a long ribbon-like tongue.

7. In the interior of Australia the light rains evaporate almost as soon as they hit the ground.

8. Life in Australia has been relatively undisturbed for perhaps 200 million years.

9. Primitive eucalyptus trees had flat, upward-facing leaves.

10. All eucalyptus trees in the world spring from seeds originally brought from Australia.

Effect

Eucalyptus leaves fall as they die, not according to any season.

Marsupials bear their young in less time and with less trouble than do higher mammals.

The koala bear is now becoming very rare in Australia.

Austalia's summer is around Christmas, while its winter is around July.

There are no great river systems in Australia.

The echidna or spiny anteater can quickly lick up ants.

The forms of plant and animal life have remained more or less as they were in the past. Therefore, Australia is sometimes called the land of "living fossils."

There is little vegetation in the interior of Australia.

Eucalyptus woods are much valued for furniture making and in the manufacture of plywoods.

Today eucalyptus trees are found in many dry, warm parts of the world, such as southern California, Peru, Greece, Turkey, and Egypt.

(Continued on following page)

11. Eucalyptus trees are all hardwoods and many have beautiful grained timber.

In an adjustment to a warming climate, eucalyptus trees learned to point their leaves downward and turn the edges of their leaves to the hot sun.

12. Australia has countless varieties of unique plants and flowers.

The mother kangaroo controls the flow of her milk to her baby by muscular effort.

13. Some Australian marsupials have long prehensile tails.

Botanists are fascinated by Australia.

14. Some Australian marsupials have a membrane of skin between forelegs and body.

Some Australian marsupials are able to hang from trees.

15. A baby kangaroo is not even able to suckle its mother's milk.

Some Australian marsupials can easily glide from tree to tree.

Answer Key

AUSTRALIA

Cause	*Effect*
1. Since Australia is in the Southern Hemisphere, the seasons are the reverse of those in the United States.	3. Eucalyptus leaves fall as they die, not according to any season.
2. There are no permanently snow-capped mountains in Australia.	4. Marsupials bear their young in less time and with less trouble than do higher mammals.
3. Eucalyptus trees are a variety of evergreen trees.	5. The koala bear is now becoming very rare in Australia.
4. Marsupials have no placenta or membrane through which the young draws sustenance before it is born.	1. Austalia's summer is around Christmas, while its winter is around July.
5. The koala bear can eat only certain kinds of eucalyptus leaves	2. There are no great river systems in Australia.
6. The echidna or spiny anteater has a long ribbon-like tongue.	6. The echidna or spiny anteater can quickly lick up ants.
7. In the interior of Australia the light rains evaporate almost as soon as they hit the ground.	8. The forms of plant and animal life have remained more or less as they were in the past. Therefore, Australia is sometimes called the land of "living fossils."
8. Life in Australia has been relatively undisturbed for perhaps 200 million years.	7. There is little vegetation in the interior of Australia.
9. Primitive eucalyptus trees had flat, upward-facing leaves.	11. Eucalyptus woods are much valued for furniture making and in the manufacture of plywoods.
10. All eucalyptus trees in the world spring from seeds originally brought from Australia.	10. Today eucalyptus trees are found in many dry, warm parts of the world, such as southern California, Peru, Greece, Turkey, and Egypt.

(Continued on following page)

11. Eucalyptus trees are all hardwoods and many have beautiful grained timber.	9. In an adjustment to a warming climate, eucalyptus trees learned to point their leaves downward and turn the edges of their leaves to the hot sun.
12. Australia has countless varieties of unique plants and flowers.	15. The mother kangaroo controls the flow of her milk to her baby by muscular effort.
13. Some Australian marsupials have long, prehensile tails.	12. Botanists are fascinated by Australia.
14. Some Australian marsupials have a membrane of skin between forelegs and body.	13. Some Australian marsupials are able to hang from trees.
15. A baby kangaroo is not even able to suckle its mother's milk.	14. Some Australian marsupials can easily glide from tree to tree.

RELATIONSHIP BETWEEN READING AND WRITING

As stated earlier in this handbook, one of the contemporary topics in reading that is currently being researched extensively is the *relation between reading and writing*. Emphasis on writing skills also can greatly add to improvement in reading comprehension. Although this emphasis can be begun at the emergent literacy stage, it can be greatly refined and extended at the middle-upper reading levels.

To understand why improvement in writing skills may also lead to improvement in reading skills, one has to understand the basic characteristics of both reading and writing.

NOTE: They have a number of the same basic characteristics, and the *child who is a good reader may be a good writer although this is not always the case.*

The remainder of Section 6 presents a number of practical suggestions and activity sheets that can be used by the reading teacher to effectively stress the relationships between reading comprehension and writing and thus improve ability simultaneously in both areas.

Writing on a Daily Basis

One of the easiest ways of doing this at the middle-upper levels is simply to have children write on a regular basis either in a personal journal, on self-selected topics, or on assigned topics. As in the case of reading skills, writing skills improve most effectively with motivated practice. For example, Peoria,

Illinois, District #150 requires all students in both the primary and intermediate grades to write on a daily basis for one-half hour. Some of the written products then are scored by the teachers on a *holistic or global basis* using a scale of 1-5. They are normally not scored with a red pencil for mechanics as is the typical practice in the intermediate grades and above. Carol Sissell, the language arts coordinator for the school district, came to my graduate class in the fall of 1988 to teach my students how to do holistic scoring of written products. Most of the students were amazed to discover that their scores did not vary more than *1* point on an essay when using the scoring system of 1-5.

Summarization Skills

Many different types of *summaries* can be used to relate reading and writing instruction and also to improve reading comprehension. It is obvious that the traditional summary simply consists of having the middle-upper level student read a narrative or expository passage and then write a summary of one or more paragraphs. To be used most effectively as a technique for improving reading comprehension, the students should be given instruction in the proper techniques of writing a summary. Normally the traditional summary contains mainly the main ideas from the material written in a cohesive, concise manner.

Several unique variations of the traditional summary can be used to improve reading comprehension on at both the middle and upper levels, and the following provides two ready-to-use examples.

Students should learn that summarizing is a very important life skill that adults often must use. Summarization is a form of retelling, but it is more focused and precise than the retelling which was just discussed. Students should learn to discriminate between good summaries and poor summaries. To help students learn this important skill, the teacher can present passages and examples of summaries, and then the students can select which is the best summary of several that are provided. Students also should determine what elements constitute the best summary, and why the other summaries do not meet the criteria of a satisfactory summary.

Sample Activity Requiring the Selection of a Good Summary

The following pages present a reading passage and exercise based on some of the characteristics of foxes. After reading the passage, the student is to select the best summary of the passage and indicate why it is the best summary. You can duplicate and use this activity at about the fourth-grade reading level if it seems applicable, or use it as a model for making your own activity of this type.

ACTIVITY SHEET FOR SELECTING THE BEST SUMMARY
OF A PASSAGE
(Approximately fourth-grade reading level)

Name ————————————   Grade ———   Teacher ————————

Read this passage about foxes to yourself. Later you will be asked to pick *the best summary of the passage from three choices and tell why each choice is or is not a good summary.*

THE WILY FOX

The wily, sly fox has had a reputation for being cowardly for many years. Instead, it combines caution with curiosity. The cunning fox can leap over or run along stone walls, run in circles, or employ tricks of various kinds to confuse the hounds that are trying to catch it. One wily fox that was being chased along a railroad embankment is said to have jumped aboard a passing railroad flatcar and ridden away to safety.

The diet of the fox has been studied extensively and it has been found that foxes eat many different types of food depending upon how hungry they are. For example, they eat anything from earthworms to strawberries. They enjoy frogs but never eat toads, feast on lizards, and find many insects tasty. They also eat ground squirrels, birds and their eggs, and a wide variety of berries, fruits, and grasses. It is interesting to learn how a fox eats an egg. The fox holds the egg in its front paws, and then licks out its contents without spilling a single drop. The fox relies on its hearing when seeking the large earthworms that are known as "night crawlers." When a night crawler wriggles to the surface, the bristles along its body rub against the grass stems and the fox hears it and pulls it out of the ground without breaking it. The fox can even hear a mouse running under several inches of snow in the winter.

A mother and father fox do not enjoy digging their own den but prefer to move into a burrow abandoned by some other animals. If they must, the foxes make their own den by digging in loose, sandy dirt. The mother fox who is called a *vixen* has six to eight babies, which are called *kits*. Each kit weighs only 4 ounces and is blind and totally helpless at birth. The kits' mother gives them excellent care and never leaves them alone for about ten days. The kits leave the den when they are about a month old. Both mother and father fox find food for the kits, and the kits lick the older foxes' mouths to get at the food. After about six months, each member of the fox family goes its own way.

Following are three summaries of the passage about the fox. Read each one to yourself and put an *X* in front of the *best summary* of the passage. Then write on the lines under each summary why that summary is, or is not, a good summary.

Summary One

———— The mother and father fox are very good parents and give their kits plenty of food to eat. The kits leave the den when they are about one month old.

————————————————————————————————

————————————————————————————————

Summary Two

_____ The fox is a clever animal with a varied diet. It raises its family in a den in the ground.

_____

_____

Summary Three

_____ The wily fox uses many tricks to fool its enemies. One fox is said to have jumped on a railroad flatcar and ridden away from its enemies to safety.

_____

_____

Answer Key

(The answers included here are only for illustrative purposes.)

Summary One

_____

This summary only tells about the baby foxes and how they live.

Summary Two

__X__

This summary tells about all of the information that was found in the passage.

Summary Three

_____

This summary tells only about the tricks that the fox can use.

GIST PROCEDURE (GENERATING INTERACTIONS BETWEEN SCHEMATA AND TEXT)

The *Gist Procedure* was developed by James W. Cunningham to improve students' abilities to comprehend the gist or main ideas of paragraphs by providing a prescription for reading from group sentence-by-sentence production to individual entire-paragraph gist production. He states that it is an effective instructional tool for guiding student summary writing, which then can improve their learning from content material.

There are two versions of the Gist Procedure: a paragraph version and a short passage version. Very briefly, here are the steps of these two versions:

Paragraph Version

1. *Select the appropriate paragraphs*—Select several paragraphs containing three to five sentences which have a gist or main idea.

2. *Students read the first sentence*—Have the students read the first sentence of the paragraph so that they can retell it in their own words. The

sentence can be displayed on the chalkboard or an overhead transparency with 15 blanks underneath it. The students then write their summaries on the blank lines.

3. *Students generate their summaries*—Students retell in a statement of 15 or less words what they read in the sentence.

4. *Reading the first two sentences*—The students read the first and second sentences and retell them in the same number of words used for the first sentence alone.

5. *Generating a summary of sentences one and two*—The students then should generate a single sentence of no longer than 15 words which summarizes both sentences one and two.

6. *Continue with the procedure for the remainder of the paragraph*—The procedure is continued with the addition of each new sentence until the students have produced a single statement of 15 words or less which best summarizes the paragraph.

7. *Moving beyond a sentence-by-sentence approach to a paragraph approach*—Students are encouraged to produce their own gist statements on an individual basis across a variety of different types of paragraphs.

Short Passage Version

1. *Choosing appropriate passages*—The reading teacher selects a short passage of an appropriate level of difficulty, each with a gist or main topic and containing three to five paragraphs. The passage is then placed on an overhead transparency.

2. *Reading the paragraph*—All of the paragraphs are covered over except for the first one. Twenty blank spaces are written on the chalkboard, and the students are told to read the paragraph so that they can retell it in their own words in one statement of 20 words or less.

3. *Students generate summaries*—When students have finished reading the paragraph, the transparency is removed and the students are told to start writing their summaries. Writing one word per blank, students dictate and edit the statement until it is complete. They are told to dictate the summary from memory. The 20-word rule should be enforced by the teacher.

4. *The students read and summarize subsequent paragraphs*—The reading teacher erases the chalkboard and the students read and summarize the first two paragraphs in not more than 20 words. The same procedures are used throughout the entire passage.

5. *Generating summaries for the entire passage and developing independence in the use of this procedure*—This strategy should be used with many different types of short passages until students become competent at efficiently producing gist statements. The students then probably should

respond to the entire passage rather than paragraph-by-paragraph. Students should be encouraged to produce gist statements on an individual basis.[21]

Sample Activity Sheet Using the GIST Procedure

The following pages present a sample activity using the Gist Procedure at approximately the sixth-grade reading level. It can be duplicated and used in its present form if it seems applicable or can be used as a model of this type of procedure. It is important to remember that this procedure should not be used very often as it is intense, and students may easily grow tired of it.

---

[21]James W. Cunningham, "Generating Interactions Between Schemata and Text," in *New Inquiries in Reading Research and Instruction*, edited by J. A. Niles and L. A. Harris. Thirty-First Yearbook of the National Reading Conference (Washington, D. C.: National Reading Conference), pp. 42-47. Used with permission of the author.

ACTIVITY SHEET USING THE GIST PROCEDURE
(Approximately sixth-grade reading level)

Name _____   Grade _____   Teacher _____

Read the following paragraphs about Charles Russell, the American cowboy artist, to yourself. After you have read each paragraph, you will be asked to write a summary of what you have read.

CHARLES RUSSELL—AMERICAN COWBOY ARTIST

Charles Marion Russell became one of America's famous artists, and to this day is known as the "cowboy artist." Although he came from a cultured, wealthy St. Louis family, from the time he was a small boy he dreamed of going to that mysterious land out West known as the frontier. At that time Charles's family owned a large farm named Oak Hill, and he spent many daytime hours hiking in the woods, sketching pictures, or climbing trees trying to look out West toward the fascinating frontier.

Now *write a summary of the paragraph in no more than 20 words.* You can work with a partner if you want to.

_____   _____
_____   _____
_____   _____
_____   _____
_____   _____
_____   _____
_____   _____
_____   _____

While he was growing up, Charles was a quiet boy who did not talk very much. However, his hands were never still, and he was either sketching pictures or modeling with his beeswax. From the beginning, Charles had no interest in school since he did not enjoy following rules and doing exactly as he was told. When he misbehaved, he was punished severely by being hit with a willow stick by his teacher. Charles later was sent to a school in the city, but he did no better there since all he dreamed about was going to the Western frontier as soon as possible.

(Continued on following page)

Now *write a summary of the two paragraphs in no more than 20 words*. You can work with a partner if you want to.

_____   _____
_____   _____
_____   _____
_____   _____
_____   _____
_____   _____
_____   _____
_____   _____

In desperation Charles's family sent him to art school. However, since he did not understand how drawing cones, cubes, and geometrical figures could help him to become an artist, he did not enjoy art school either. Instead he spent most of his days on the Mississippi River levee sketching the river men, the trappers, and the fur traders and dreaming about going West to live in Montana. Indeed he was so obsessed with going to the West, that he headed West with a friend when he was almost 13. He worked on a farm not far from his home for a time, and then went home again to his family's farm.

Now *write a summary of the three paragraphs in no more than 20 words*. You can work with a partner if you want to.

_____   _____
_____   _____
_____   _____
_____   _____
_____   _____
_____   _____
_____   _____
_____   _____

Charles's family tried sending him to school one last time. This was a military school in the East which had fine teachers, but very strict discipline. However, Charles spent much of his time daydreaming about traveling to the West or working on his drawings when he was in study hall supposed to be doing his schoolwork. After he stayed, at the military school for a year, Charles's father finally relented and allowed him to go West to Montana to work on a sheep ranch owned by a family friend. Therefore, at the age of 15, Charles Russell headed toward the Montana territory that had always drawn him like a magnet.

Now *write a summary of the four paragraphs in no more than 20 words*. You can work with a partner if you want to.

_____   _____
_____   _____
_____   _____
_____   _____
_____   _____
_____   _____
_____   _____
_____   _____

Charles traveled by railroad to Red Rock and then continued the journey by stagecoach. After many hours, the stagecoach stopped to let the passengers rest and walk for a few minutes, and Charles saw a white buffalo skull with nose bones split and the horns still attached. This tragic sight became his trademark, and the skull next to his signature appears on every one of his later paintings. Charles Russell remained in the West for the rest of his life, living among the Indians, working with cowboys, and painting and modeling figures of everything which he saw. He molded animals, flowers, Indian heads, and cowboys from beeswax while he rode the range. Montana, the state which he adopted, later placed a bronze statue of Charles Russell in the Hall of Fame in the Smithsonian Institute in Washington, D.C. He was a master American artist, and a segment of our country's history lives on in his work.

Now *write a summary of the entire passage in no more than 20 words*. You can work with a partner if you want to.

_____   _____
_____   _____

(Continued on following page)

Answer Key

(The following answers are included only for illustrative purposes. Many other possible summaries are acceptable.)

Charles Russell always dreamed of going out West to the frontier.

Since Charles always wanted to go West, he did not like school and sketched pictures instead.

Charles tried to achieve his dream of going out West by leaving home at 13, but it was unsuccessful.

Finally Charles achieved his dream of going West at 15 when he went to Montana to work on a ranch.

Charles became a famous Western artist and painted and modeled figures of Western objects like animals and cowboys.

GUIDED WRITING PROCEDURE

The *Guided Writing Procedure* developed by Smith and Bean is an attempt to use the *process of writing* as a way of helping students learn from textbook material. Smith and Bean state that writing fluency (the processes of writing) can be taught concurrently with the content material itself. This is an extension of the concept that the processes of reading and listening can be taught along with the content material.

The *Guided Writing Procedure* involves specific procedures that take several days of content instruction. Two general steps are involved:

Informal diagnosis of prior content knowledge and written expression.

Teaching content and written expression

Here very briefly, are the steps which the content teacher at the middle-upper level can apply while using the *Guided Writing Procedure.*

1. *Informal Diagnosis of Prior Content Knowledge and Written Expression—* Have the students brainstorm any thoughts which they have related to the content topic to be learned. For example, the following ideas related to the content topic of the *study of the constitution* could be offered:

the Confederation	the Great Compromise
the convention	framers
delegates	executive branch
ratification	legislative branch
Bill of Rights	judiciary branch
Magna Carta	cabinet

Record everything which the students say on the chalkboard or a transparency.

Next have the students vote on which ideas are the important ones and which ideas are details. Organize the ideas into an outline or a graphic organizer on the board or a transparency. The outline should help students to organize and cluster their thoughts. Have the students write one or two short paragraphs using the outline or graphic organizer as a guide. Collect these first drafts and then have the students read the text.

The teacher should examine the students' paragraphs quickly and analyze them for organization of ideas, style, and mechanics. A *Concept and Writing Checklist* can be used to record the information for each student.

Concept and Writing Checklist

+ = Acceptable
? = Cannot Tell
0 = Needs improvement

Criteria

Organization of Ideas
    Clear topic
    Supporting details/examples
    Logical flow
    Comments _____

Style
    Shows variety in:
    Word choice
    Sentence length
    Comments _____

Mechanics
    Complete sentences
    Capitalization
    Punctuation
    Spelling
    Comments _____

2. *Teach Content and Written Expression*—One or several days should have elapsed since the first draft. The teacher then displays an actual student's draft or a composite of several first drafts on the board or a transparency. One probably should be used that contains inaccurate information as well

as inappropriate writing criteria. The class or group should use the check-list and text information to edit the illustrative paragraph.

Each student should then use the checklist to help analyze his or her own first drafts. They should edit for both content and written inaccuracies. Then the second draft is collected, and a follow-up quiz is given on the material read. The reading teacher should examine the second drafts and compare them to the checklist results.

The *Guided Writing Procedure* is a fairly unique way to introduce and teach content material. Students may examine examples of text written by professional authors also. This will be done in the activity sheet which follows.[22]

Sample Activity on the Guided Writing Procedure

The following pages present a sample activity based on some aspects of the Guided Writing Procedure. Obviously, not all of the elements of this technique can be included in an activity sheet since some of them must involve oral and group activities. However, this example should serve as a model of how a part of the procedure can be adapted to the activity sheet form. You can duplicate and use it in its present form if it seems applicable for your students.

---

[22]Carl Smith and T. W. Bean, "The Guided Writing Procedure: Integrating Content and Writing Improvement," *Reading World* 19 (January, 1980) pp. 290-298. Used by permission of the College Reading Association.

ACTIVITY SHEET ON THE GUIDED WRITING PROCEDURE
(Approximately sixth-grade reading level)

Name _____ Grade _____ Teacher _____

Read the following passage about *honeybees and pollination* silently. Although it is factually correct, it contains some inaccuracies in the organization of ideas, style, and writing mechanics.

Here is a checklist that you may want to use in analyzing this passage. You should complete the checklist after reading the passage. You may refer back to the passage if you wish, and you also may work with one or more partners in completing the checklist.

Concept and Writing Checklist

+ = Acceptable
0 = Needs improvement
? = Cannot tell

Criteria

ORGANIZATION OF IDEAS

Clear topic _____

Supporting details/examples _____

Logical flow _____

Comments _____

STYLE

Shows variety in:

Word choice _____

Sentence length _____

Comments _____

MECHANICS

Complete sentences _____

Capitalization _____

Punctuation _____

Spelling _____

Comments _____

HOW HONEYBEES WORK

Honeybees are very important in the polination that occurs in flowers and is necessary for their survival. Honeybees live in large colonies containing 30,000 to 80,000 adult bees and each colony has a big female bee which is called a queen and the queen bee lays as many as 1,500 eggs a day.

Most all of the bees in the colone are small females. They cannot lay eggs. They are called worker bees. The worker bees do all the work in the colony. Some worker bees feed the queen. Some clean the hive. Some guard it. Some worker bees make or repair honey-combs where the honey is stored and the queen lays her eggs. As the young hatch out, some workers take care of them and give them food and still other workers keep making trips out of the hive to find food and bring it back.

Worker bees find two kinds of food in flowers and one is the powdery dust called polen which is yellow but some kinds of flowers have white and red and blue or black pollen. Polen grains are small and each kind has its own shape.

Many flowers also make a sweet, sticky liquid called necter. It is a mixture of sugar and water. Necter is the raw material from which bees make hony, and it is their flower food. Adult bees feed on necter and sometimes on pollen and the young feed on honey and pollen and pollen is rich in protein, fats, minerals, and vitimins and the young need these in order to grow.

The honeybees you see on flowers are always worker bees and they visit flowers to collect food. They must colect enough food to feed the colony in colder weather when there are no flowers in bloom.

All bees have six legs, wings, hairy bodys, and feelers. Each worker has two hairy baskets on their hind legs. These are where she stores the pollen. A worker moves from flower to flower to collect pollen. At each flower she scrapes pollen with her legs and mouth parts and more pollen sticks to her body hairs. The worker bee cleans herself and arranges her pollen and rests on a flower and huvers in the air and flies from one flower to another. Her legs are lines with stiff hairs and they serve as brushes and the bee uses the hairs to collect pollen from her body—she uses her mouth parts to moisten the pollen with a little necter she has collected and the necter makes the pollen sticky and it sticks to her.

Each hind leg has a kind of comb and just above the comb each hind leg has a polen basket made of stiff hairs. The bee scrapes one hind leg down against the other, pushing pollen into the basket on the moving leg. Worker bees also collect necter which is a liquid that is carried in a special stomech called the honey stomach and is a special stomach that is in front of the stomach that digests the bees own food.

A worker bee works very hard and only lives 14 days after she starts working since she works herself to death. Her normal life span is 5 or 6 weeks. A honeybee colony uses 50 to 75 pounds of pollen each year and it takes 38,000 collecting trips to cary out a pound of pollen to the hive.

Answer Key

The passage on honeybees is factually correct. However, the responses included here are only for illustrative purposes.

Organization of Ideas

Clear topic	+
Supporting details/examples	+
Logical flow	?

Comments _____

Style

Shows variety in:

Word choice	0
Sentence length	0

Comments <u>too many and's</u> _____

MECHANICS

Complete sentences	+
Capitalization	+
Punctuation	0
Spelling	0

Comments _____

AUTHOR'S CHAIR/PEER CONFERENCING

The goal of *Author's Chair/Peer Conferencing* is to develop readers and writers who have a sense of authorship and readership which can aid them in either composing process. This can include developing in students an appreciation of the following:

What they read has been written by someone who has certain purposes in mind and control over what they have written.

When they write they have a variety of options. What they write can be interpreted in different ways by different readers.

In *Peer Conferencing* the students act as advisors and evaluators along with the teacher. The teacher may facilitate Peer Conferences, but students are given control of many of the questions and other ideas that get introduced. At the core of Peer Conferencing is *collaboration*. In a single class this procedure can involve:

coauthoring

coreading

class discussions of a peer's problem or work in progress

small group or paired sharing of work, ideas, or interests

Three variations of the group conference which can be used in this technique are as follows: *reading and writing in progress conference, end-of-book conference,* and *peer author conference.*

At any stages in the reading or writing of a story or a report, it may be appropriate to conference. For example, as readers or writers begin to read or to write a story or other written work, they can seek some input on what they are about to read or write. A writer may need some help on how to begin a report so he or she can meet with peers to receive their help. Another child might want to read a certain book, and he or she may wish to find out from classmates the appropriateness of the book. Peer conferences can occur during a reading or writing assignment. In another variation the child author of a written product is present during the peer conference and might be consulted occasionally, but another child may report on the book and answer questions about it. Thus, the child author has the opportunity to have someone else represent the book.

The *Author's Chair or Peer Conference* can result in improvement in a student's sense of readership and authorship as well as in his or her ability to evaluate and problem-solve. It also uses the child's own classmates as a good source of help. However, most teachers find it difficult to relinquish this much sense of control in empowering children to be independent. In addition, some children need considerable encouragement and practice before becoming competent in this technique. If you want more information on this technique, consult the footnote.[23]

DIALOGUE JOURNAL

The *Dialogue Journal* is a type of writing activity designed to give students the opportunity to share privately in writing their reactions, questions, and concerns about school experiences and sometimes personal matters without any

---

[23]Tierney *et al., op. cit.,* pp. 99-104.

threat of teacher evaluation. It may also give the teacher the opportunity to learn what each child is thinking and doing and then to offer help if this is possible.

Although the term *Dialogue Journal* has been coined rather recently, journals have been kept for time immemorial, ever since individuals began using writing as a means of keeping a written record of their own lives. The major difference between traditional journals and dialogue journals is the importance given to *communications between the student and the teacher. Dialogue journals* are similar to a daily letter or memo to the teacher. The students should write to the teacher and have the teacher normally attempt to write a sincere response to the student.

To illustrate the possible use of a dialogue journal, the following examples are given from dialogue journals used in a typical fifth-grade classroom:

November 10, 1991

    We made our mural for the hall by Mr. Robinson's office yesterday.

I had a hard time making the picture of the pioneer that I was supposed to paint. I hope you like our mural. Mr. Robinson said he does.

Kristin

    I thought that the mural that your committee painted was just excellent. I'm sure that all the children and teachers in our school will very much enjoy seeing it this fall.

    W. Reimer

November 14, 1991

    I liked the computer program on the Oregon Trail that I used yesterday a lot. I didn't get all the way to Oregon, but it was fun anyway. The next time I bet I'll get there.

Matt,

    I'm glad that you enjoyed that program. I bet you learned a lot about pioneer times from using it. I also am sure that you'll get all the way to Oregon next time.

    W. Reimer

It is important to allow uninterrupted time each day or several times a week for the journal writing. In most classes the child has a folder in which the material is placed. As much as possible, the journals should focus on *writing about reading, books, authors, and writing.*

Here are several cautions that always should be observed in writing dialogue journals:

1. *Protect the privacy of the journal.* Don't read aloud any part of the journal without the author's permission.

2. *Be an active reader and a sincere responder to the journal.* Write general comments and react rather than correct or criticize.

3. *Be honest with students.* Do not encourage students to tell you more than you should know or want to know and do not allow them to use offensive language.

4. *Accentuate the positive in the journals.* Encourage rather than criticize students.

5. *Make journal writing interesting and unique.* Be careful not to let this activity become tedious and boring by being sure to respond with interest and creativity.

6. *Do not promise to respond to students more often than is truly possible.*[24]

ECOLA (EXTENDING CONCEPTS THROUGH LANGUAGE ACTIVITIES)

ECOLA was developed by M. T. Smith-Burke and is an attempt to integrate reading, writing, speaking, and listening for purposes of developing a reader's ability to interpret and monitor his or her own comprehension. The major purpose of this procedure is to ensure that the interpretation that is constructed is correct. It is designed to be used at the middle-upper level with both narrative and content (expository) material.

Very briefly, here are the five main steps in this procedure:

1. *Setting a communicative purpose.* The teacher should determine what he or she would like his or her students to gain from the reading. The teacher should then decide what type of support is needed in helping the students read this material, such as formulated questions.

2. *Silent reading for a purpose and a criterion task.* Students are reminded of their purposes for reading and told that they should be able to support their interpretation with ideas from the text.

3. *Crystallizing comprehension through writing.* During this step each student and the teacher should write a response to the overall or general question or purpose for reading. Their responses are kept confidential.

---

[24]J. Joan Staton, "Writing and Counseling: Using a Dialogue Journal," *Language Arts* 57 (April, 1980), pp. 514-518.

4. *Discussing the ideas*. Students are placed into small groups and given a time limit in which they are told to discuss their interpretations and conclusions.

5. *Writing and comparing*. The last step is to have students in small groups or individually formulate a second interpretation.[25]

NOTE: Since ECOLA is very intensive, it should be used only occasionally. It may help students in formulating a written response to textual material. It also helps students refine and expand on a reader's interpretation following the discussion. Student-centered rather than teacher-directed consideration of the usefulness of reading strategies is strongly encouraged by this technique. It promotes self-monitoring of reading comprehension.

[25]M. T. Smith-Burke, "Extending Concepts Through Language Activities," In *Reader Meets Author/Bridging the Gap*, edited by J. Langer and M. Smith-Burke (Newark, Delaware: International Reading Association, 1982).

7

Materials
and Computer Software
for Improving
Reading Comprehension
Ability

The final section of the *Reading Comprehension Kit* presents a comprehensive listing of materials and computer software which can be used at the elementary and secondary school levels for improving comprehension ability.

The listing was developed through an exhaustive study of contemporary publishers' catalogs at the Teaching Materials Center of Milner Library at Illinois State University. In addition, the Computer Center in the College of Education at Illinois State University was used extensively in its preparation.

The reading teacher should find the resources included in this section extremely useful in the teaching of reading comprehension at various levels.

Various Materials to Develop Reading Comprehension

Best-Selling Chapters
By Raymond Harris
Jamestown Publishers; The Reading People
Post Office Box 9168
Providence, RI 02940

This series is available in two separate levels. The Middle Level (grades 6-8) and the Advanced Level (grades 9-college) both use chapters from best-selling novels as the focus of each lesson. After an introduction of the novel and the author, the student is to read the passage and answer a number of multiple choice questions dealing with comprehension and literary form. Questions center on skills such as setting, event order, main idea, details, retaining concepts, making inferences, developing vocabulary, and a number of other skills related to comprehension.

Reading the Content Fields
By Edward Spargo & Raymond Harris
Jamestown Publishers; The Reading People
Post Office Box 9168
Providence, RI 02940

This series of books and optional read-along cassettes deals with the specific challenges of developing reading comprehension skills in the content areas of science, social studies, mathematics, English, and the practical arts. Each three-part lesson starts with an introduction of the subject area. Next, a complete lesson deals with how to develop these skills, and, finally, a sample exercise is provided for practice.

Basic Thinking Skills
By Anita Hared
Midwest Publications
Post Office Box 448, Dept. 17
Pacific Grove, CA 93950

This series, which deals primarily with material appropriate for grades 3-8, was developed to promote analytical thinking skills in reading comprehension (through the use of interpretive as well as literal questions following reading passages) along with skills in math, writing, science, and test taking. Following directions is also an important part of this series.

Reading for Understanding 2 & 3
By Telia Gunning Thurstone
Science Research Associates, Inc.
155 N. Wacker Drive
Chicago, IL 60606

Each kit contains 300 lesson cards totaling 3000 individual exercises. These exercises take the form of paragraphs with literal and interpretive multiple choice questions. Divided into 100 levels of difficulty, these kits have been used successfully in developing reading comprehension skills from third grade through adulthood. Level 2 is for reading levels 3.0 to 7.0, while Level 3 is recommended for reading levels above 7.0. Both kits also include record books, and pre- as well as post-test forms.

Keys to Understanding Mankind
By Sandra Nina Chaplain & JoAnn Butom Kaplan
Creative Teaching Press, Inc.
10701 Holder Street
Cyprus, CA 90630

This is a series of 55 open-ended reading task cards developed to teach students "basic philosophical concepts about" while furthering reading comprehension and critical thinking skills. The cards are designed with three major components: (1) A statement or question to relate the reading to; (2) Specific points to consider after reading; and (3) An illustrated model of thinking to respond to. This series can be adapted to fit any age level.

Guinness Book of World Records READING Comprehension Program
By Society for Visual Education, Inc.
1345 Diversey Parkway
Chicago, IL 60614

This highly motivational program is divided into second, third, and fourth grade reading levels dealing in the areas of "vocabulary development, literal comprehension, and interpretive thinking." The program is comprised of 120 vocabulary-controlled reading exercises, four question-and-answer filmstrips with guides, score sheets, and cassette narration, a copy of the latest Guinness Book of World Records, and Guinness Challenge certificates and scoreboard.

Teaching Reading Comprehension
By Roger Farr
National Education Association
1201 16th Street, N.W.
Washington, D.C. 20036

This 30-minute cassette tape is geared towards educators at all levels concerned with reading comprehension. Dr. Farr suggests strategies to be used by classroom teachers and offers a variety of discussion questions related to the cassette in order to encourage further thought into the teaching of reading comprehension.

Selections from the Black, Third Edition
By Edward Spargo, Editor
Jamestown Publishers; The Reading People
Post Office Box 9168
Providence, RI 02940

These four books focus on literature by black writers. Book One deals with reading levels 6-7; Book Two with 8-9; Book Three with 10-11; and Book Four with 12-college. Reading comprehension exercises following each unedited passage help students develop abilities in "recalling and organizing facts, retaining concepts, understanding main ideas, drawing conclusions, making judgments and inferences, recognizing tone, understanding characters, and appreciating the literary forms." These books also contain lessons on developing study skills.

Critical Reading Skills Series
By Jamestown Publishers; The Reading People
Post Office Box 9168
Providence, RI 02940

A six-book series (each with 21 stories) "arranged on three reading levels, from grade 6 to grade 8." These books, with their motivational passages and eye-catching illustrations, allow students to develop their reading comprehension skills through finding the main idea, recalling facts, making inferences, and using words precisely after being presented with new vocabulary words in context. Charts for figuring and recording reading rate and a progress graph are also included with each book.

Reading the Newspaper
By Margery S. Miller, Ed.D. & Karen K. Allan, Ph.D.
Jamestown Publishers; The Reading People
Post Office Box 9168
Providence, RI 02940

This provocative series using both reading and writing as a means to develop reading comprehension draws information from the lesson books and local newspapers. The newspaper is used to be read for information, entertainment, and interpretation. Questions take the form of "two vocabulary, two literal, and two inferential" comprehension questions. Students also have the opportunity to learn more about "recognizing main ideas and details in headlines, isolating quotes in a news article, identifying fact and opinion in editorials and reviews, etc. . . ." and many other reading skills.

Comprehension Skills Series
By Jamestown Publishers; The Reading People
Post Office Box 9168
Providence, RI 02940

A series of specialized skills books for students with particular problems developing comprehension skills. Each lesson specifically identifies and explains an area of reading comprehension, follows it with practice exercises (passages and specific comprehension skill questions), and moves on to new skills. Cassettes are also available as an enhancement of the next to help students "read along." Skills cross such areas as main idea, conclusions, making judgments and inferences, and recall and organization skills, among others.

Comprehension Crosswords
By Lawrence B. Charry, Ed.D.
Jamestown Publishers; The Reading People
Post Office Box 9168
Providence, RI 02940

This series of crossword puzzle books (10) is designed for students from grades 3 through 12. These "noncompetitive, self-challenging" puzzles call on students to follow directions, use context clues, draw conclusions, improve spelling, strengthen recall and visual memory of words, and become familiar with homonyms and rhymes. Each book contains 24 spirit masters with mini-lessons to accompany each puzzle and the specific skill it stresses.

Best Short Stories
By Raymond Harris
Jamestown Publishers; The Reading People
Post Office Box 9168
Providence, RI 02940

This series, which comes in a separate Middle Level (grades 6-8) and Advanced Level (grades 9-college), is developed to teach the basic elements of literature while expanding reading comprehension. Each unit begins with an introductory section which discusses the author and establishes the story. Each story is followed by a number of multiple choice questions divided by skills along with discussion guides and writing exercises. The comprehension skills cover a variety of areas including recognizing words in context, keeping events in order, recognizing tone, isolating details, understanding characters, and retaining concepts.

Reading for Content and Speed
By Carol Einstein
Educators Publishing Service, Inc.
75 Moulton Street
Cambridge, Massachusetts 02138

This four-book series centers on such high-interest subjects as sports, science, biography, history, and hobbies. Each passage of the book is followed by four questions; "Two ask for recall of main ideas, and two ask the student to draw conclusions from what has been read." The books are to be used with students grades 3-6, and each contains answer sheets and progress charts.

Wordly Wise Reading
By Kenneth Hodkinson
Educators Publishing Service, Inc.
75 Moulton Street
Cambridge, Massachusetts 02138

All the books in this series deal in some way with "magic," therefore creating a high-interest content for students in grades 2-4. All the stories in this series are original stories designed by the author in order to stimulate critical thinking. After reading the stories the students finish exercises that "require inferential comprehension, and ask them to do some original writing." Literal comprehension skills are also reinforced through the use of exercise questions and "follow the maze" activities. The series is divided into two books, each available separately.

Early Reading Comprehension in Varied Subject Matter
By Jane Ervin
Educators Publishing Service, Inc.
75 Moulton Street
Cambridge, Massachusetts 02138

This is a series that is made up entirely of workbooks created to be used in developing comprehension skills. The workbooks are fully illustrated and progress in difficulty: first, introducing the skills (recalling main idea and details, sequencing, and developing vocabulary) and then reading the passage (in the form of stories, articles, and poems), and answering the questions. Also stressed is the idea that students can learn to answer questions with brief, more efficient answers as the student progresses through the different skill levels.

Clues for Better Reading
By Diane Lapp and James Flood
Curriculum Associates, Inc.
5 Esquire Road
N. Billerica, MA 01862

This series, which was created for grades 1-9, contains contemporary writing that is high-interest with large colorful pictures. The comprehension skills which are stressed through multiple choice, true/false, cloze, matching, and short written answers cover a variety of areas. The series is broken down into three kits, each drawing from the following areas of comprehension development: following directions, sorting and classifying, main idea, details, emotions, sequencing, "what's next?" questions, inferring, predictions, fantasy/reality propaganda, and reading maps, charts, graphs, and schedules. The kits contain 80–100 story cards, charts, lesson plans, and "Bonanza" supplementary activity sheets.

Listening Comprehension Skills Program
By Stan Laird
Curriculum Associates, Inc.
5 Esquire Road
N. Billerica, MA 01862

This kit is developed on the idea that "the ability to read is directly related to the ability to listen." Focusing on oral reading and listening skills, this kit works on developing such skills as inferring word meanings, identifying moods, restating, sequencing, predicting, judging validity, inferring author's purpose, and several others. Skill areas are separated by Tab Cards, each area designed as a "self-directed" activity. Overlapping levels cover grades 1-10, each level with manuals, activity cards, answer keys, response sheets, and student listening questionnaires.

Reading Attainment System Books
By Opportunities for Learning, Inc.
20417 Nordhoff St., Dept. 75B
Chatsworth, CA 91311

These books are designed especially for students who have been experiencing reading difficulty. Each set in this series contains 50 books along with a Teacher's Guide. The books concentrate on vocabulary and thinking skills "through comprehension questions and vocabulary exercises" in different content areas (such as history, geography, biology, health, consumer skills, and other related subject areas). Reading passages make up the bulk of the program and are followed by a variety of types of questions, both literal and interpretive, growing in complexity as the series progresses.

Caught Reading Program
By Opportunities for Learning, Inc.
20417 Nordhoff St., Dept. 75B
Chatsworth, CA 91311

As the name implies, this series is made up of high-interest stories and follow-up activities. This series was especially made for reading levels 4-7 and interest levels 6-adult, so it is appropriate for older readers in need of remediation. The kit is made-up of several 300-400 word stories, a glossary of "Words You Ought to Know," topics for discussion and supplemental writing assignments, and comprehension questions dealing with main idea, supporting details, inferential thinking, and similar activities.

Codebusters
By Opportunities for Learning, Inc.
20417 Nordhoff St., Dept. 75B
Chatsworth, CA 91311

This unique series, developed for use by upper-elementary and junior high school students, makes reading a game through the use of a special "decoder" for checking answers to comprehension questions. Large illustrations accompany the books and make them pleasant to view. The comprehension questions that follow the short stories gradually become more difficult, moving into more interpretive as well as literal questions. Each individual set has 10 36-page books, 10 question cards, and 3 decoders.

Improving Your Reading with Cartoon Strips
By Opportunities for Learning, Inc.
20417 Nordhoff St., Dept. 75B
Chatsworth, CA 91311

This series of workbooks was designed for underachieving readers as a high-interest way to teach reading comprehension. The reading level of this series is 2-5 and covers areas of comprehension such as "main ideas, making inferences, drawing conclusions, recognizing important details, and grasping the tone of a selection." After reading comic strips by well-known cartoonists, the students answer questions related to the comprehension areas listed. A very motivational set of workbooks for fun and learning.

Starting Comprehension: Stories to Advance Reading and Thinking
By Ann L. Staman
Educators Publishing Service, Inc.
75 Moulton Street
Cambridge, Massachusetts 02238

This group of workbooks is designed for young readers at the preprimer to second grade level. These twelve workbooks have four basic different types of lessons on (1) vocabulary exercises, (2) literal comprehension questions, (3) inferential comprehension questions, and (4) organizational comprehension questions and exercises. The teacher's manual that accompanies this series helps the teacher to select which of the two teaching strands (Phonetic-Analytic, and Visual-Gestalt) is most appropriate for each lesson objective.

Reasoning and Reading
By Joanne Carlisle
Educators Publishing Service, Inc.
75 Moulton Street
Cambridge, Massachusetts 02238

This series is available in several levels for differing grades of students. The Beginning Level is designed for grades 3-5, Level 1 for 6-7, Level 2 for 8-9. Each workbook builds on skills of reading comprehension gradually increasing in detail and difficulty. This series concentrates on building comprehension through word meaning, sentence meaning, paragraph meaning, and reasoning skills. Each of these areas is further divided into more precise comprehension skills such as time order, cause and effect, main idea, supporting details, and distinguishing fact from fiction.

Materials to Build Content Area Comprehension

Energy Horizons
By Christina G. Miller and Louise A. Berry
Educators Publishing Service, Inc.
75 Moulton Street
Cambridge, Massachusetts 02238

This series is divided into two workbooks; Book 1: Energy Sources, and Book 2: Electrical Energy. The main purpose of these two books is to help students develop more successful reading comprehension in the area of science. Stressed by these books are critical thinking skills, recalling details from the passages, and developing a strong vocabulary (bold-faced in text, and included in glossary), related to the content area of science. Concepts designed for grades 3-6.

The Story of Western Civilization
By Alan W. Riese and Herbert J. La Salle
Educators Publishing Service, Inc.
75 Moulton Street
Cambridge, Massachusetts 02238

This series of three fully illustrated workbooks deals with the development of reading comprehension in the content area of history. The three workbooks, "How Civilization Began," "Greece and Rome Build Great Civilizations," and "The Middle Ages," were designed to be used with students in grades 4-8. Each contains "carefully controlled language levels" so that readers of all levels will benefit without being overly bored or frustrated. The workbooks can be taught in any order, although sequentially is best. All passages are followed by comprehension questions asking for recall and development of vocabulary, among others.

The Story of the U.S.A.
By Franklin Escher, Jr.
Educators Publishing Service, Inc.
75 Moulton Street
Cambridge, Massachusetts 02238

The four workbooks in this series are developed in the area of United States History and are as follows: (1) "Explorers and Settlers," (2) "A Young Nation Solves Its Problems," (3) "America Becomes a Giant", and (4) "Modern America." Each chapter is introduced with new vocabulary and captioned illustrations. Each workbook comes with its own teacher's guide and deals with the comprehension skills of recall as well as a variety of different questions and formats (literal mostly). Designed for students grades 4 through 8.

Return to Azltan
By Alan W. Reise and Beverly Rodgers
Educators Publishing Services, Inc.
75 Moulton Street
Cambridge, Massachusetts 02238

This is an interesting book which uses the content area of history, in this case the history of Mexico and Mexican-Americans, to be used as a base for developing reading comprehension. Developed for students in grades 4-8, this book includes both English as well as Spanish vocabulary development skills, along with both objective, literal questions, and short answer interpretive questions. A valuable resource in a multicultural classroom.

Listening Comprehension: Grades 1-3
By B. Cheney Edwards and Susan J. Hohl
Educators Publishing Services, Inc.
75 Moulton Street
Cambridge, Massachusetts 02238

This kit begins with a series of seven inventories to determine weaknesses in students' listening skills. These inventories cover the following areas of reading comprehension: "following directions, sequencing, using context in listening, finding main ideas, forming sensory images from oral description, sensing emotions and moods through word usage and delivery, and making inferences and drawing conclusions." The Kit then uses games and activities to help correct any weaknesses that were found, and these games and activities are also helpful in listening, remembering, imagination, and verbalization skills.

Reading Milestones
By Stephen P. Quigley, Ph.D. and Cynthia M. King, Ph.D. (Editors)
Dormac, Inc.
Post Office Box 1699
Beaverton, Oregon 97075

This extensive series of readers and workbooks covers reading levels from pre-primer through 4.0. As a "language based" series, it uses a developmental progression through vocabulary, reading comprehension, decoding, and inferential reading skills. The reading comprehension area of the series deals with main idea, locating details, sequencing, cause and effect, making interpretations, drawing conclusions, word meaning through context, predictions and inferences, and judgments and generalizations. The color coded levels and brightly illustrated books span so many areas of reading that the series can be adapted to be used by a variety of students with different strengths and weaknesses.

Macmillan Instant Activities Program
By Macmillan Company
6 Commercial Street
Hicksville, New York 11801

This kit is a series of sections on different subject matters all bound in a three-ring binder. The kit includes sections not only on reading, but also on grammar and spelling, science experiments, and nature studies, math, and bulletin boards among others. In the reading section there are many varied activities such as posters, games, and activity sheets. The students learn to find main ideas, supporting details, draw inferences, and find facts while completing riddles, puzzles, and mystery stories. Designed for use with students in grades 3 through 6, this motivational series can be beneficial if used in whole or in part, for the reading section alone.

The Primary Teacher's Ready-to-Use Activities Program
By The Center for Applied Research in Education
C.S. 995
Hicksville, New York 11802

This interdisciplinary kit provides hundreds of reproducible activities to build skills in each content area, all organized by subject and bound in a three-ring binder for easy use. The reading section is subdivided into three parts: (1) Vocabulary, (2) Perceptual Skills & Word Analysis, and (3) Comprehension. Other sections include math, language arts, music, art, science, social studies, and health & safety. Activities utilize a variety of stimulating illustrations and formats, from games, crosswords and word searches, to true-false, multiple choice, fill-ins and sentence completions. Designed for K-3 students, the high-interest activity sheets develop reading comprehension and other skills across the curriculum.

TR Reading Comprehension Series
By DLM Teaching Resources
Post Office Box 4000
One DLM Park
Allen, Texas 75002

This series of workbooks and soft-bound texts is designed to teach "50 key comprehension skills" to readers in grades 2 to 7 who are reading below their appropriate reading level (one to three grades below). Specifically, this series concentrates on the following areas: "1) context and references, 2) form, 3) topic, 4) main idea, 5) details, 6) sequence, 7) spatial relationships, 8) comparison, 9) cause and effect, 10) author's purpose and technique, and 11) study skills."

Comprehension Through Active Involvement
By Marjorie Slavick Frank and P.J. Hutchins
DLM Teaching Resources
Post Office Box 4000
One DLM Park
Allen, Texas 75002

This series is made-up of four easy to read workbooks ranging in readability levels from 2.0 to 4.9. The format of the series is as follows: (1) Preview, (2) Reading selection (high-interest passages for first and second grade readers 150-200 words, and third and fourth grade readers 300-400 words), (3) Comprehension activities (with multiple choice questions, help in picking-up language cues, and open-ended questions), and (4) Writing practice. Teaching strategies are also included to facilitate learning.

Graphical Comprehension
By Jamestown Publishers; The Reading People
Post Office Box 9168
Providence, RI 02940

This workbook is used as a resource for instructing students in the skill of graphical literacy. The reading levels most appropriate for this workbook are 7 through 10, although its interest level stretches through college. Each lesson in the workbook begins with a description of a graph, followed by exercises in understanding how to read and create similar graphs.

Macmillan Reading Spectrum
By Macmillan Publishing Company
966 Third Avenue
New York, New York 10022

This reading program covers several extensive areas of reading development—such skills as sight word recognition, word attack skills, vocabulary development, oral reading, dictionary usage, comprehension skills, and study skills. The eighteen self-directed and self-corrective booklets cover a vast number of varied comprehension skills by presenting a story passage, character list, and comprehension questions requiring recall and interpretation. Set A focuses on grades 2 through 6, while Set B is for grades 3 through 8.

Critical Steps to Effective Reading and Writing
By Zenobia Verner and Bill Minturn
DLM Teaching Resources
One DLM Park
Allen, Texas 75002

The workbooks in this program each deal with a specific area. The ten workbooks are as follows: (1) Details and Sentences, (2) Details and Paragraphs, (3) Order and Sequence, (4) Main Idea and Sentences, (5) Main Idea and Paragraphs, (6) Cause/Effect and Sentences, (7) Cause/Effect and Paragraphs, (8) Fact and Opinion, (9) Evidence and Prediction, and (10) Evaluation and Purpose. This program also comes with transparencies to correlate with workbook activities. This series is recommended for students in grades 5 through 12.

Beginning Reasoning and Reading
By Joanne Carlisle
Educators Publishing Service, Inc.
75 Moulton Street
Cambridge, Massachusetts 02138

The four workbooks in this series, (1) Beginning Word Meaning, (2) Beginning Sentence Meaning, (3) Beginning Paragraph Meaning, and (4) Beginning Reasoning Skills, all work on developing more and more complex comprehension skills. The exercises in these workbooks include writing exercises to enhance the reading exercises. The exercises themselves are designed for students in grades 3 through 5 and "All of the books encourage each student to take an active role in the reading process."

Workbooks for Reading Comprehension
By Opportunities for Learning, Inc.
20417 Nordhoff St., Dept. 75B
Chatsworth, CA 91311

This series of five 20-page workbooks provides reading activities to promote the skills of comprehension through story passages and the follow-up questions and activities dealing with "finding main ideas and details, determining sequence, drawing conclusions, and predicting outcomes." Broken down into three available sets, this series is appropriate for reading levels 2.0 (Set A), 2.5 (Set B), and 3.0 (Set C).

Comprehension Motivators
By Opportunities for Learning, Inc.
20417 Nordhoff St., Dept. 75B
Chatsworth, CA 91311

This set of reading comprehension worksheets is designed for motivation through the use of high-interest short reading passages, and large illustrations. The comprehension skills stressed by these worksheets include the following: "finding main idea, using context clues, drawing conclusions, and other thinking skills." The two sets in the series focus on different reading levels. Pack A deals with levels 1 through 4, while Pack B deals with materials for levels 3 through 6. Each Pack consists of six books, each with 20 duplicating masters.

The Reading Machine
By Opportunities for Learning, Inc.
20417 Nordhoff St., Dept. 75B
Chatsworth, CA 91311

This highly motivational series combines a variety of different activities and materials for the development of reading comprehension skills in reading levels 2 through 8 (interest levels 9 through 13 years). This multisensory kit includes the integration of "magazines, audio cassettes, and duplicating masters." The colorful illustrations in the magazines help to make them high interest, along with such activities included within them as games and riddles. The ten audio cassettes have story narrations on one side and comprehension activities on the other. The duplicating masters deal with "listening, following directions, and auditory and visual memory skills."

Critical Reading for Proficiency
By Opportunities for Learning, Inc.
20417 Nordhoff St., Dept. 75B
Chatsworth, CA 91311

This book is specifically designed to offer a variety of reading passages in varied content areas to help prepare students for standardized tests. Suggested for use with students in grades 8 through 12, such comprehension skills as "finding the main idea, sequence, cause and effect, author viewpoint, fact or opinion, comparison, outlining, word meanings from context, and more," help students prepare for the type of reading comprehension necessary for success in taking standardized tests.

Reading Comprehension: Tricky Picture Stories
By Opportunities for Learning, Inc.
20417 Nordhoff St., Dept. 75B
Chatsworth, CA 91311

These three kits deal with the reading comprehension skill of prediction. Recommended for students in grade 4 and up, these kits use cards with detailed illustrations and attempt to predict fact and fiction from their context. The student then turns the cards over to read about the illustrations and determine how accurate their predictions were. Each of the 48 8½" × 11" cards includes comprehension questions in a variety of different areas (main idea, sequence, vocabulary, etc.). The three kits are as follows: (1) American Literature, (2) Animals, and (3) Great Americans.

Word Wise I, II, and III: Better Comprehension Through Vocabulary
By Isabel L. Beck, Margaret G. McKeown, and Steven F. Roth
DLM Teaching Resources
One DLM Park
Allen, Texas 75002

This computer software program for teaching better reading comprehension through vocabulary development, is formatted as a highly motivational game. This program has built-in speech handicap capabilities so that students can not only compete against each other, but the computer, too (with a fair chance of winning either way), a system to track student progress. The kit itself contains five 5¼″ diskettes, eight "blackline masters of fun-to-play reinforcement activities," a key chart, teacher's manual, and vinyl binder. The computer challenges students to match vocabulary to definitions, explanations, and examples (NOTE: Word Wise works only with Echo or Cricket speech peripherals, also available from DLM.)

Bridges to Understanding
By Susan Sheridan and Lynn Springfield
DLM Teaching Resources
One DLM Park
Allen, Texas 75002

This kit is designed for use with students in the primary grades who are working on the development of reading and writing skills. Emphasizing the connection between oral speech and the written language, these materials offer students the opportunity to tell or write their own original stories after reading from the kit's booklets, examining one of the kit's 22″ × 17″ posters of a story illustration, or role-playing the story plot. This series allows the students to develop understanding of the story and to prove their comprehension through their writing and role-playing. The six booklets contain samples of actual language collected from more than 600 children, therefore providing realistic language.

The Kim Marshall Series in Reading
By Kim Marshall
Educators Publishing Service, Inc.
75 Moulton Street
Cambridge, Massachusetts 02138

This series is divided into two books, providing the student reader with reading passages followed by literal and interpretive comprehension questions. Designed for grades 4 through 6, Book 1 contains 92 stories while Book 2 contains 94. The format of the two books is such that the story is half a page long in one column of the page, with the accompanying questions in the column next to it. The questions also ask for student responses such as feelings and opinions.

Five-Minute Thrillers
By Opportunities for Learning, Inc.
20417 Nordhoff St., Dept. 75B
Chatsworth, CA 91311

This set of books (100 books-five books each of 20 titles) and cassettes (20) deal with the reading levels 3-0 through 4-0 and interest levels 7 through 12. Each story is of high interest and contains about 1,000 words per passage, yet is easy to read and only takes minutes to complete. Some subject matters dealt with in these passages are outer space aliens, vampires, and other strange subjects. The comprehension questions that follow each passage are varied according to the subject matter. "Punchy, unexpected twists" at the end of these stories encourage critical thinking skills.

Reading Enrichment for the Gifted Student
By Opportunities for Learning, Inc.
20417 Nordhoff St., Dept. 75B
Chatsworth, CA 91311

This kit, which deals with developing such reading comprehension skills as using context clues, making inferences, finding main ideas, finding facts, and just overall "creative thinking" skills, is designed for reading levels grades 6 through 10. Especially designed for gifted readers, it is best used to help improve test-taking skills. The sets (four in all) are comprised of comprehension cards followed by exercises to check for comprehension. Each set contains 50 cards.

Magic Message Reading Books
By Opportunities for Learning, Inc.
20417 Nordhoff St., Dept. 75B
Chatsworth, CA 91311

Cloze skills are emphasized in this highly motivational set of books. As the students "work through skill-specific reading problems," they have the use of a decoder section to find the secret hidden message. Students will be forced to check their own work, since one mistake makes the message remain "secret." Each book has 32 pages, available in sets of 10 consumable books. The first set is designed for use with reading levels 2 through 3, and the second for reading levels 4 through 5 (interest levels span 2 through 6).

Bookmark Reading Filmstrips
By Harcourt Brace Jovanovich, Inc.
6277 Sea Harbor Drive
Orlando, FL 32821

The filmstrips and audio cassettes in this series are designed to correlate with classroom activities by reinforcing such critical reading skills as "recognizing main ideas and details, drawing conclusions, and interpreting characters' feelings and motives." These filmstrips also deal with study skills such as "dictionary use, following directions, and reading maps, graphs, and charts."

Single Skills
By Walter Pauk, Ph.D.
Jamestown Publishers; The Reading People
Post Office Box 9168
Providence, RI 02940

This series focuses on grades 3 through 12 dealing with the reading comprehension areas of (1) subject matter, (2) main idea, (3) supporting details, (4) clarifying devices, and (5) vocabulary in context. The series is made up of books containing high-interest reading passages (approximately 150 words) followed by questions to develop the comprehension skill of the lesson. This series can be purchased as 60 books on a single grade level or as 60 books spanning all ten grades.

Essential Skills Series
By Walter Pauk, Ph.D.
Jamestown Publishers; The Reading People
Post Office Box 9168
Providence, RI 02940

This series contains two books in each reading level grades 3 through 12. The books use passages on nature and follow them with six comprehension questions, one from each of the following areas: (1) subject matter, (2) supporting details, (3) conclusions, (4) clarifying devices, (5) vocabulary in context, and (6) main idea. Each book begins with a lesson to help define and teach the six essential skills being focused upon.

Six-Way Paragraphs
By Walter Pauk, Ph.D.
Jamestown Publishers; The Reading People
Post Office Box 9168
Providence, RI 02940

These books span the reading levels grades 4 to 8 in the middle level book and continue grades 8 through 12 in the advanced level book. Each of the 100 "factual high-interest passages" are followed by questions dealing with (1) main idea, (2) subject matter, (3) supporting details, (4) conclusions, (5) clarifying ideas and devices, and (6) vocabulary in context. The diagnostic chart in the back of each book allows the students to record their answers and chart their own strengths and weaknesses.

Cloze in the Content Area
By Opportunities for Learning, Inc.
20417 Nordhoff St., Dept. 75B
Chatsworth, CA 91311

This set of three duplicating master workbooks uses the content areas of science, social studies, and math to help the classroom teacher develop literal comprehension skills and also in using syntactic and semantic cues. Each book of 60 masters uses a variety of short reading selections for grades 2.0 through 7.9. The books are available singly or together.

Reading Comprehension Card Kits
By Opportunities for Learning, Inc.
20417 Nordhoff St., Dept. 75B
Chatsworth, CA 91311

These eight different sets of reading comprehension cards deal with the following areas of interest: (1) Aviation, (2), Dogs, (3) Marguerite Henry's Horses, (4)

Crime Fighters, (5) Cars and Cycles, (6) Fads, (7) Special People, and (8) Escape. Designed for reading levels 3.0 through 4.4, each card contains full-color photos, reading selections with ranges from 400 to 675 words, and reading comprehension questions on the back. Each kit contains 75 reading cards along with instructional guides and progress charts.

Just Clues: Experiences in Reading Comprehension
By Opportunities for Learning, Inc.
20417 Nordhoff St., Dept. 75B
Chatsworth, CA 91311

These two reproducible books are designed to be used with grades 2 through 4 and 4 through 6. By providing the reader with clues such as photographs, fragment materials, and written clues, they encourage students to use reading comprehension skills of "noting detail, classifying, drawing inferences, sequencing, identifying the main idea, and recognizing cause and effect." Follow-up questions and activities are included with the books for further instruction in these skills.

Computer Software to Develop Reading Comprehension

Hide 'N Sequence
By John D. Perron, Ph.D., and Victoria Hanson
Sunburst Communications
39 Washington Avenue
Pleasantville, New York 10570
(Available for 48K Apple II and Commodore 64.)

This colorful program gives the student a passage to read and a choice among 3 sentences to complete the passage. While the program develops reading and writing skills through sequencing, it also allows for students to enter their own sentences into the computer. Designed for reading levels 3 through 12, the kit includes one teacher disk, one student disk, a backup, and a teacher's guide (divided into grades 3-5, 5-8, and 8-12).

Word-A-Mation
By Glenn Kleiman, Jillian Dorman, and J.B. Shelton
Teaching Tools Software, Inc.
Sunburst Communications
39 Washington Avenue
Pleasantville, New York 10570
(Available for 64K Apple II.)

This computer software program is for grade levels 4 through adult, and is used to develop vocabulary working with such concepts as synonyms, antonyms, homophones, tense, spelling, and categories. The kit includes one disk, a backup, and a teacher's guide.

The Puzzler
By Queen's University at Kingston, The Scarborough Board of Education, and the Frontenac County Board of Education, Ontario Canada
Sunburst Communications
39 Washington Avenue
Pleasantville, New York 10570
(Available for 48K Apple II, Commodore 64, 128K IBM PC or Pcjr., 256 Tandy 1000, and 32K TRS-80.)

This computer software program is designed for students at grade levels 3 through 6. The program gives the students one of five stories to read. The students must interpret the reading passages and make inferences to solve the story puzzle. The student must therefore read for comprehension. The kit has one disk, a backup, and a teacher's guide.

Mickey's Magic Reader
By Neil Larimer and Mary Anne Hermann
The Walt Disney Company
Sunburst Communications
39 Washington Avenue
Pleasantville, New York 10570
(for 64K and Apple II)

This computer software program was designed for students in grades 1 and 2. Mickey Mouse takes students through the variety of comprehension skills within this program, such as sentence comprehension, understanding words in context, the use of interactive stories where the student chooses what happens next, and simple riddles. The motivational program uses colorful graphics to reinforce correct answers. The kit includes one disk, a backup, and a teacher's guide.

Tiger's Tales
By Mary Anne Hermann and Eric Grubbs
Sunburst Communications
39 Washington Avenue
Pleasantville, New York 10570
(Available for 64, Apple II, or Commodore 64)

This early reading comprehension program was designed to be used by students in kindergarten through second grade. In the form of interactive stories, students are introduced to a cat named Tiger and after reading the passage are required to use problem-solving skills to decide what to do next. Students develop in the areas of vocabulary (through a picture-to-word matching section) as well as in following directions. The colorful graphics are motivating and the problem can be accessed through the regular keyboard Muppet Learning Keys, and (in the Apple II) Touch Window. The kit includes one disk, a backup, and teacher's guide.

A Wrinkle in Time
By Dean VanDeCarr and Janice Kanter (Croton Schools, New York)
Sunburst Communications
39 Washington Avenue
Pleasantville, New York 10570
(Available for 48K, Apple II, and Commodore 64)

Designed after the award-winning book of the same title, this computer software program is recommended for grades 4 through 8. As the students read the passages on the screen, they must make decisions as to what comes next. The program also develops the concepts of main ideas and recalling details while working on sequencing. The kit comes with one book, one disk, a backup, and a teacher's guide.

Dr. Disk's Adventure
By Infotech Manitoba Educational Technology Program
Sunburst Communications
39 Washington Avenue
Pleasantville, New York 10570
(Available for 64K and Apple II)

This interactive reading program was designed for students in grades 4 through 8. The reading comprehension skills of vocabulary development and decision skills based on your reading lead you through the stories. Along with the reading skills, this program is also designed to teach computer literacy skills. Successful students earn a Computer Operator's Certificate. The kit includes one disk, a backup, poster, and a teacher's guide.

Charlotte's Web
By Mary Anne Hermann and Neil Larimer
Sunburst Communications
39 Washington Avenue
Pleasantville, New York 10570
(Available for 64K and Apple II)

This computer software program is designed to follow the story of the same name. The animated graphics of this program test students' understanding of such concepts as main ideas, specific details, character profiles, and vocabulary. The original story won a Newbery Award, and the program brings the story to life for students in grades 3 through 6. The kit comes with one book, one disk, a backup, and a teacher's guide.
**Also available are other Newbery titles in similar software formats, also for the 64K and Apple II . . .

Island of the Blue Dolphins
Designed by Martha Nichols and Peter Wierzbicki
Grades 5-8

Mrs. Frisby and the Rats of NIMH
Designed by Dean VanDeCarr and Janice Kanter
Grades 4-8

Mr. Popper's Penguins
Designed by Mary Anne Hermann and Neil Larimer
Grades 3-7

The Oregon Trail
By Apple Computer, Inc.
Copyright MECC
3490 Lexington Avenue, North
St. Paul, MN 55126

This computer software program is designed as a covered wagon trip across the United States to California in 1848. The student is required to read the situation on the screen and react to it in a way that will best benefit getting his group to California alive and in good health. The colorful and detailed graphics allow the student to learn the history of the Oregon Trail while at the same time learning problem-solving skills, foreshadowing, and new vocabulary. The program allows a variety of situations to occur which focus on an interest level (and reading level) appropriate for intermediate grade students through adults. Map reading is also incorporated into the program.

Compu-Read
By Opportunities for Learning, Inc.
20417 Nordhoff St., Dept. P A
Chatsworth, CA 91311
(For use with Apple 48K)

This computer software program is designed to "rapidly help increase reading comprehension and retention." The four program topics are: (1) "Character Recognition," (2) "High-Speed Word Recognition," (3) "Synonyms and Antonyms," and (4) "Sentence Comprehension." The computer itself has an automatic adjustment system that will adjust the program to fit the difficulty level at which the student works best. The kit contains one disk.

How to Read in the Content Areas
By Opportunities for Learning, Inc.
20417 Nordhoff St., Dept. P A
Chatsworth, CA 91311
(For use with Apple 48K)

This computer software program is designed for students in grades 5 through 6 and concentrates on reading comprehension skills as related to the content areas of social studies and literature. The reading comprehension skills concentrated on are: "vocabulary building, detecting main ideas and inferences, recalling important facts, ideas, and details, and applying these skills to the content areas." Also helpful for remedial students in grades 7 through 8. Includes 1 disk and 5 reproducible Activity Masters per title.

Main Idea Maze
By Opportunities for Learning, Inc.
20417 Nordhoff St., Dept. P A
Chatsworth, CA 91311
(For use with the Apple 48K)

The computer software program is for the development of the main idea in the reading passages presented. There are 150 different passages included which are presented to the students in a game format. The program is also designed to be self-directed for the students and very motivational. Best for grades 2 through 8. Kit contains one disk with a backup.

Scholastic Reading Comprehension
By Scholastic Inc.
P.O. Box 7502
2931 East McCarty Street
Jefferson City, MO 65102
(For Apple 64K)

This computer software program was designed to teach reading comprehension skills to students in grades 4 through 6. This interactive program centers on such skills as "literal recall of facts, understanding main idea, searching for key words, putting events in order, sentence meaning, inferential thinking, who, what, where, when, why, and how, and drawing conclusions." Passages represent both classic and contemporary literature. The program offers HELP features, grade specific passages, and a recordkeeping feature.

Twistaplot Reading Adventure Series
By Scholastic Inc.
P.O. Box 7502
2931 East McCarty Street
Jefferson City, MO 65102
(For use with Apple 48K Computer)

These highly motivational computer program stories offer the students colorful graphics and interesting characters. Drawing from many of the content areas, this program offers students the opportunity to make problem-solving decisions as to the story plot. Critical thinking skills, story mapping, and plot construction are all key components of this series. Designed for students in grades 4 through 8.

Memory Castle
By Rochester School District, Rochester, Minnesota
Sunburst Communications
39 Washington Avenue
Pleasantville, New York 10570
(For Apple II 48K, Commodore 64, 128K IBM PC or Pcjr, 256K Tandy 1000, and 32K TRS-80.)

This computer software program uses colorful graphics to develop skills in remembering instructions and following directions while at the same time developing memory skills. The program offers strategies for students to use while they experience the adventure on screen. Designed for grades 5 through adult, it comes with one disk, a backup, and a teacher's guide.

Ace Reporter, Detective & Explorer
By Opportunities for Learning, Inc.
20417 Nordhoff St., Dept. P A
Chatsworth, CA 91311
(For use with Apple 48K)

These computer software programs offer reading comprehension skills such as drawing conclusions, recognizing main ideas and using critical reading and thinking skills. The programs also allow the student the opportunity to practice creative writing. Designed for use in grades 2 through 6, the kits include one disk, a backup, and one teacher's guide per title. Reading passages ask students to solve problems in the stories and "check all pertinent leads."

GAPPER: Reading Comprehension
By Opportunities for Learning, Inc.
20417 Nordhoff St., Dept. P A
Chatsworth, CA 91311
(For use with Apple 64K)

This reading comprehension program uses the cloze technique for grades 3 through 12. Students read the passages on the screen and fill in the empty areas in the passages. The program makes use of the student's "word structure, spelling, grammar, and meaning in context." Some important features are an automatic readability analysis, record keeping, and differing difficulty levels. The kit includes one disk, a backup, and a teacher's guide.

New Kid on the Block
By Opportunities for Learning, Inc.
20417 Nordhoff St., Dept. P A
Chatsworth, CA 91311
(For use with the Apple 48K)

This computer software program introduces the character of "Jodi," and covers reading comprehension skills such as understanding the main idea, cause and effect, inferencing, etc., along with literary skills such as recognizing theme, author's purpose, tone, mood, and characterization. The program also includes "diagnostic record keeping" to recognize students who are experiencing problems. For grades 5 through 7, the program kit includes one disk.

Comprehension Skill Builders
By Opportunities for Learning, Inc.
20417 Nordhoff St., Dept. P A
Chatsworth, CA 91311
(For use with Apple 48K)

These reading comprehension programs deal with "Sequence," "Inference," and "Following Directions" in an entertaining game format. "Sequence" is designed for two players while the other two titles are designed for use with from two to six players. As the students follow through the programs, they are asked to prove their comprehension of the passages by answering questions. The reading levels of these programs are from 3.5 to 5.0. One disk is included with each title.

Time Capsule Reading Skills
By Opportunities for Learning, Inc.
20417 Nordhoff St., Dept. P A
Chatsworth, CA 91311
(For use with Apple 48K)

Three reading levels are available in this title, 2.0-3.5, 3.5-5.0, and 5.0-6.5. This game format allows students to travel through eleven different "time periods" with over 300 reading comprehension questions dealing with such areas as main idea, context clues, author's purpose, details, sequence, structural analysis, inference fact or opinion, cause and effect, and word meanings. All scores are recorded by the program, difficulty level can be changed and additional questions can be added. One disk available per title.

Reading for Meaning
By Opportunities for Learning, Inc.
20417 Nordhoff St., Dept. P A
Chatsworth, CA 91311
(For use with Apple 48K)

This computer software program uses Mother Goose rhymes as a means to teach reading comprehension skills. It is available at Level I and Level II, both for students in grades 3 through 4. Level 1 deals with such things as facts, details, and sequencing. Level II deals with such items as inferencing, prediction, conclusions, and main ideas. Each level comes with two disks and a teacher guide.

Main Idea Gold Rush
By Opportunities for Learning, Inc.
20417 Nordhoff St., Dept. P A
Chatsworth, CA 91311
(For use with Apple 48K)

This computer software program is designed to be used with two players. The competitive game format challenges the students to identify the main idea of each paragraph in order to advance further toward their goals. The system "records up to 200 student files, raw scores and percent correct." Available for students in grades 3 through 4 and 5 through 6. Kit includes one disk with a backup.

StickyBear Reading Comprehension
By Opportunities for Learning, Inc.
20417 Nordhoff St., Dept. P A
Chatsworth, CA 91311
(For use with Apple 48K)

This reading comprehension computer software program is most effective when used with grades 2 through 4. Students answer comprehension questions covering a variety of reading skills after reading over 30 different stories in the software program. Teachers can also add stories of their own. The kit includes 1 disk, a poster, "Stickybear Stickers", and a user's guide.

Reading Comprehension Series
By Opportunities for Learning, Inc.
20417 Nordhoff St., Dept. P A
Chatsworth, CA 91311
(For use with Apple 48K)

This series includes three separate titles for grades K through 1 ("Scuffy & Friends"), 1 through 2 "Kittens, Kids & a Frog"), and 3 through 5 ("Chariots, Cougars & Kings"). Stories are accompanied by full-color graphics and are followed by comprehension questions dealing with such things as identifying details, sequencing events, predicting outcomes, identifying main ideas, defining cause and effect, and identifying pronouns. This kit also includes a record-keeping function and comes with two disks and one teacher's guide per title.